IMAGES
of America

AROUND BANGOR

IMAGES
of America

AROUND BANGOR

Cindy LaPenna

ARCADIA
PUBLISHING

ISBN 978-0-7385-3902-7

Published by Arcadia Publishing
Charleston, South Carolina

Printed in the United States of America

Library of Congress Catalog Card Number: 2005931166

For all general information contact Arcadia Publishing at:
Telephone 843-853-2070
Fax 843-853-0044
E-mail sales@arcadiapublishing.com
For customer service and orders:
Toll-Free 1-888-313-2665

Visit us on the Internet at www.arcadiapublishing.com

Dedicated to my grandfather Frederick, an immigrant and quarryman.

Contents

ACKNOWLEDGMENTS

Many people are responsible for bringing this book to fruition. A very special thank you to Walter Emery of the Slate Belt Museum in Mount Bethel for lending his time, knowledge, and photographs freely and without hesitation.

Thanks too, to Barbara Brandt, director of the Bangor Public Library, for doing the same. Thank you to Rita Shope and the staff of the Hunter Martin Museum in Martin's Creek and the employees of Martin's Creek Grocery and Deli for the connections; to David Drinkhouse, June Jones of the Flicksville Historical Society, and especially Frank Ferruccio for freely providing the Jayne Mansfield photographs from his personal collection; Dave Butler and the staff of the Stroudsburg Foto Shop provided the photographic expertise. And thanks to Aunt Lucy Mullinger for the information and to Rudy Corazza for his help and support. You are all true professionals. I feel certain that I could not have completed this project without the help of all of you, but even if I could have, I know it would not have been half as enjoyable.

The following people have also contributed their time, photographs, and expertise: Mike Serbon and the staff of the Pennsylvania State Archives in Harrisburg; Jane Moyer, librarian; Colleen Cunningham Lavdar, executive director, and the staff of the Northampton County Historical and Genealogical Society in Easton; and the Slate Belt Heritage Center in Bangor.

A special thank-you, too, goes to my editor, Erin Loftus, for being flexible and answering all of my questions, and to Arcadia Publishing for providing this opportunity to publish.

This project has made me realize the importance of documenting and preserving those moments in time we will come to call "history." All of you have contributed to that process in your own way, and for that and all your help, you deserve a pat on the back and have my deepest gratitude.

The images in this volume are courtesy of the Slate Belt Heritage Center (SBHC), Northampton County Historical and Genealogical Society (NCHGS), the Slate Belt Museum (SBM), the Bangor Public Library (BPL), the Pennsylvania State Archives (PSA), the Hunter Martin Museum (HMM), the Flicksville Historical Society (FHS), David Drinkhouse, Frank Ferruccio, and the author's collection.

Introduction

Bangor, Pennsylvania, and its surrounding Slate Belt towns are located in Northampton County, nestled in the Blue Ridge Mountains, and are within a few miles of the Delaware River. The town of Bangor was formed from two land areas, Uttsville and New Village, and remained primarily a farming community for many years, until a gray rock put it on the map.

Millions of years of evolution deposited silt and other sediments in the area to form the Martinsburg Formation and give the area its greatest asset—slate. Bangor was fortunate enough to have the upper, or soft, layers of this formation run through it. The soft members are perfect for fashioning slate items such as roofing shingles and blackboards, which is what Bangor eventually became known for.

Although there is some controversy about the exact dates and people involved in slate's discovery, geologists and many others accept the discovery of slate in 1836, on the property of James M. Porter near Slateford, as a starting point. From there, quarrying spread to Bangor, thanks largely to the efforts of Welshman Robert Morris Jones, who is generally regarded as Bangor's founder.

Bangor would eventually become known worldwide for its long-lasting, quality slate. European immigrants, such as the English, Italians, Germans, and especially the Welsh, who were already skilled quarrymen, flocked to the area in search of economic opportunity or to escape religious persecution and other restrictions. It did not matter that life for the immigrants in a new land and in the damp quarries was hard and, at times, dangerous, with long hours, low pay, and hours spent walking many miles to work. These varied cultures, each with their own unique customs and contributions, eventually blended together in the Slate Belt community.

Over the years, as the area grew and expanded, it became home to a major railroad company, produced a movie star, and was the subject of a study on heart disease. The town had much to celebrate. Unfortunately the quarry industry did not fare as well. Not one of the original quarries, nearly 100 in all, located throughout the area at various times, exists today.

One quarry, Dally Slate, which opened in 1948 in Pen Argyl, continues to produce slate flooring and other products, and a few businesses make and sell items such as slate clocks, magnets, and other decorative products. Many of the quarries, now covered over with landfill, are virtually unrecognizable in addition to being obsolete, as new businesses spring up around and on top of them.

Economics, wars, new products, and stricter immigration eventually combined to bring about the demise of the quarry industry, but the industrious people of Bangor and the Slate Belt—undaunted—opened silk and, later, garment mills to provide for themselves. They became entrepreneurs in a variety of businesses and services that the expanding area needed. During the 1960s, a thriving garment industry, primarily of made up of blouse mills, provided employment to the area, until it, too, petered out toward the end of the 1970s. It is hoped that the photographs and contents of this book will capture the facts and spirit that was once Bangor and the Slate Belt, because today the area is not much different from the rest of the world.

Bangor is now primarily a town of small businesses with some light industry and professions, but the majority of its residents commute to work in other towns and in the nearby states of New Jersey and New York, while trying to preserve the good qualities that once made the communities sought after and unique.

One

Old Countries, New Lands

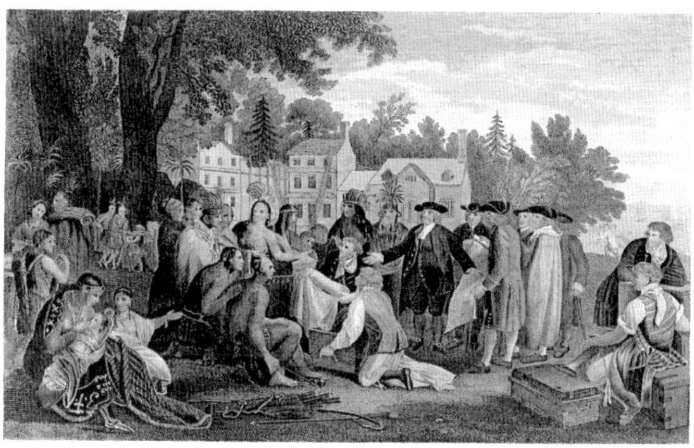

Northampton County, home to Bangor and the Slate Belt, came into being as a result of William Penn's treaty with the Lenape Indians known as the Walking Purchase of 1737. Although Penn treated the Lenapes fairly, his sons, John and Thomas, did not. In debt, they convinced the Lenapes that their father had bought their land but never completed the purchase. The purchase, which never actually transpired, was to include land accumulated "as far as a man could walk in a day and a half." Three "walkers" were hired to secure the land, but only one, Edward Marshall, completed the walk from present-day Wrightstown, in Bucks County, to Slateford. The deception of the Walking Purchase is said to be partially responsible for the Delabole Massacre of the Keller family during the French and Indian War. (Author's collection.)

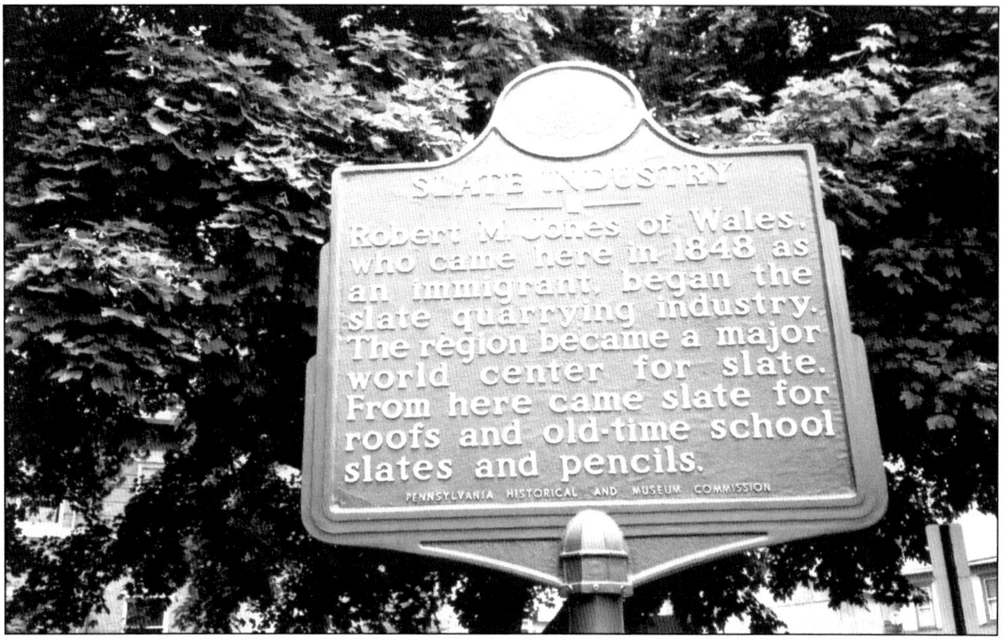

This historical marker on the corner of North First Street in Bangor commemorates the scope and importance of the slate industry to the area and the man generally regarded as helping it flourish, Robert Morris Jones of Wales. Jones opened the old Bangor Slate Quarry in 1866 and, in 1874, became the first chief burgess of the newly incorporated borough of Bangor. (Author's collection.)

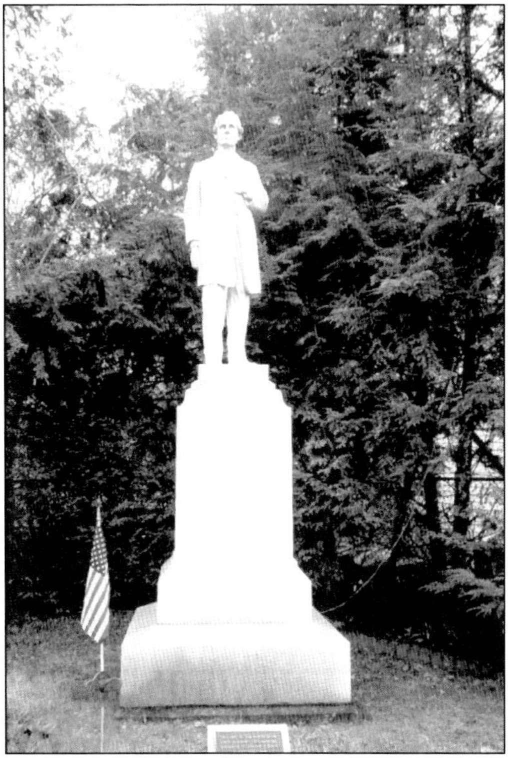

This statue of Robert Morris Jones stands in Founder's Park. Jones, the son of a Calvin-Methodist minister, was born in 1822 in Bethesda, Caernarvonshire, Wales. He studied geology and moved to Slatington, Pennsylvania, in 1846. Jones fought in the Battle of Gettysburg and was regarded as an intelligent, caring visionary. He died suddenly on January 20, 1886, while on a business trip to Philadelphia with his children. (Author's collection.)

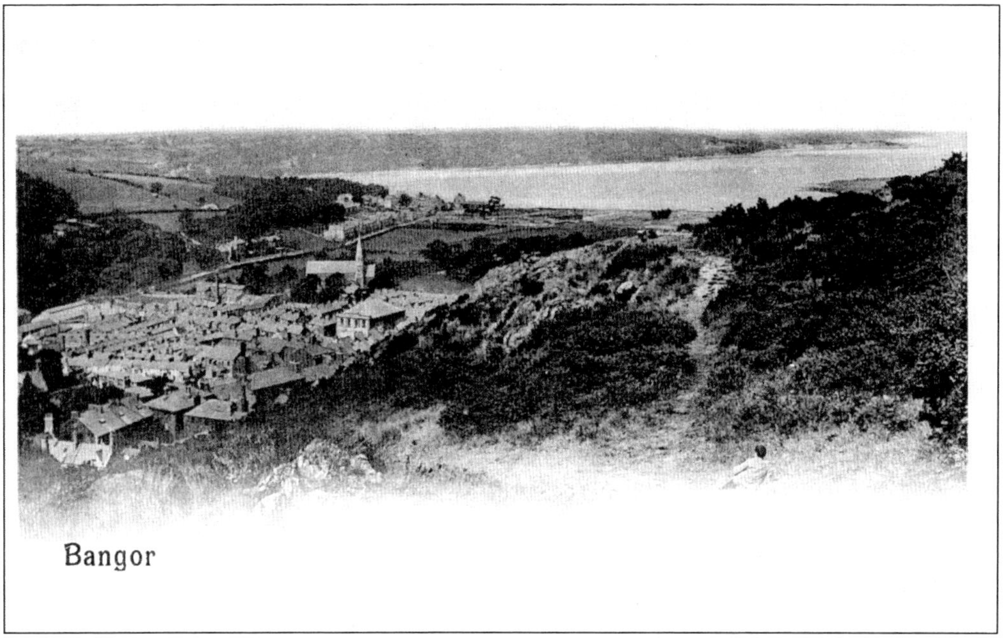

These are two countryside scenes of Bangor, Wales (above), and Bangor, Pennsylvania (below). It is said that Robert Morris Jones named his new home in Pennsylvania "Bangor" because the quarries and surrounding land reminded him of Bangor, Wales. Many World War II servicemen who visited Bangor, Wales, while stationed in England have commented on the similarities, as have many tourists. The most obvious similarity is the way the two areas are surrounded by mountains. Bangor, Wales, is surrounded by the Snowdonia Mountains, with their many peaks and valleys, while the Slate Belt is surrounded by the beautiful Blue Ridge Mountains. (Author's collection.)

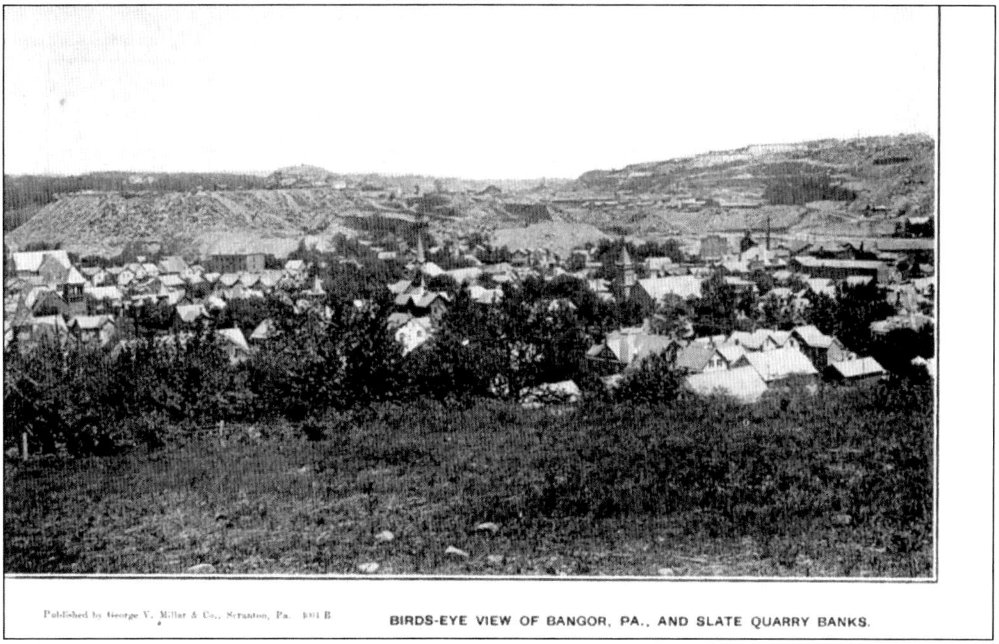

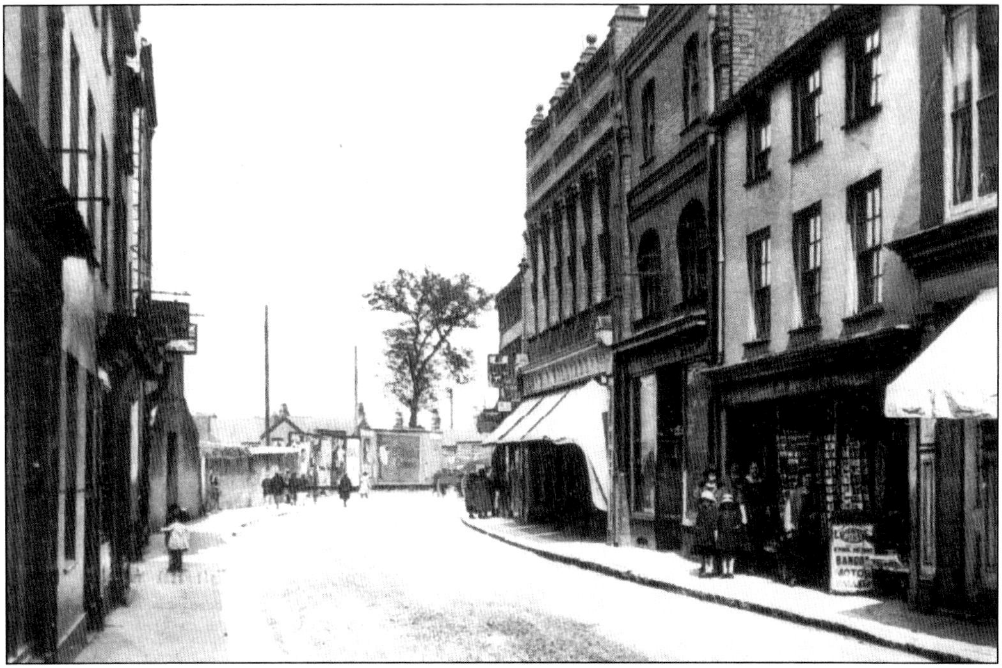

These are photographs of High Street in Bangor, Wales (above), and Main Street in Bangor, Pennsylvania (below). Both streets are the business areas of the towns. Main Street has undergone only minor changes from the way it looked in this 1930s photograph. Most of the buildings are still standing today, even if the types of businesses operating within them have changed. The First National Bank, which can be seen in the right-hand corner, has nearly always been a banking institution, serving the financial needs of the community. The tall building on the left at the end of the street is the housing unit known as the Real Estate Building, which still operates today as the Century House. (Courtesy SBHC.)

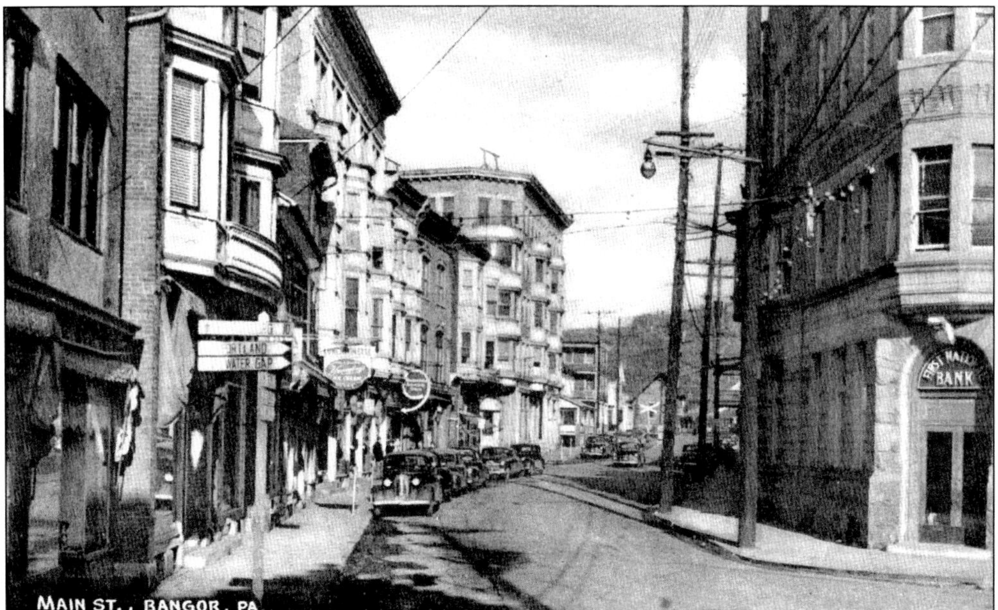

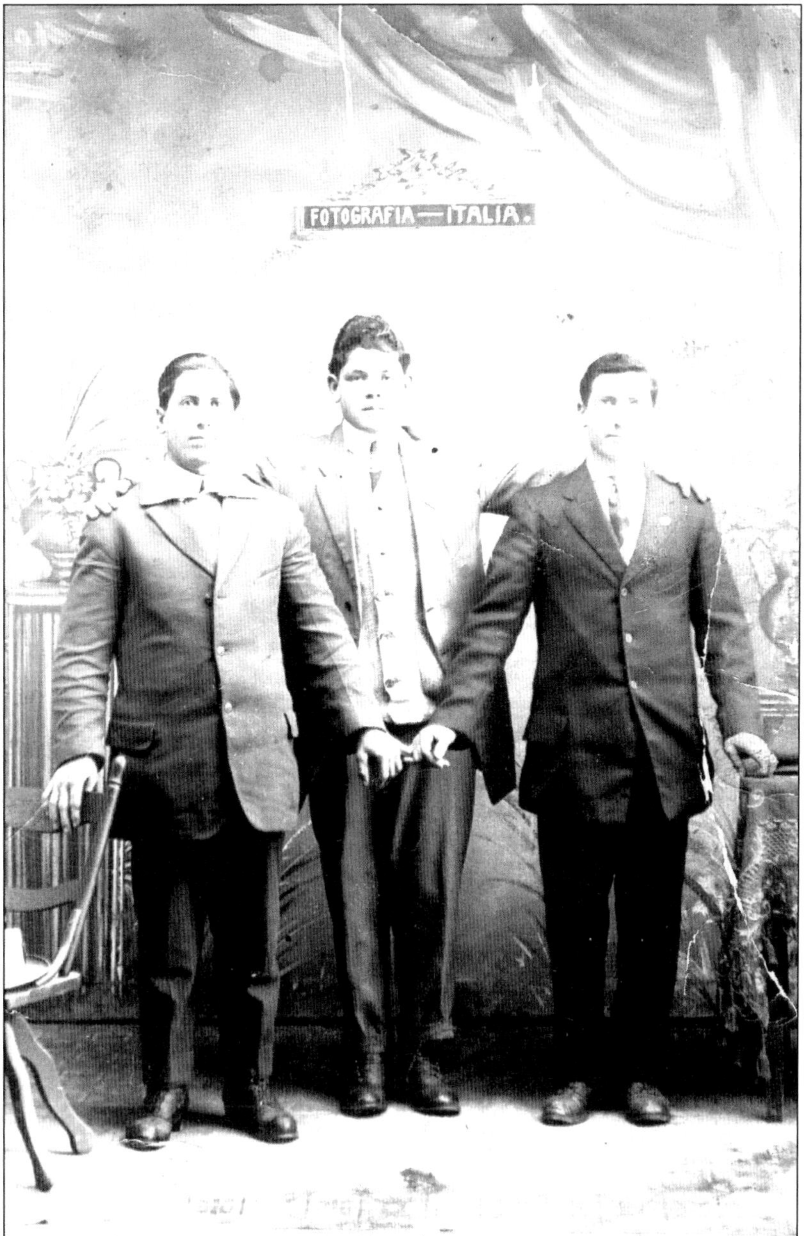

An Italian immigrant poses with friends in the 1920s. The Italians, along with the Welsh and Cornish and Pennsylvanian Germans, comprised the biggest immigrant groups to Bangor and the Slate Belt in the early 19th century. There were also small groups of Scotch-Irish, French Huguenots, and African Americans, as well as some Jewish businessmen. Life for the immigrants was not easy. Survival meant long hours of physical labor, such as that found in the quarries or factories, which sometimes paid meager wages. Many immigrants rose early in the morning and walked many miles to their jobs, often literally encountering "sticks and stones" for taking work away from local townspeople. In addition, many ethnic groups were antagonistic to one another or in personal conflict, trying to decide how much of their old ways they would retain or leave behind. (Author's collection.)

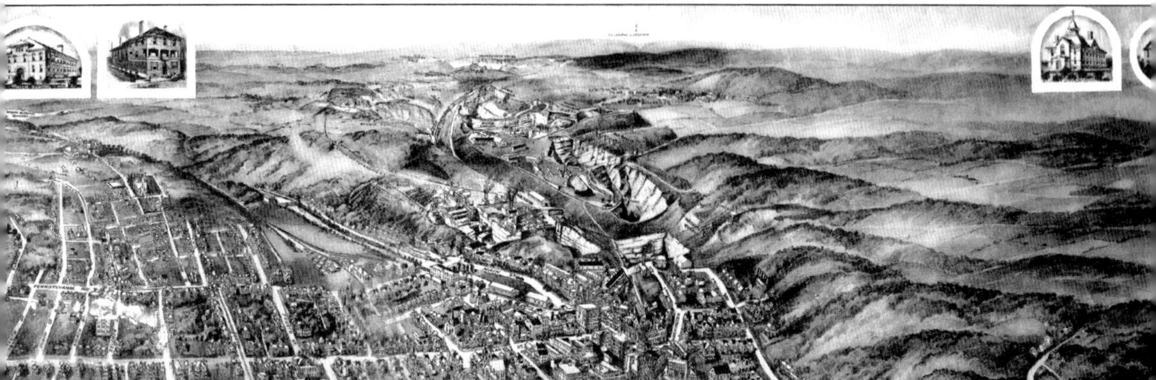

This map of Bangor, showing an aerial view of the area in 1918, can be used as a guide for places mentioned throughout the book. Note the proliferation of quarries in the background and their proximity to one another. By 1918, much of the town had expanded and developed from a sleepy community with a handful of homes and businesses into a bustling area of businesses and residences thanks to the discovery and success of the slate industry. Although there were still many changes to come, by this time, the people and businesses had become somewhat more established than in earlier days, when changes to the landscape were more frequent. (Author's collection.)

Two

Rock Solid Foundation

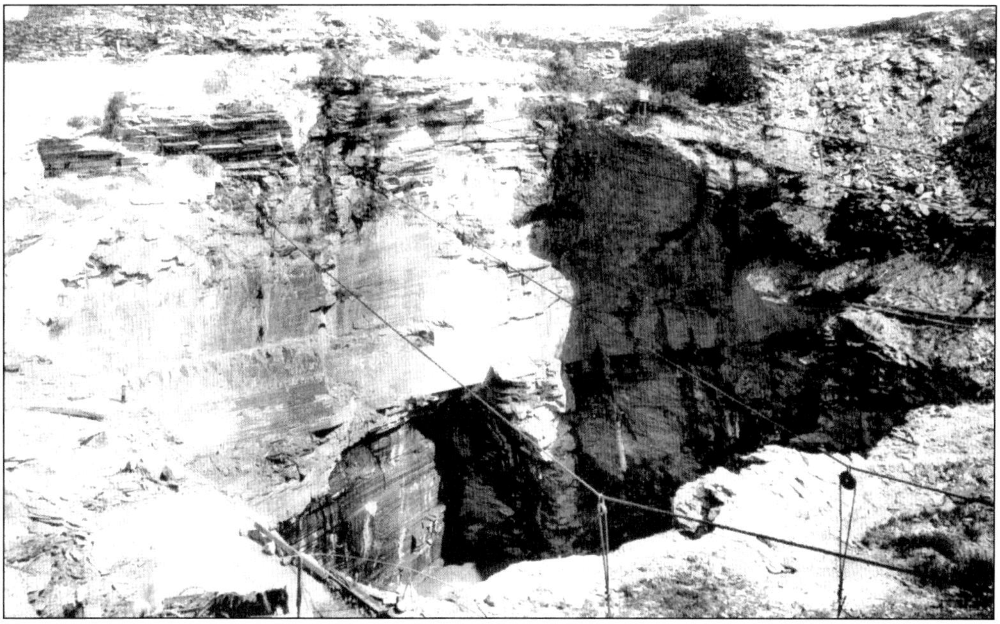

The Old Bangor Quarry is shown here around 1900. Old Bangor Quarry was one of the first quarries opened and, at one point, one of the largest quarries of the Bangor Group. Note the horse in the lower, left-hand corner. Horsepower was used to haul slate and slate waste in and out of the quarries before the invention of more modern machinery. (Courtesy NCHGS.)

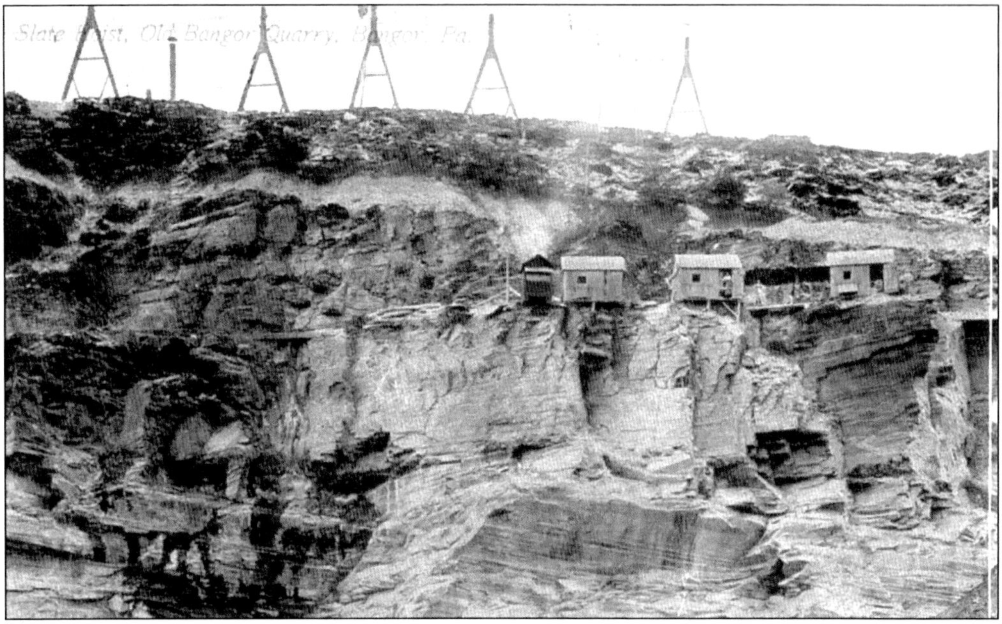

These *c.* 1910 views of the Old Bangor Quarry show slate hoist operations (above) and workers preparing newly extracted, raw blocks of slate for processing into roofing squares. Although the quarry, opened by Robert Morris Jones and Philip Labar, was responsible for helping the Bangor area to expand, the quarry itself operated only sporadically. In 1866, Labar sold his interests to Samuel Straub and Dr. Jacob P. Scholl of the Old Bangor Slate Company, and Jones served as the company superintendent. In 1924, the quarry was sold to the Amalgamated Slate Quarries in Easton, Pennsylvania. It closed for good in 1931. (Author's collection.)

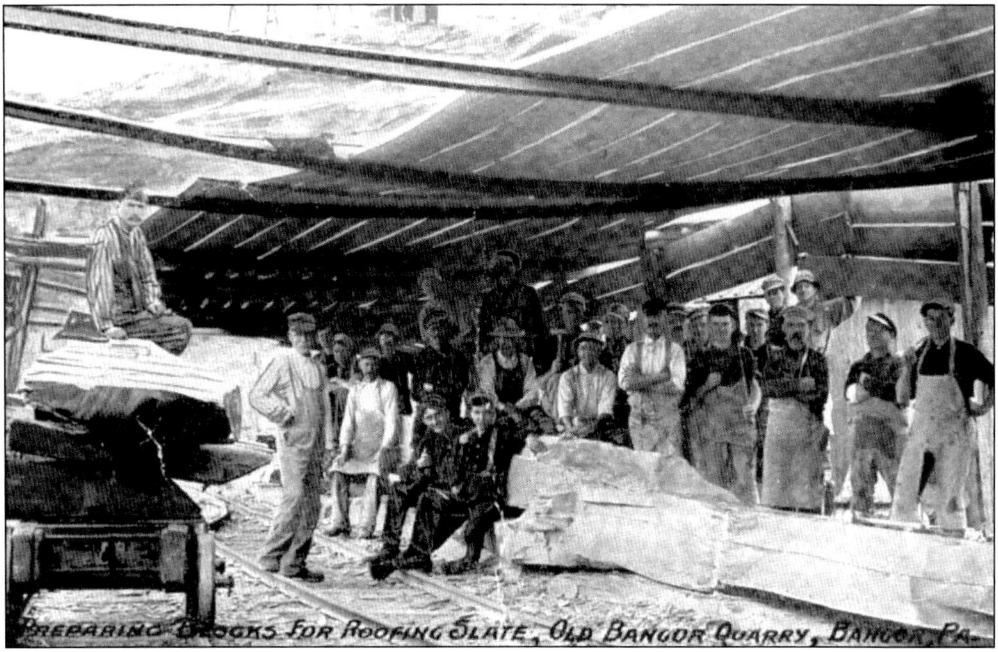

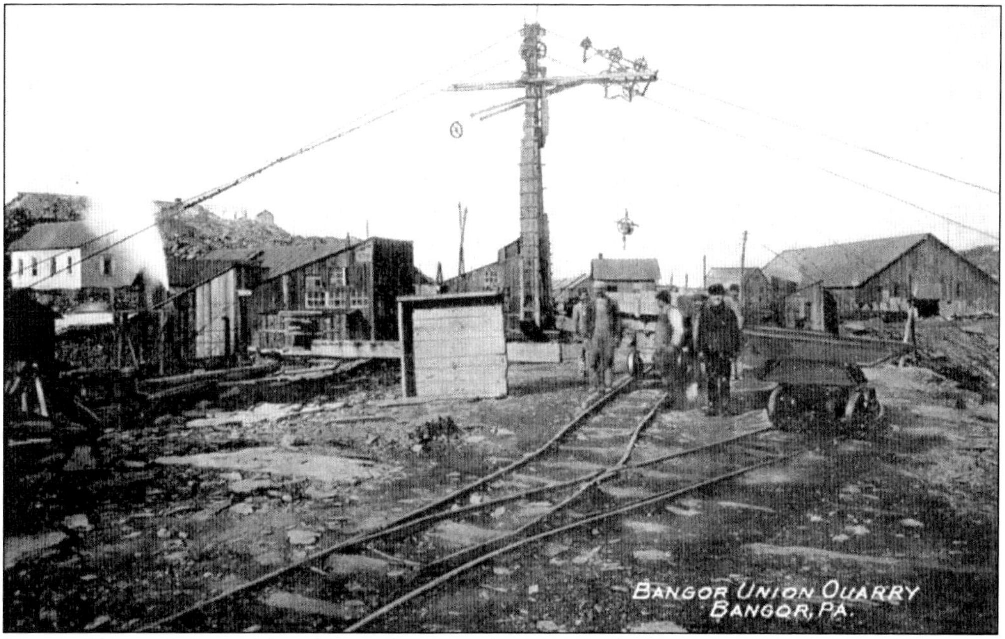

Bangor Union Quarry (above) was the second quarry to be opened in Bangor. It sat in close proximity to the Old and North Bangor Quarries and was originally called Elmira and later Wheeler Quarry. The Columbia Bangor Quarry (below) was located one mile northeast of Bangor on the Bangor–East Bangor Highway. It was opened in 1832 by Samuel Taylor and was the third-largest quarry of the Bangor Group. In 1870, it was taken over by David Howell, and in 1889, the owners were Thomas Ditchette, James Blake, and George Mutton. It closed in the 1930s after a mud slide and cave-in. (Author's collection.)

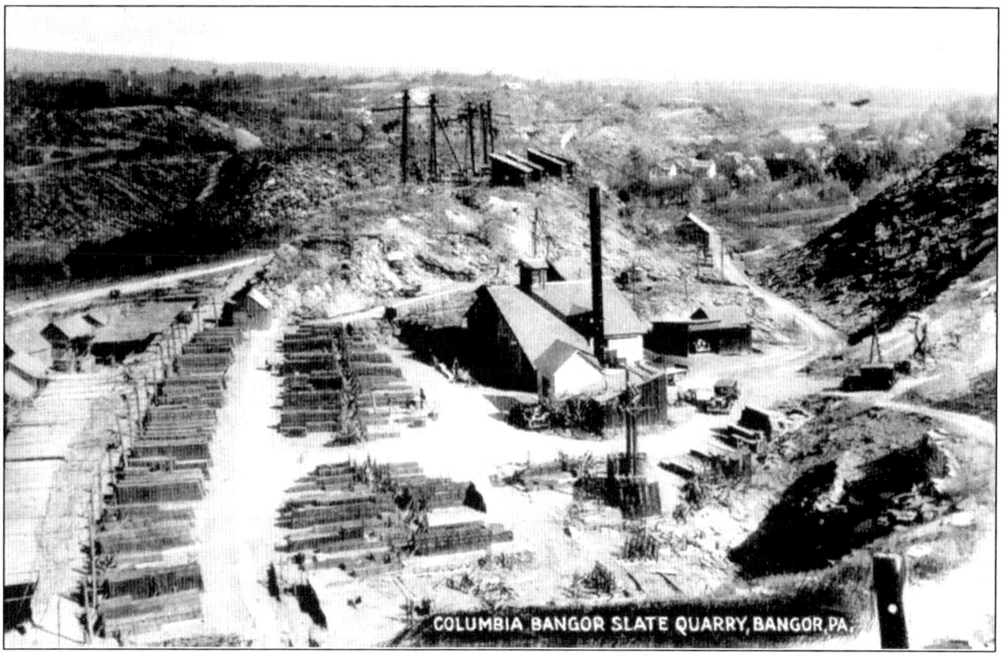

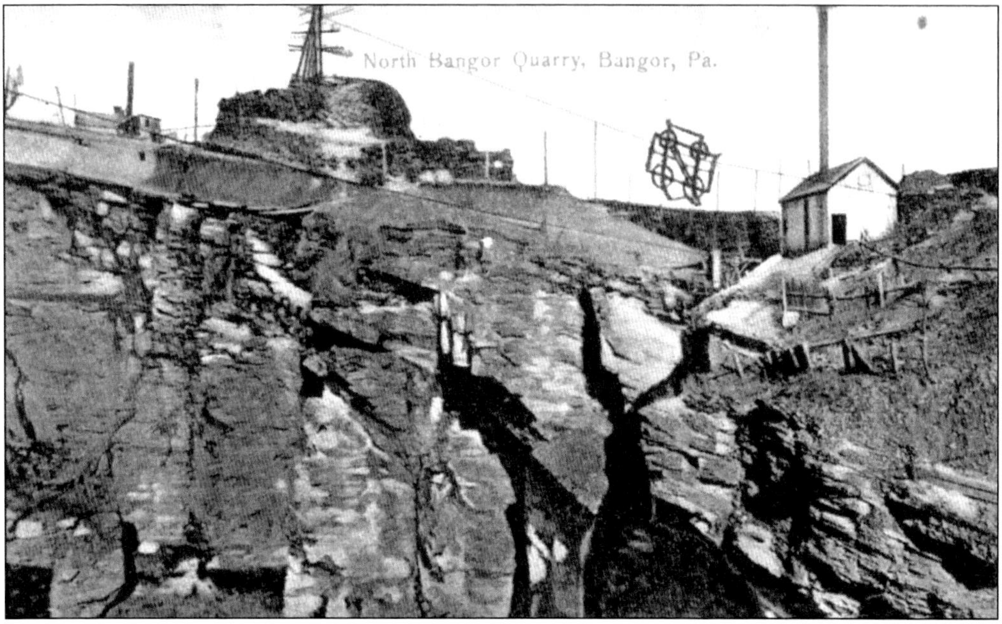

This is the North Bangor Quarry, which was opened in 1871 by Robert Morris Jones and Adam R. Reese. It was one of the longest operational quarries. Charles A. Smith, the last owner, closed the quarry for good on September 21, 1973, on his 65th birthday. Smith's father and grandfather ran the quarry before him. The quarry employed several hundred men, including the author's grandfather. (Courtesy SBHC.)

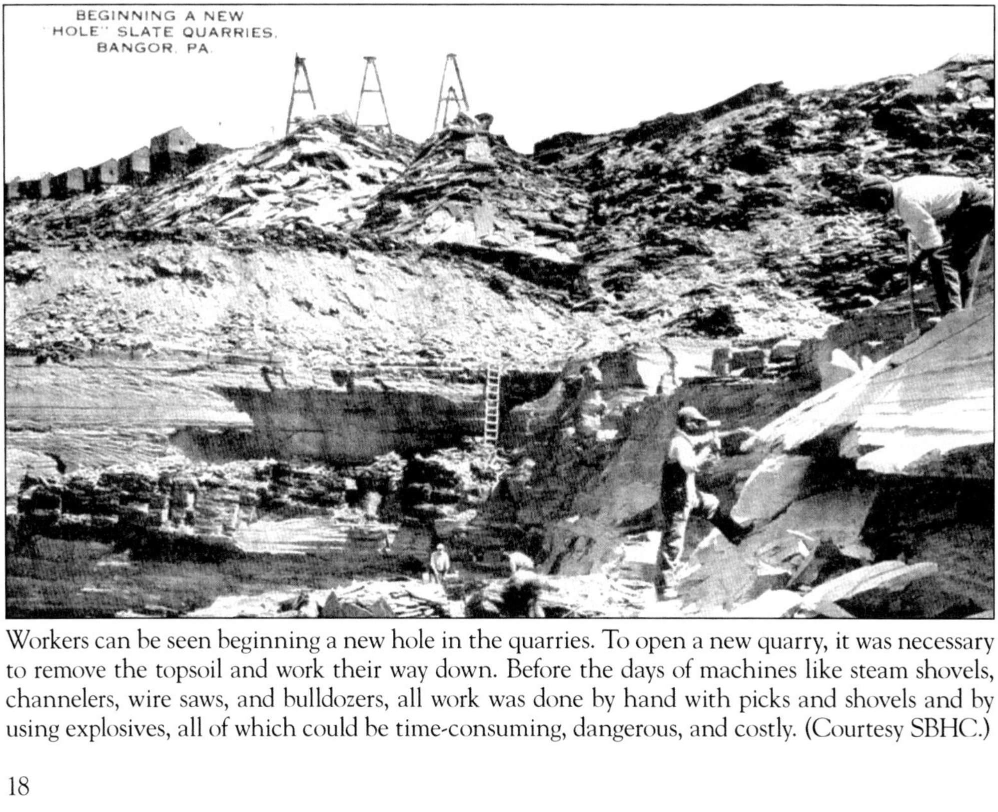

Workers can be seen beginning a new hole in the quarries. To open a new quarry, it was necessary to remove the topsoil and work their way down. Before the days of machines like steam shovels, channelers, wire saws, and bulldozers, all work was done by hand with picks and shovels and by using explosives, all of which could be time-consuming, dangerous, and costly. (Courtesy SBHC.)

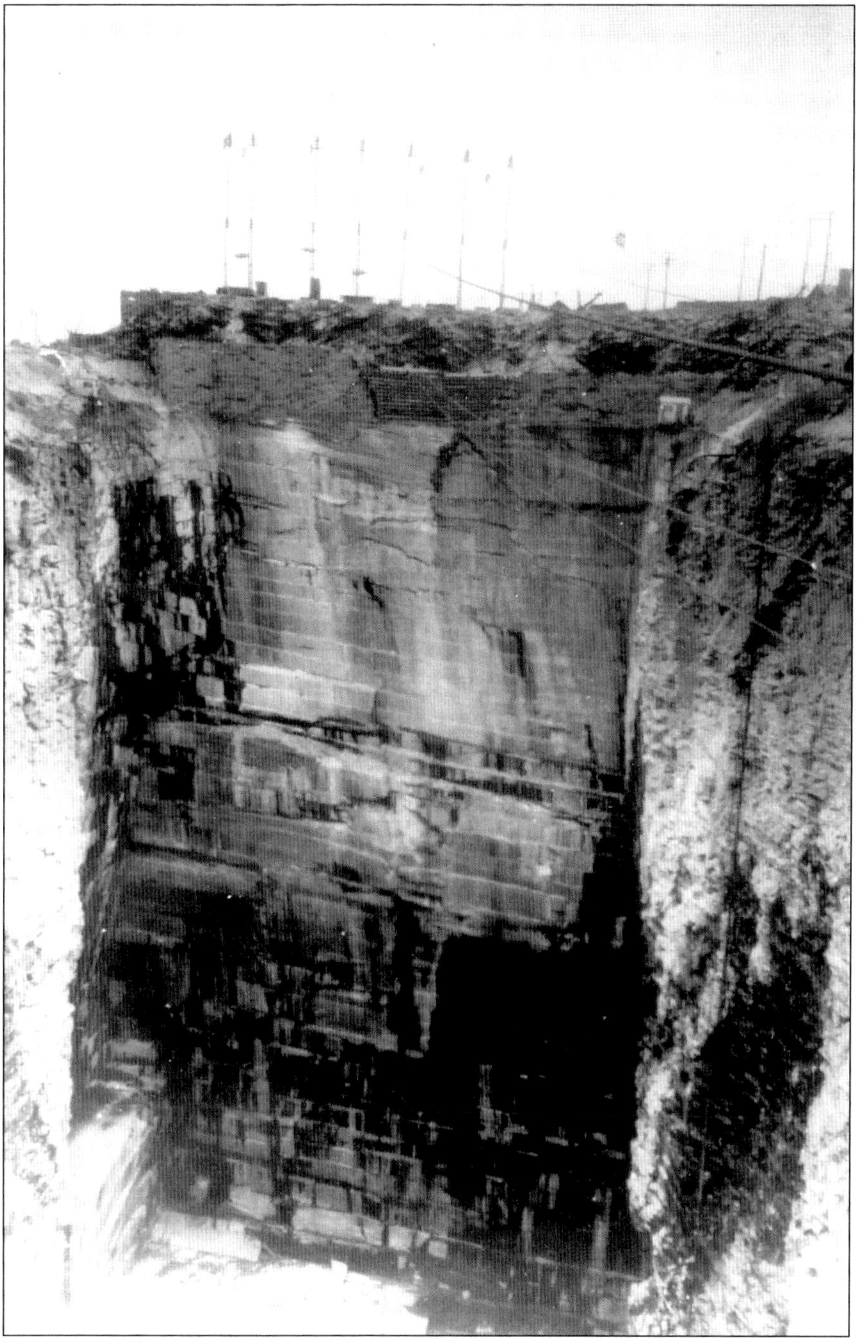

This shows the depth and beds typical of many quarries. This is likely a quarry from the Pen Argyl Group. Because quarries were dug to follow the beds, Pen Argyl quarries were generally vertical and deep, as opposed to the Bangor quarries, whose beds were wider and shallower. Note the shanty at the top of the pit on the right. This was a signaler's, or motion, shack involved in the hoisting operations. A worker in the quarry would call or motion to a "signal boy" in the shanty, usually a young boy, who would then signal the engineer that the slate block was ready to be hoisted out. The signaling was done by voice or a system of bells. (Courtesy SBM.)

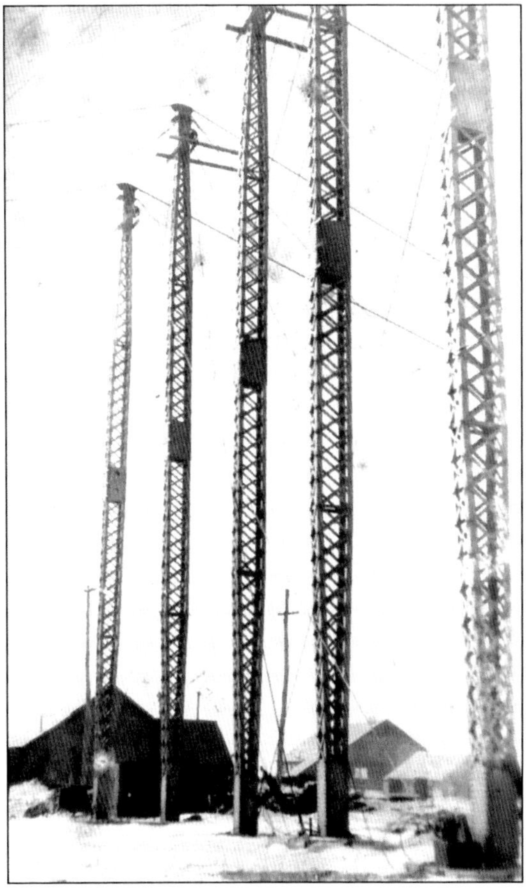

Both of these pictures show quarry landings, where slate was taken after the raw slabs were extracted from the quarries. The hoisting masts in the photograph to the left were usually made of wood or steel and were anchored by heavy ropes. A system of cables spanned the quarry opening to help remove the slate from the quarry pits. Carriers were attached to the cables and a chain was suspended from the cables directly to the blocks of slate. Before removal from the quarry pit, the blocks were marked according to their intended use as roofing shingles, millstock, blackboards, or waste. They were then loaded on trucks or four-wheel trams, shown below, and pushed by hand to the shanties or mills for processing. (Courtesy SBHC.)

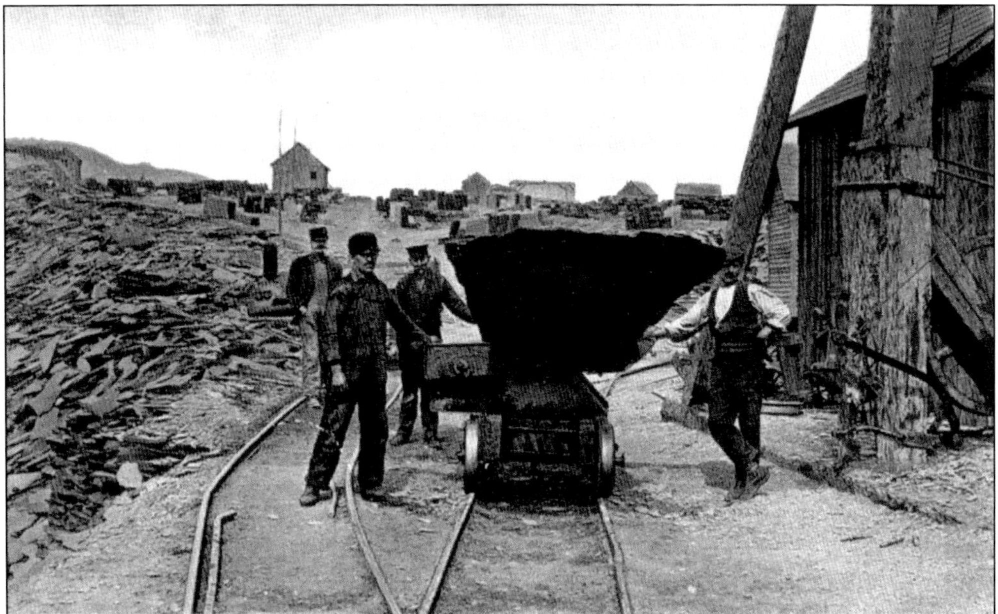

A Block of Slate on the Landing, Bangor, Pa.

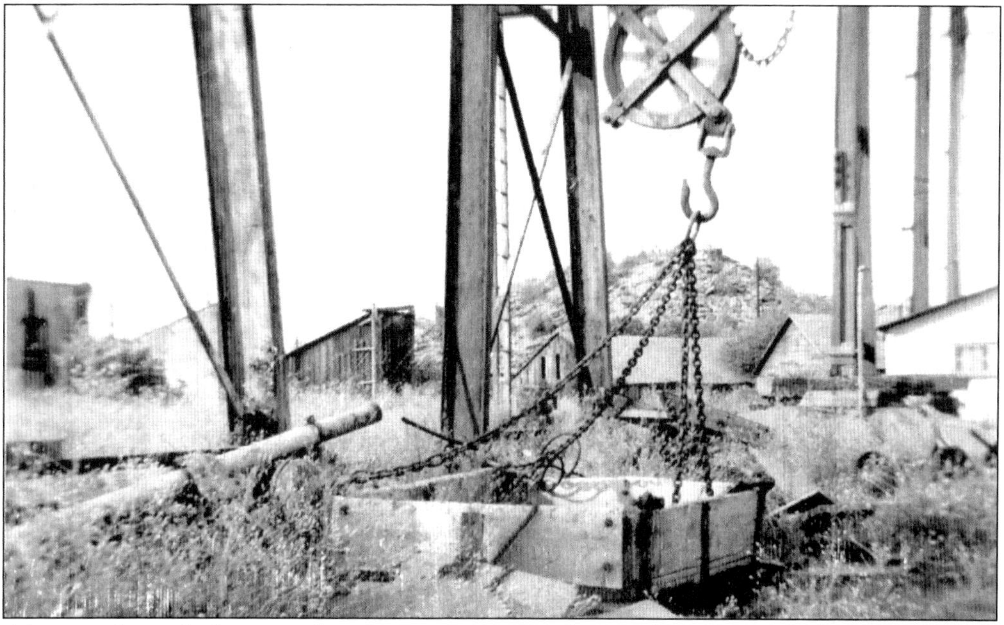

A hoisting box, which was used to transport men in and out of the quarry pits, is shown here. The boxes were sometimes called man boxes. The boxes were attached to a hoisting cable and several men would generally stand inside of them and be lowered into the quarry, often times swinging and swaying. (Courtesy BPL.)

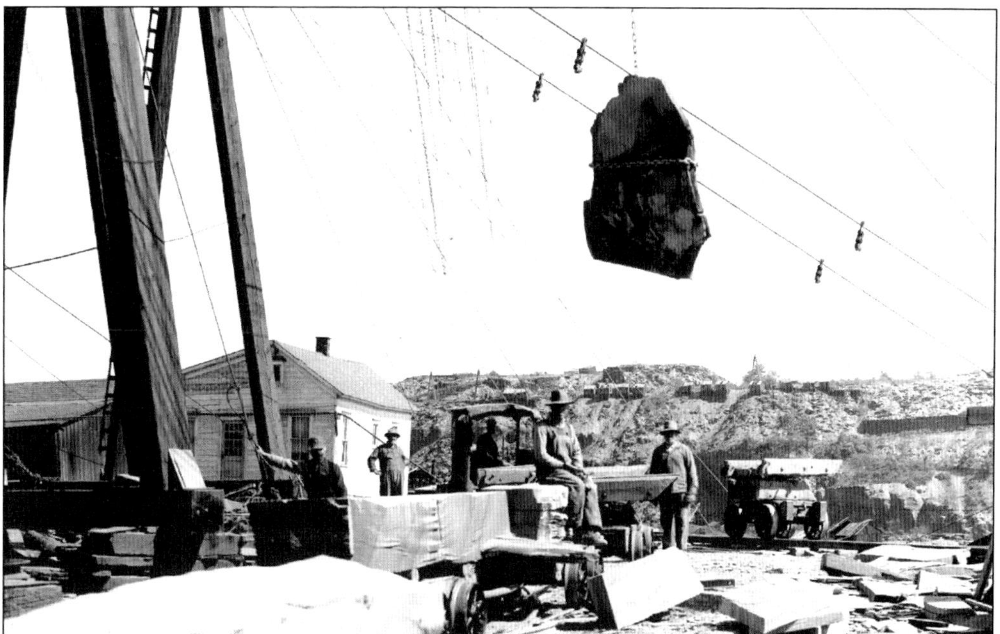

Workers pose for the camera at an unknown quarry. The yard shows both unworked slabs of slate on the left and a newly extracted piece of slate on the carriers and hoisting cables. The slate was then taken to the mill on the left or to the shanties on the hill, where it was split, trimmed, and finished into products like roofing shingles or blackboards. (Courtesy BPL.)

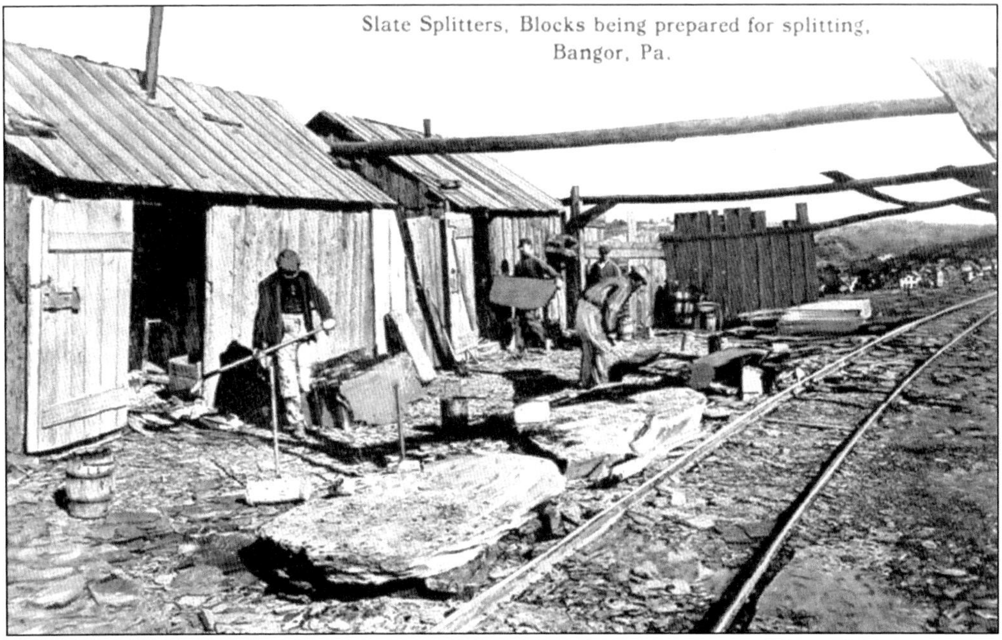

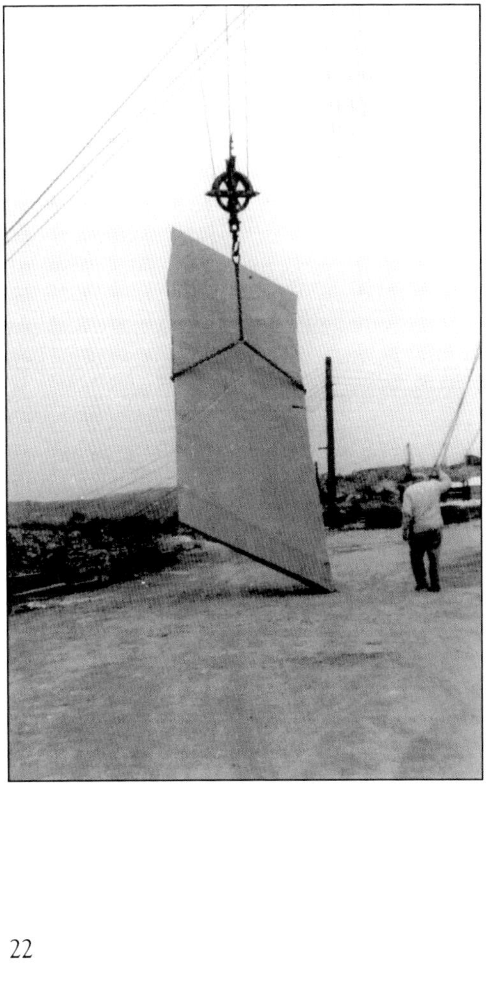

After slate was extracted from the quarries, the rough slabs were given to splitters. After the splitters swabbed the blocks with water, a wide-bladed, flexible chisel was worked into the slate along its cleavage, the structure of the rock that permits splitting, and tapped with a mallet. In the photograph below, a worker guides a block of slate to its destination for further processing. The slabs of slate could easily weigh anywhere from three to seven tons. (Above, courtesy SBHC; left, courtesy SBM.)

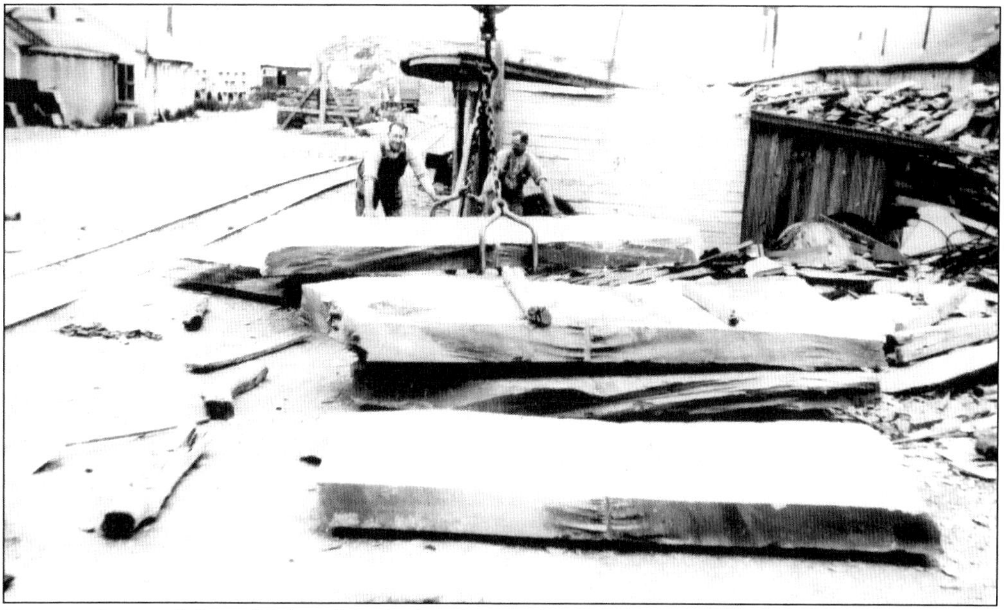

Herman Segetti, left, and Edward Oxford, right, are shown at the old blackboard mill in 1925. The blackboard mill was located on the grounds of the North Bangor Quarry along North Main Street in Bangor. The bottom photograph shows, from left to right, Danny Tedesco, George Stoddard, and Edward Oxford at the mill. The Mack "Bull-Dog" solid wheel truck in the background was used to take 28 square feet of slate to the railroad in one shot before the days of tractor trailers. (Courtesy SBM.)

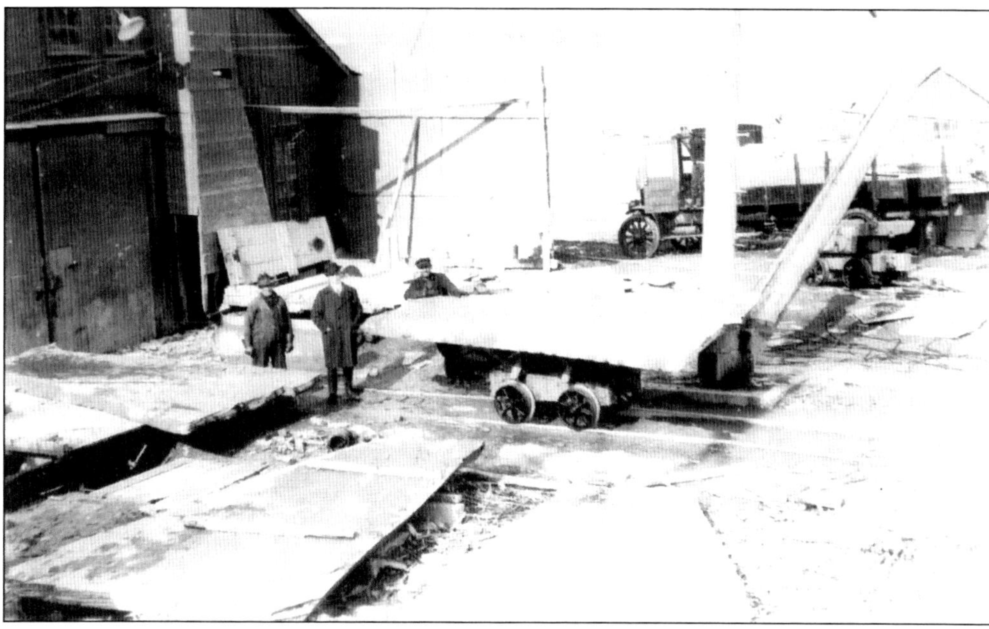

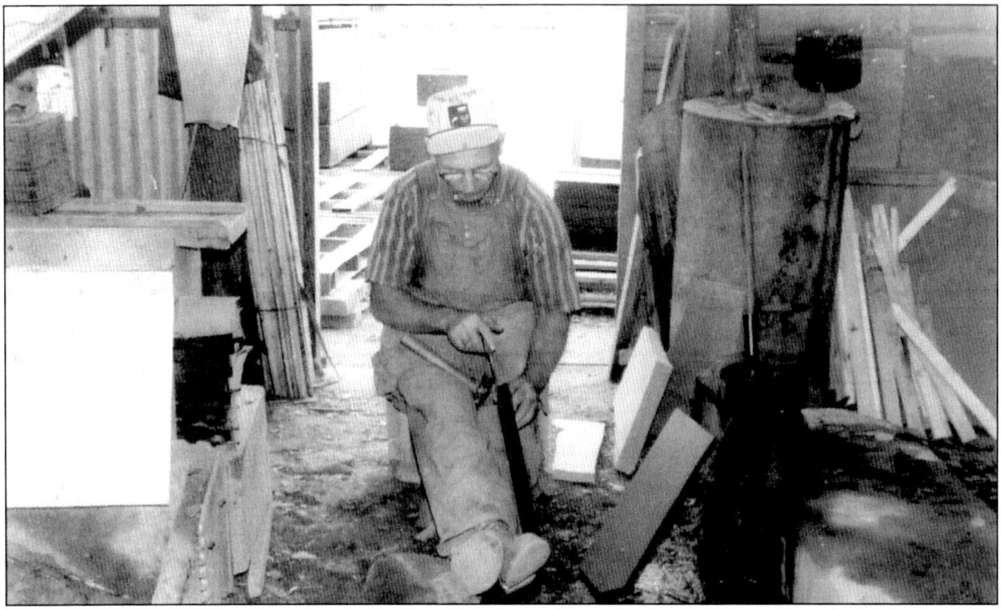

A worker, perhaps Tisiano Ulliana, is shown splitting slate at a roofing and flagging mill operation in 1965. It was customary for splitters to sit on a low stool, like the one shown here, and lean the slate against their leg, the smoothest side up. A good piece of slate, in the hands of a skilled splitter, could be split with a few taps of a hammer and chisel. (Courtesy SBM.)

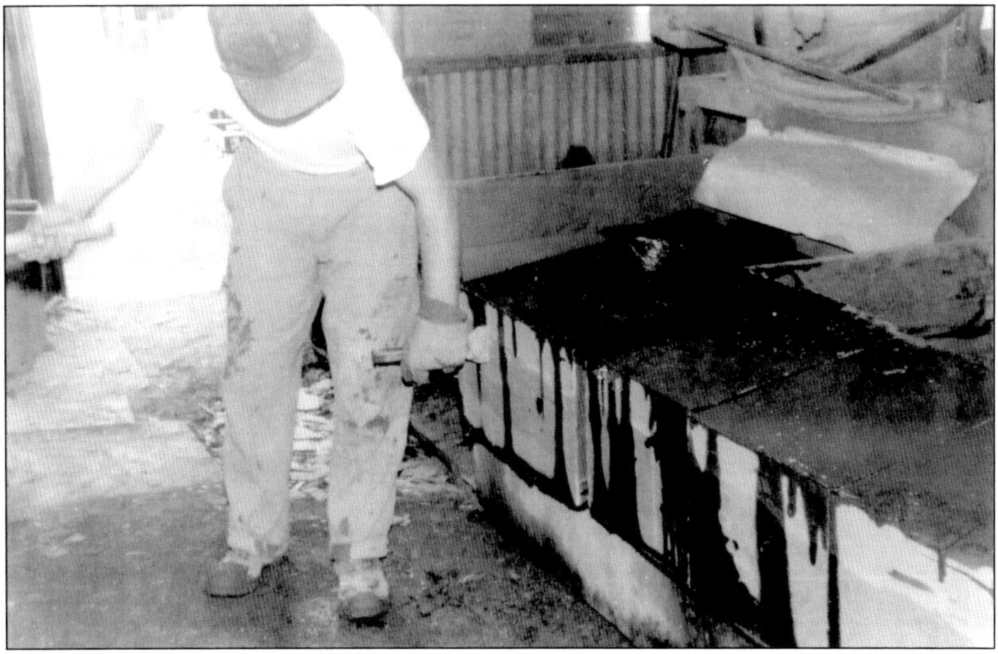

This unknown worker can also be seen splitting slate. Note the water on the blocks. It was necessary to keep the slate wet at all times for it to be split properly. This made for damp working conditions, particularly in the early days of quarrying, when health problems related to the cold and dampness were not uncommon. (Courtesy SBM.)

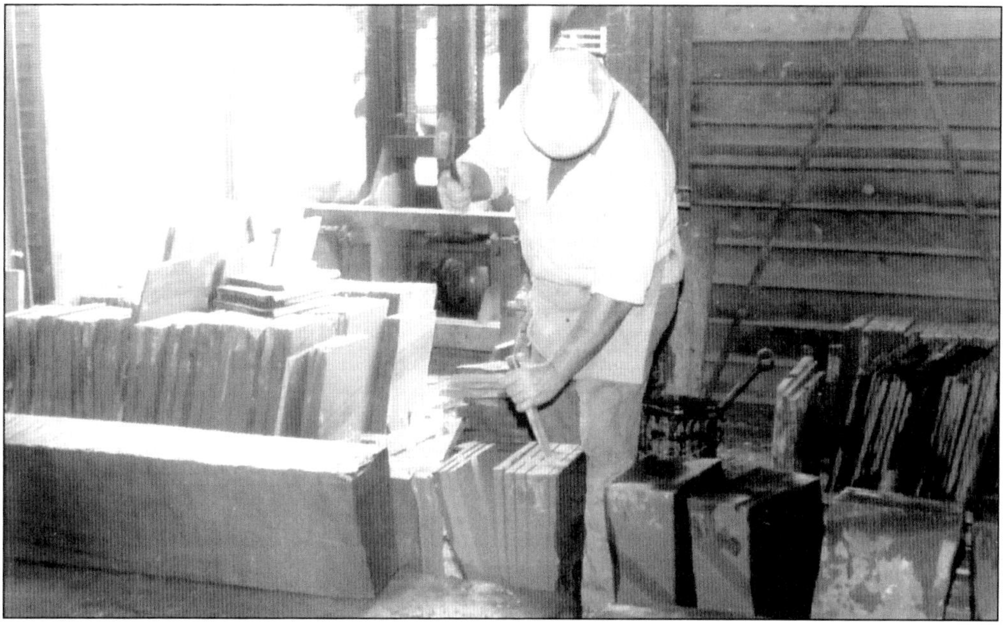

A worker is shown here splitting ribbon flagging, irregular pieces of regular thickness. Ribbons were caused by a large concentration of carbon and were desirable for millstock and decorative items only. Ribbons appeared as dark streaks, which interfered with the smooth one-color surfaces like those on blackboards or roofing shingles. Ribbons disintegrated more rapidly than the rest of the slate, which also made them undesirable. (Courtesy SBM.)

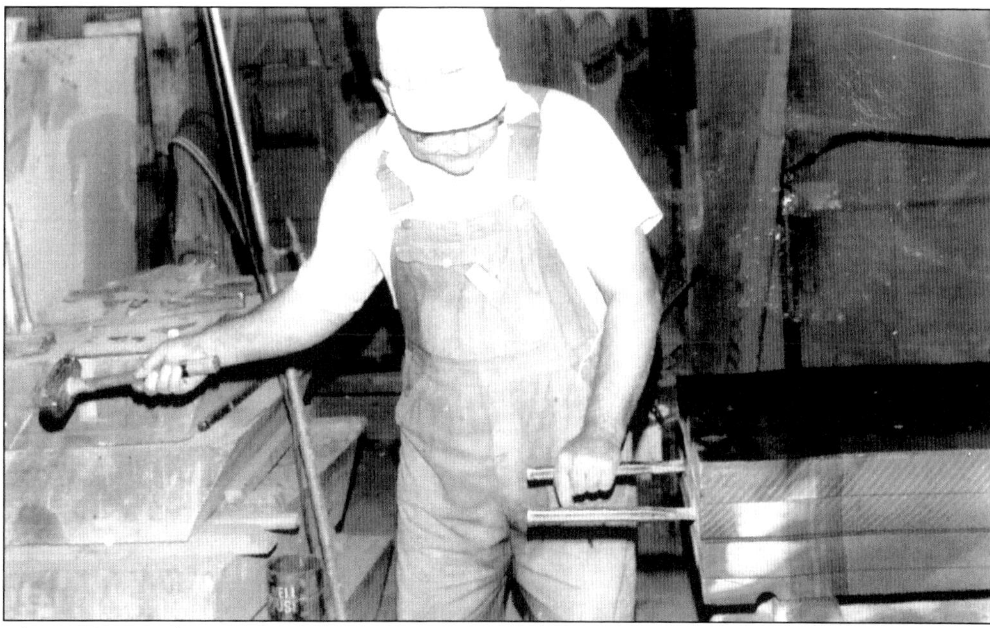

This worker is splitting structural slate. Structural slate was slate other than roofing shingles, such as blackboards, that could be used for homes and businesses. Bangor slate was used for an amazing range of items that included blackboards, fireplace mantels, steps, and even urinals and burial vaults. Structural slate was also split with hammers and chisels, but the dimensions did not require the thinness of roofing slate. (Courtesy SBM.)

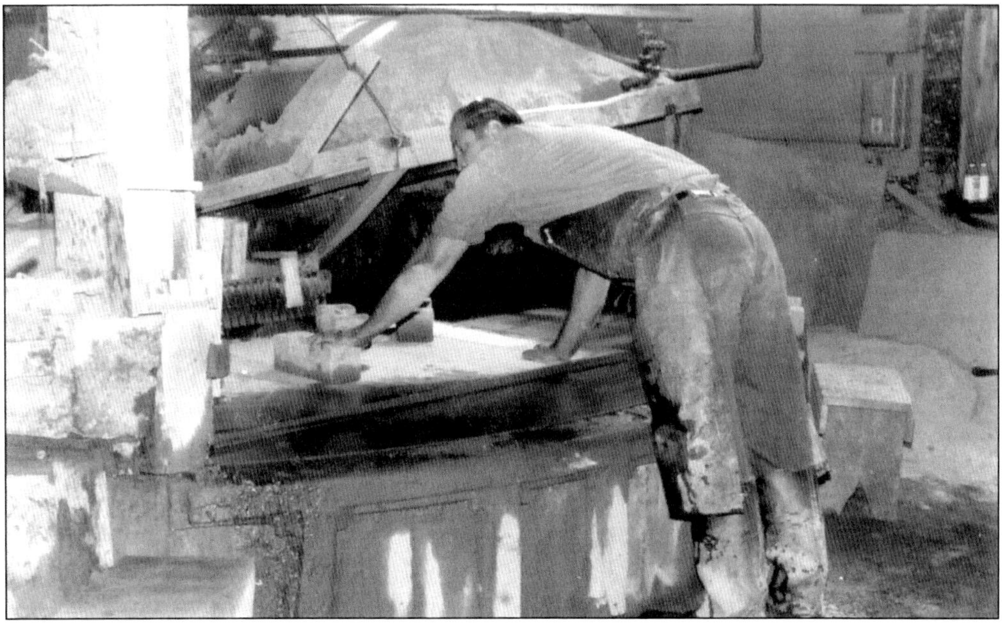

A worker is seen in the photograph above sand rubbing structural slate by hand at a rubbing bed. The sand acted as an abrasive that was used to smooth and polish the slate and can be seen here in the form of a polishing stone. This buffing process was later done by machine. In the photograph below, a Carborundum wheel is used to cut slate to a smaller dimension. The axle in the background allows the wheel to move back and forth. (Courtesy SBM.)

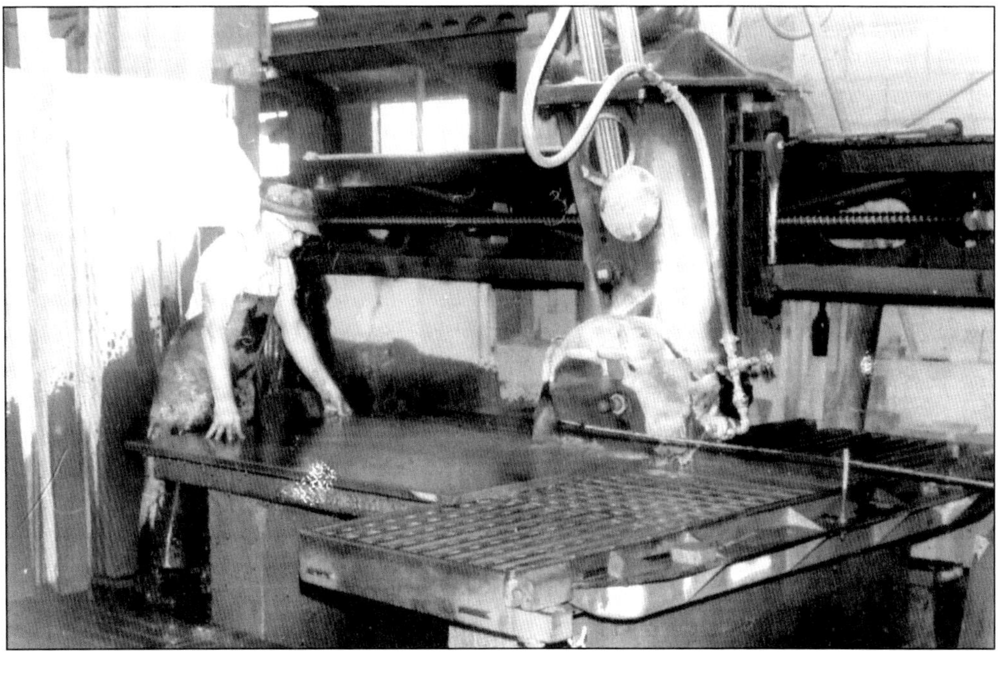

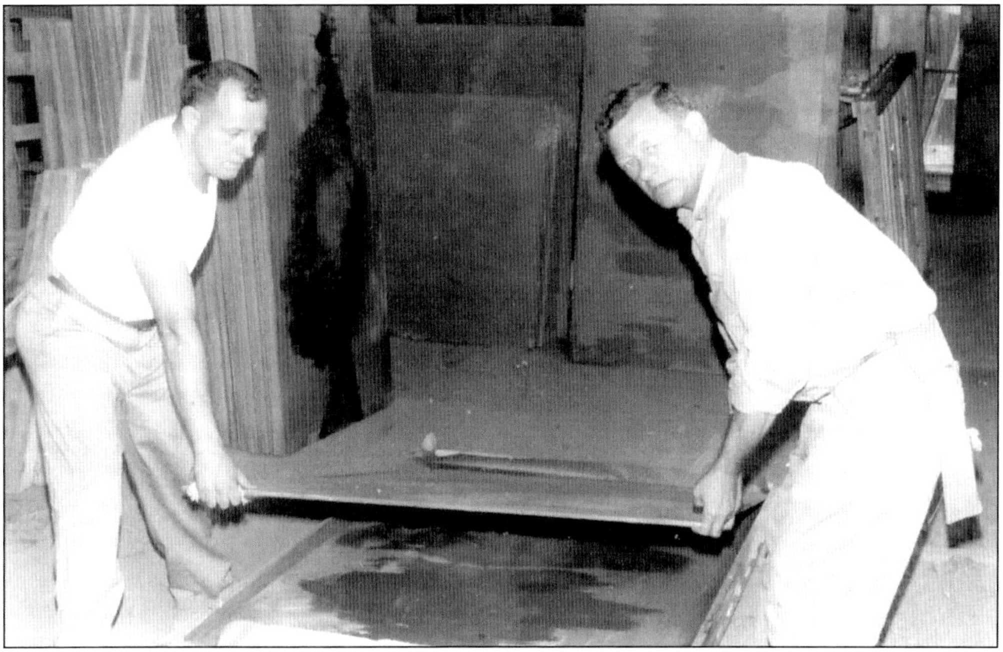

Workers are shown finishing blackboards around 1960. Blackboards were split to their desired thickness, like roofing slates, but greater care was needed because the slabs were generally larger in size. Blackboards were stored upright in racks but needed to be crated and shipped more cautiously to avoid damage. They, along with other mill products, were usually stored in rooms or separate quarters on the premises that were connected to the factory by rail. Bangor blackboards were considered some of the best in the world. One educational journal from the 1930s recommended them for the classroom because they were "likely to outlast the school building." (Courtesy SBM.)

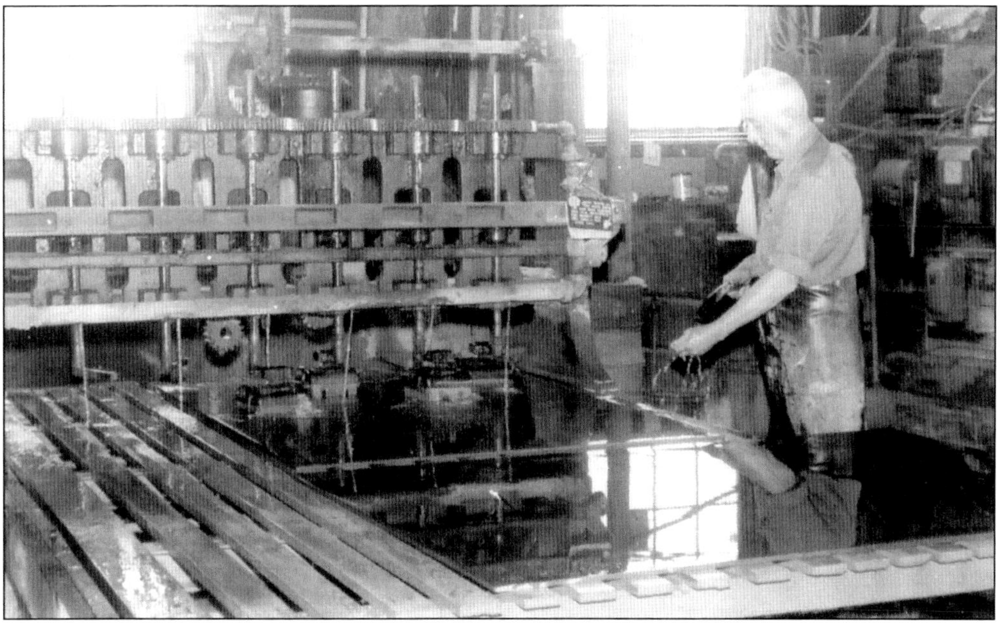

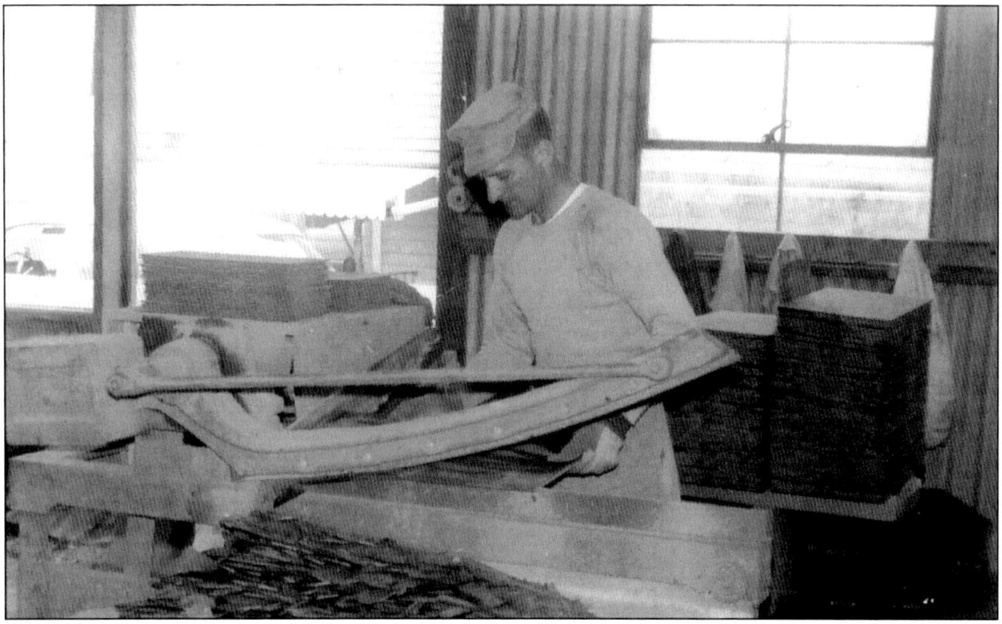

A worker is seen here trimming, or dressing, slate, a process that was done after the slate had been split. The splitter's untrimmed slate or chips were given to the trimmer, who cut them to required lengths. The trimming machine consisted of a long blade that was operated by a foot pedal. Metal plates helped gauge the dimensions. The foot pedal was eventually replaced by power-driven machines. (Courtesy SBM.)

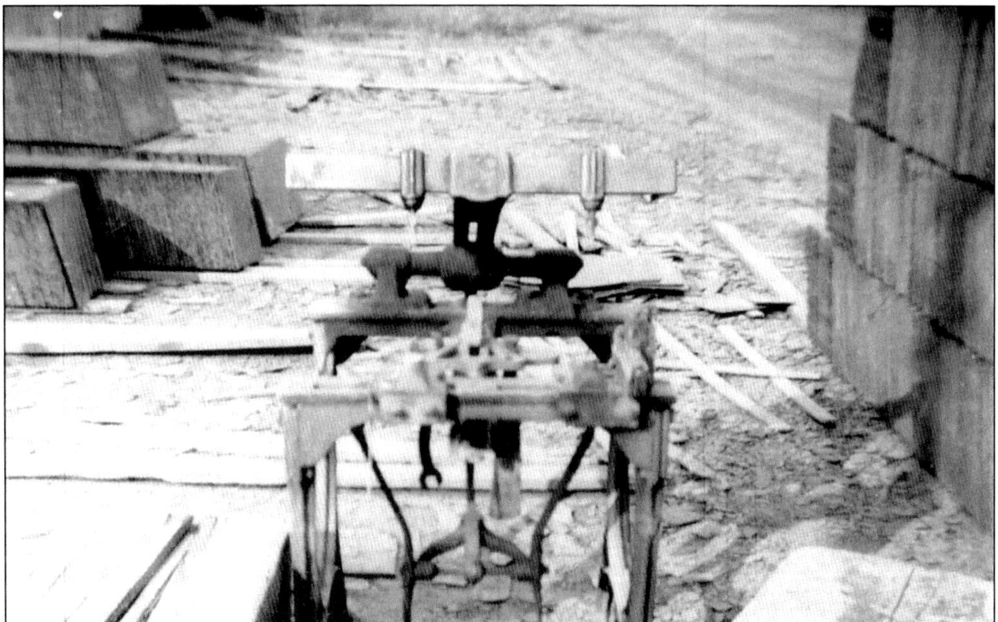

After slate was trimmed, it was punched with holes, using a punch press like the one here, which was also operated by a foot pedal. Two metal punches poked holes in the slate about a third of the way down and approximately two inches from the side. Nails were later sunk into the slate so it could be fastened to the roof. (Courtesy BPL.)

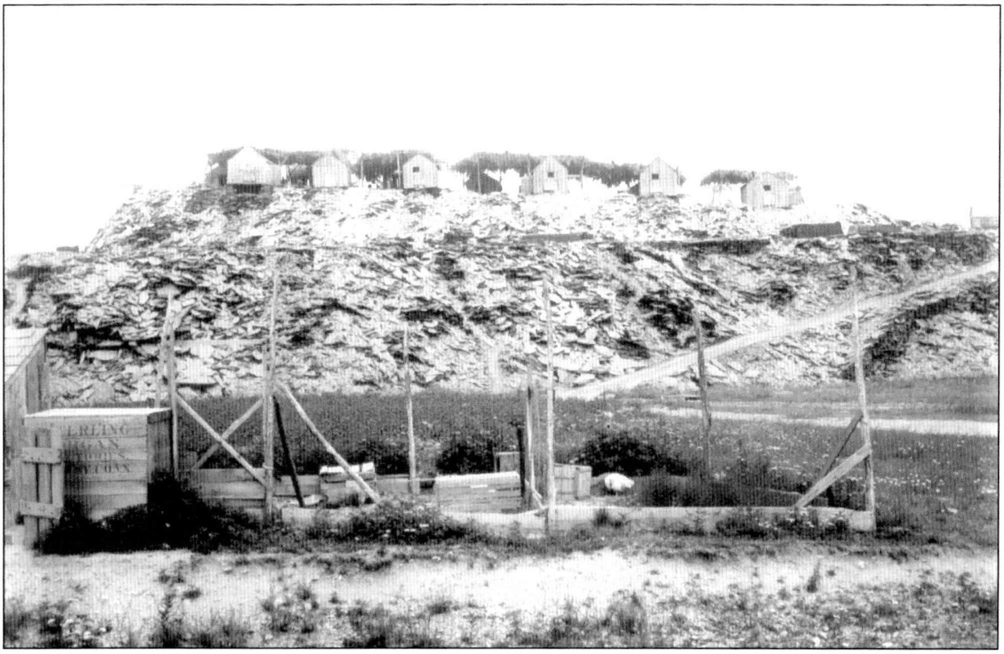

Shanties were always present in the quarries. They were typically 10-by-10-foot structures that sat on top of the waste piles at the edge of the quarries. They sat some distance from the larger, structural slate mills, so as to distribute the waste from the two processes. They were simply constructed, so they could be moved or raised as needed. (Courtesy NCHGS.)

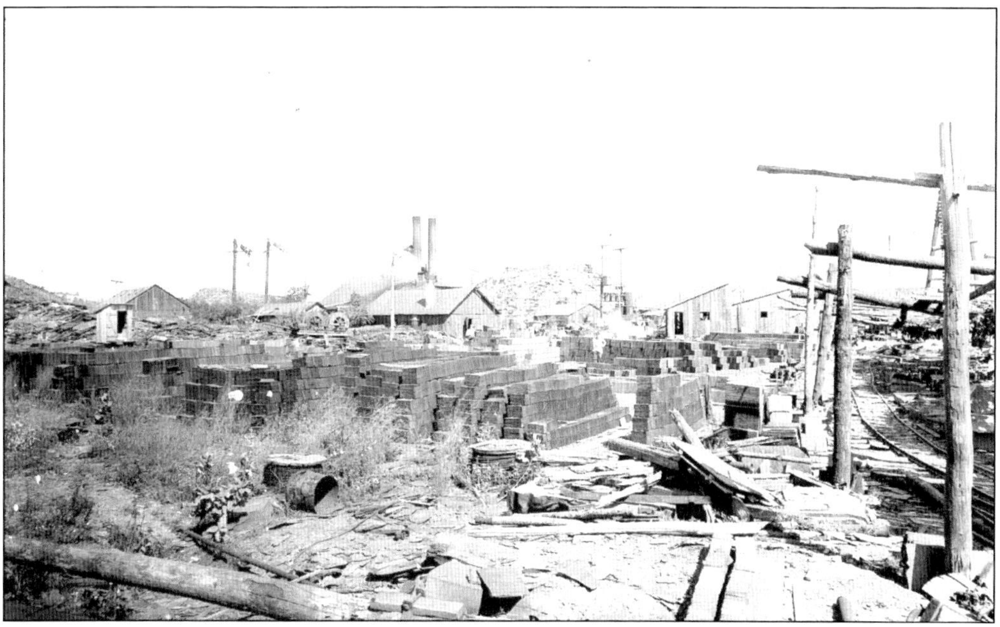

The roofing shingles seen here have been cut to the standard three-sixteenths of an inch and are awaiting shipment to various markets. Roofing slate reached its peak production in 1903, but Pennsylvania continued to be one of the biggest producers of slate, with production in excess of $5 million. (Courtesy BPL.)

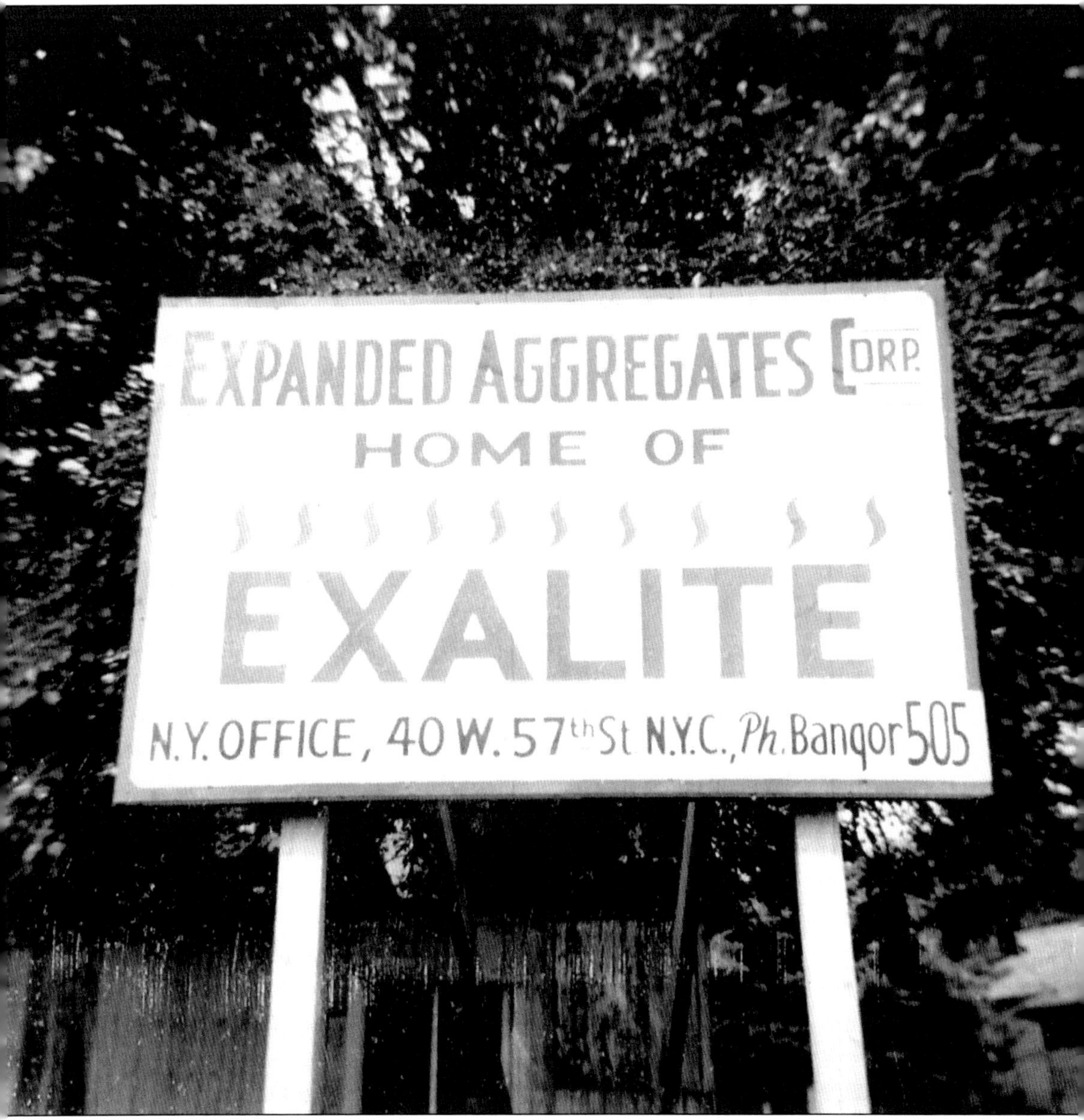

This sign advertises Exalite, a new product that grew out of experimentation at Pennsylvania State University in 1947. Exalite was produced from slate waste that was crushed and then conveyed by belts to furnaces, where it was heated at high temperatures. The extreme temperatures would cause the crushed slate to pop like popcorn. The end result was a lightweight product used as an aggregate for concrete and in mineral wools, pottery, and clay products. (Courtesy BPL.)

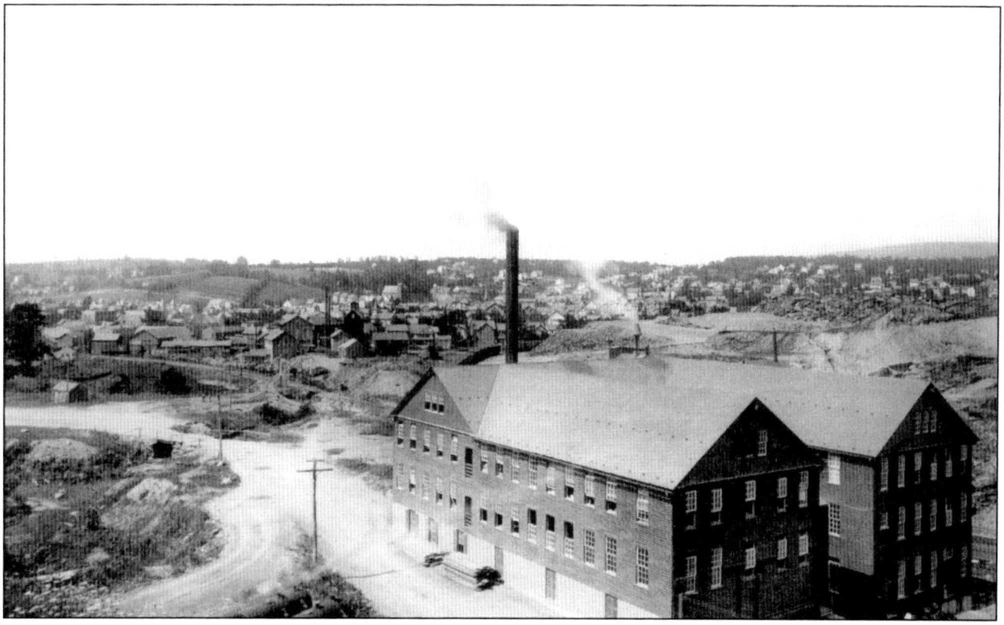

Opened in 1881, the Hyatt Slate Factory was located on the East Bangor Highway, near Washington Quarry. The Hyatt was one of several slate factories in the area that produced personal-sized blackboards and structural slate items. A similar factory, the Griffin Factory, operated in Flicksville. The Hyatt burned three weeks after it opened and then again years later, after which it closed for good. (Courtesy NCHGS.)

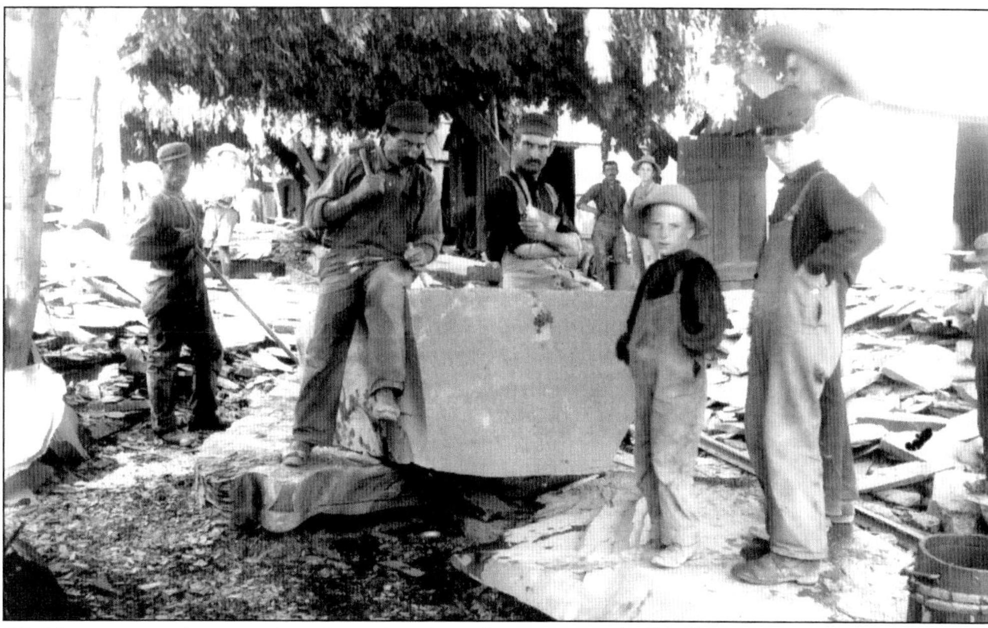

Children were often employed in the slate factories as "hollibobbers," sometimes spelled as hollybobbers. Their job was to make the slate splitter's job easier by keeping the slate wet. This was done by wrapping a piece of burlap around a stick, dipping it in water, and swabbing the blocks. The Hyatt Slate Factory and Griffin Slate Factory employed many child laborers. (Courtesy NCHGS.)

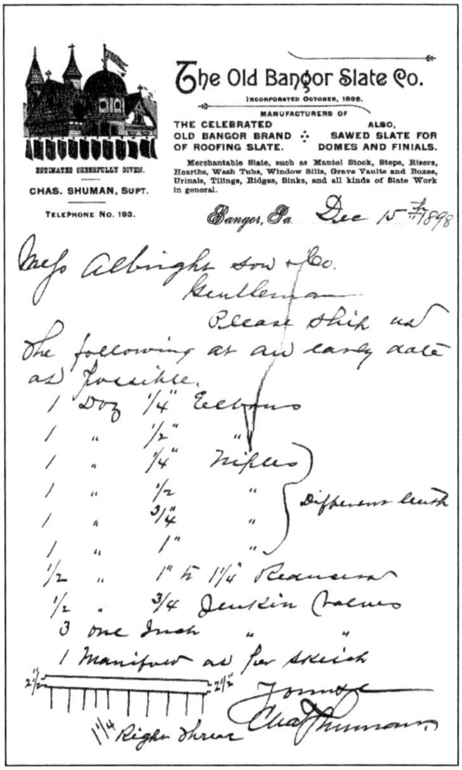

The Old Bangor Slate Co.

Incorporated October, 1886.

Manufacturers of

THE CELEBRATED OLD BANGOR BRAND OF ROOFING SLATE.

ALSO, SAWED SLATE FOR DOMES AND FINIALS.

Merchantable Slate, such as Mantel Stock, Steps, Risers, Hearths, Wash Tubs, Window Sills, Grave Vaults and Boxes, Urinals, Tilings, Ridges, Sinks, and all kinds of Slate Work in general.

Estimates Cheerfully Given.

CHAS. SHUMAN, Supt.

Telephone No. 193.

Bangor, Pa. Dec 15th 1898

Messrs Albright Son & Co.

Gentlemen

Please ship us the following at an early date as possible.

1 Doz 1/4" Elbows

1 " 1/2" "

1 " 1/4" Nipples

1 " 1/2 "

1 " 3/4 " } Different length

1 " 1" "

1/2 " 1" to 1 1/4 Reducers

1/2 " 3/4 Jenkin Valves

3 one Inch " "

1 Manifold as per sketch

2 1/2 — 2 1/2

1 1/4 Right threads

Yours &c

Chas Shuman

This is an original invoice from one of Bangor's slate factories, the Old Bangor Slate Company, dated December 15, 1898. It shows the array of structural products that were produced, including decorative, scalloped slate used on roofing domes of some of the houses and businesses, which can still be seen in the area. Bangor founder, Robert Morris Jones, was superintendent of this company in 1866. (Author's collection.)

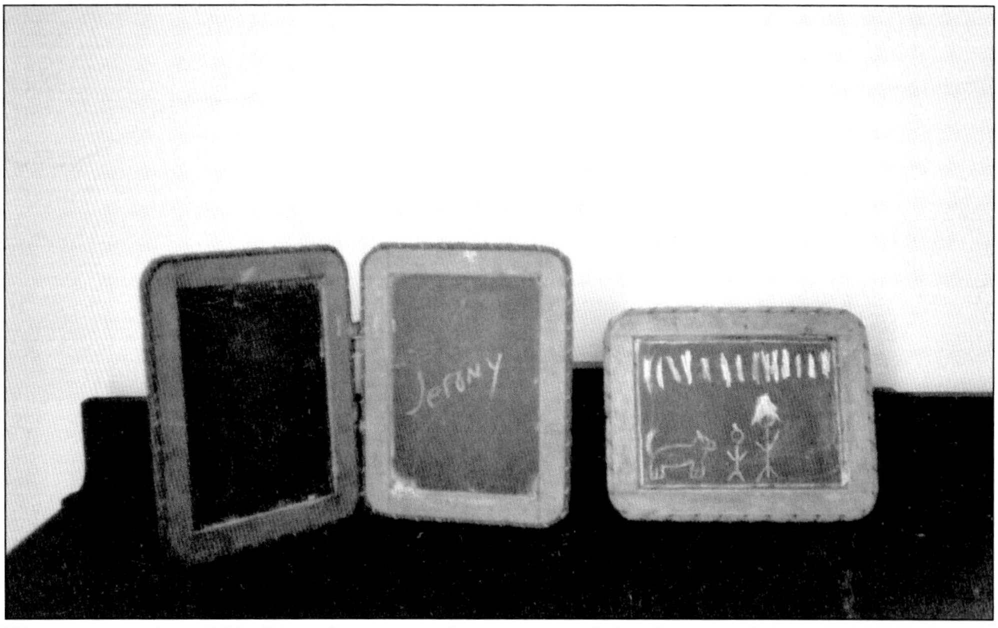

These personal-sized blackboards were made in many of the factories. Many times, they were more readily available than paper, and children used them in school, writing on them with slate pencils. Slates trimmed with ribbon, like those here, were quieter when closed. The board of health eventually outlawed use of these slates, deeming them unsanitary because the children would spit on them to clean them. (Author's collection.)

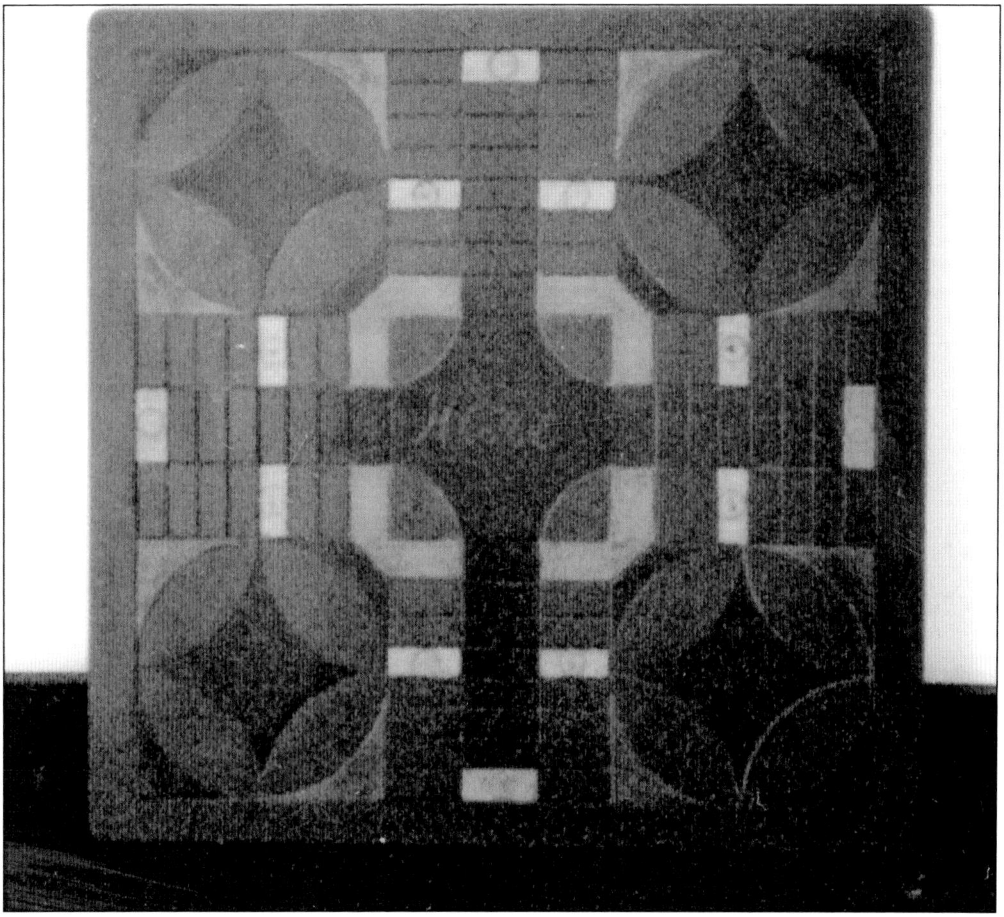

Slate was not always used just for commercial purposes. "Slaters" often used slate to make decorative items like this mosaic (above) and a slate bible (below). Items such as these, as well as beautifully, intricately carved fans, were often given as gifts or as a sign of affection. The more detailed and intricately carved the item was, the greater the skill of the crafter. (Author's collection.)

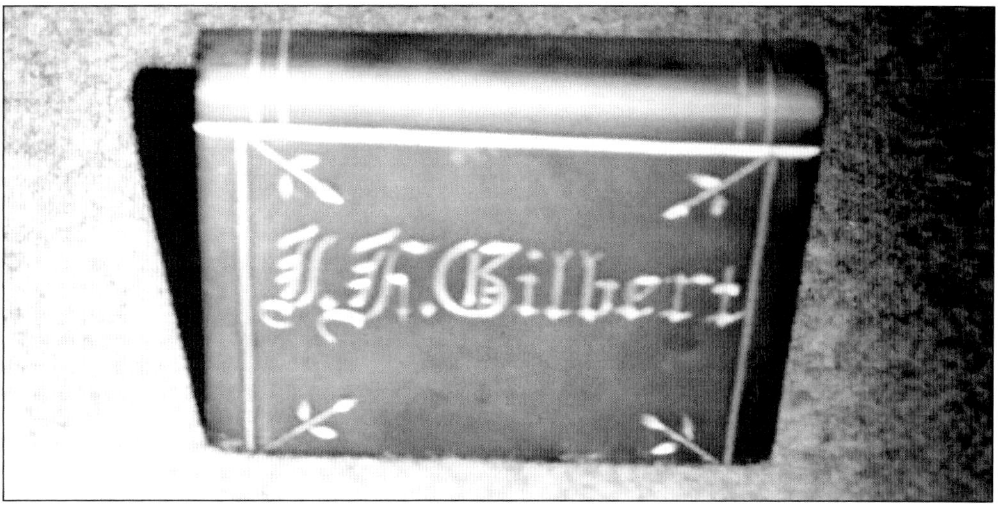

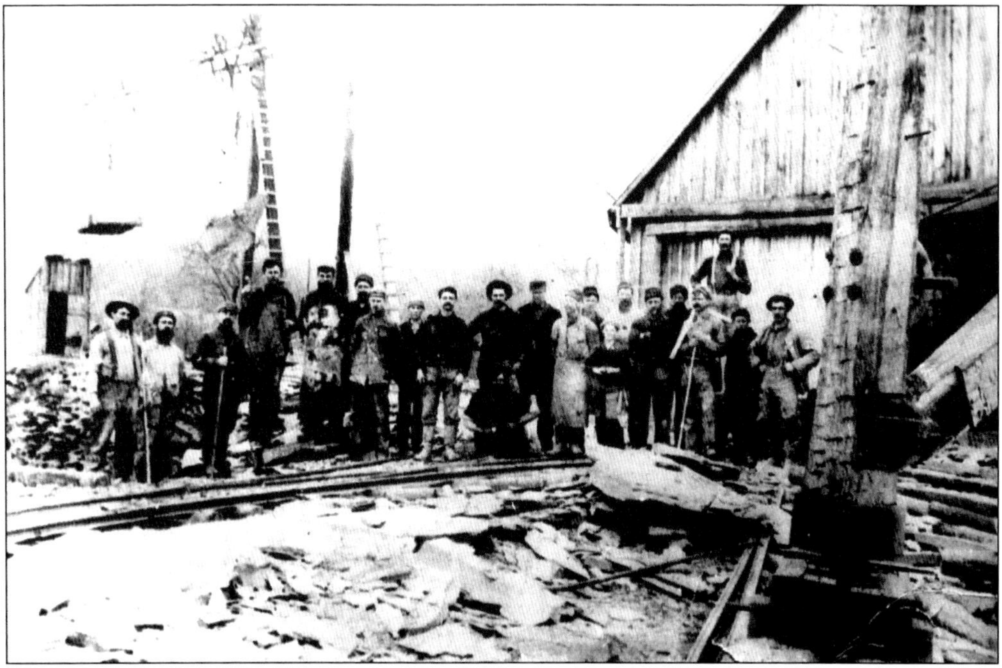

Workers stand outside an old blackboard mill (above) around 1900. The mill was located on the premises of the North Bangor Quarry. Note the hollibobbers, or water boys, among the men. A fire destroyed the old mill, and it was replaced with the stone structure below, which sat to the left of the old building. Workers are seen in the front yard of the new mill in 1940, along with the owners, Mahlon Stoddard (second row, left) and George Stoddard (right). (Courtesy SBM.)

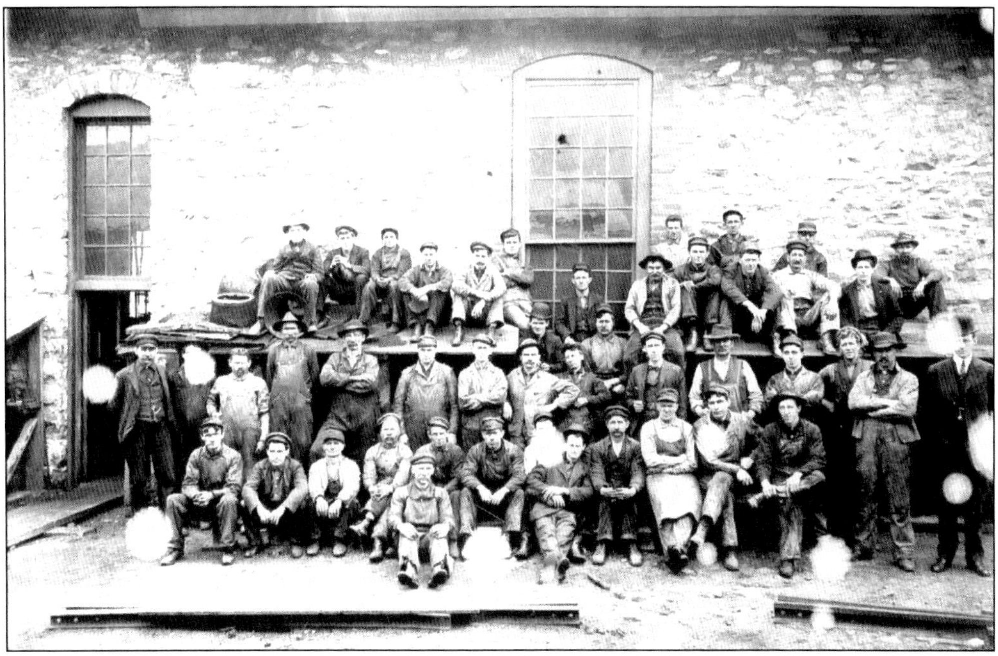

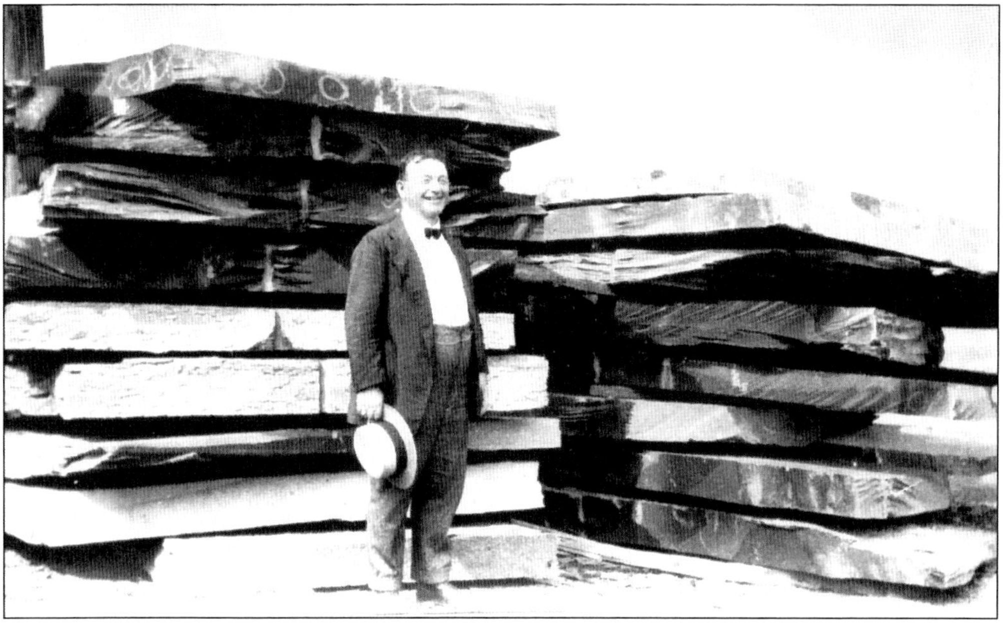

David Stoddard (above), operator of the Stoddard Quarry in Pen Argyl, is seen here around 1910. This quarry actually operated on the grounds of the Albion Quarry (below), with whom Stoddard had business interests, as the stone in his quarry came from Albion. Albion was one of the deepest quarries in Pen Argyl, measuring some 600 feet at one point in its operation. The innovative and advanced quarry was one of the first quarries to use a bar channeler in 1893, which replaced explosives as a way of getting slate from the pits. It also used steel masts on its hoisting cables. At its peak operation in 1925, it employed over 300 men and had a payroll of over $300,000. It also produced over one million square feet of blackboard. (Courtesy SBM.)

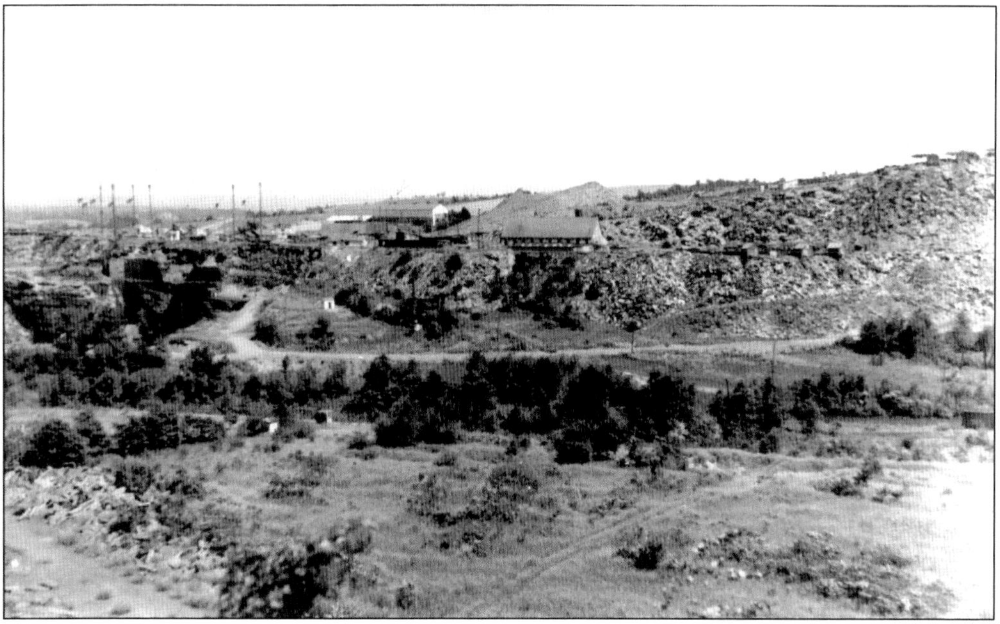

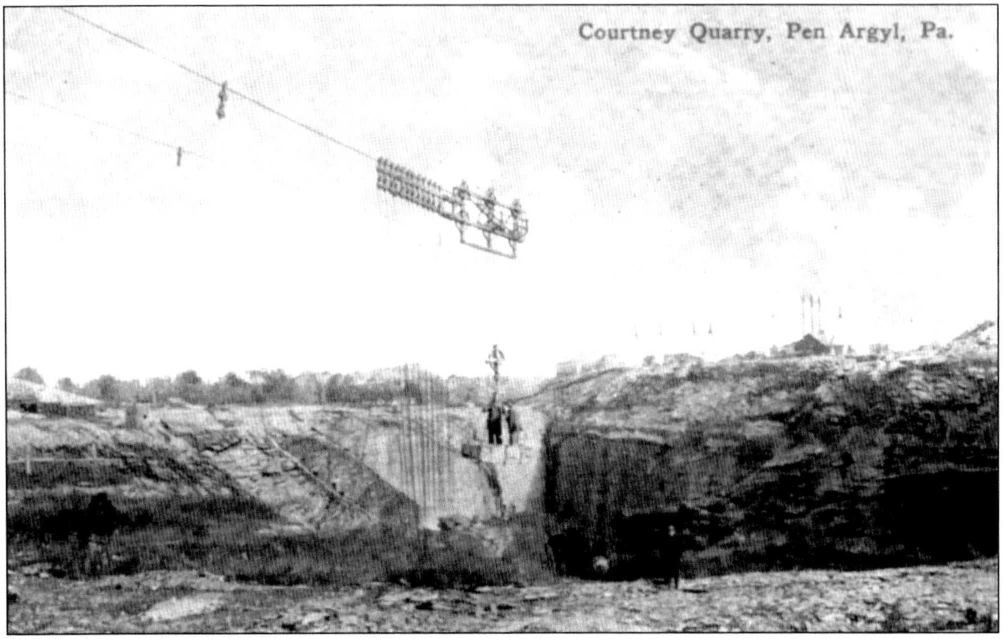

Men are lowered into a quarry pit at the Courtney Quarry (above), and a view of the Master's Quarry can be seen in the photograph below. Both of these quarries were located in Pen Argyl. The opening for Courtney was actually located within the Albion Quarry. The quarry names reflect the nationality of the English immigrants who settled Pen Argyl. (Author's collection.)

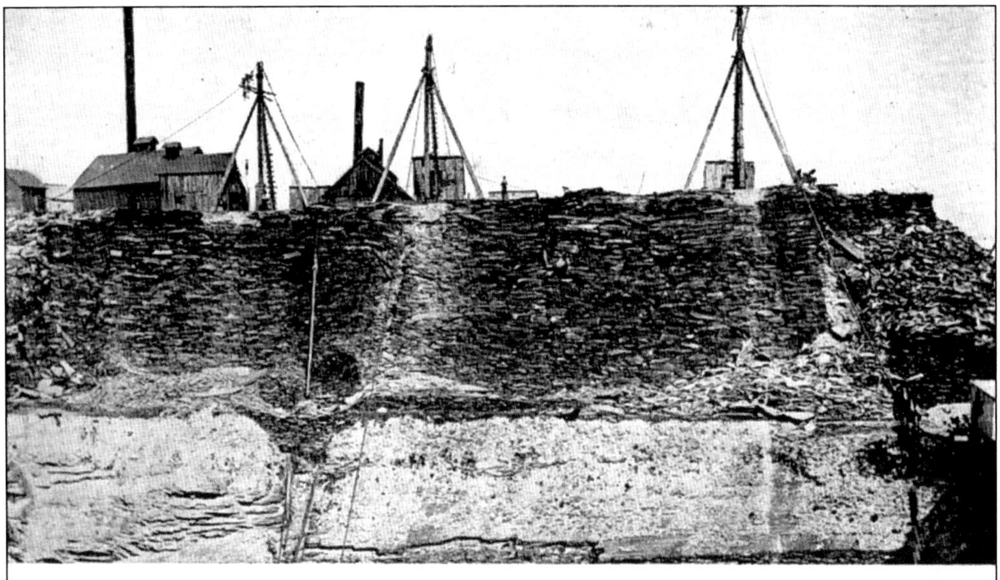

PEN ARGYL, PA. The chief industry; mining and manufacture of ROOFING SLATE. MASTERS QUARRY

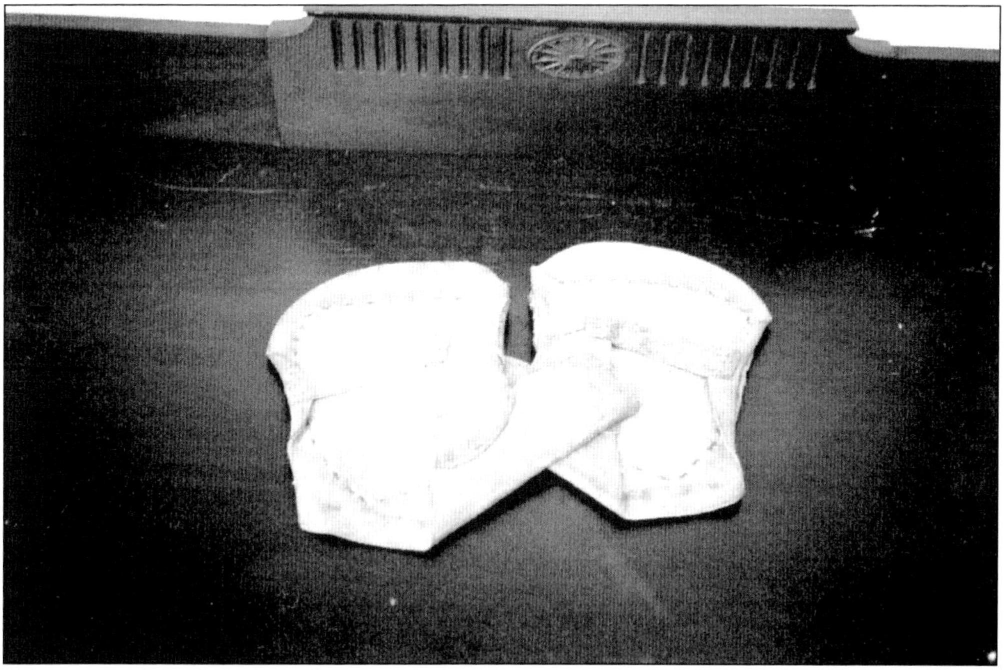

Below are some of the standard tools of the trade in most quarries. The oversized gloves might not have been fashionable, but they were necessary to protect the quarryman's hands from the ragged edges of the slate slabs. Hammers, shown on the right and left in the picture below, came in many varieties but were basically used to cut and chop slate. The T-shaped metal tool in the middle is a slater's stake, which was driven into the ground or a block of wood and used as a back support for the slate while the hammer chopped the slate to size. (Author's collection.)

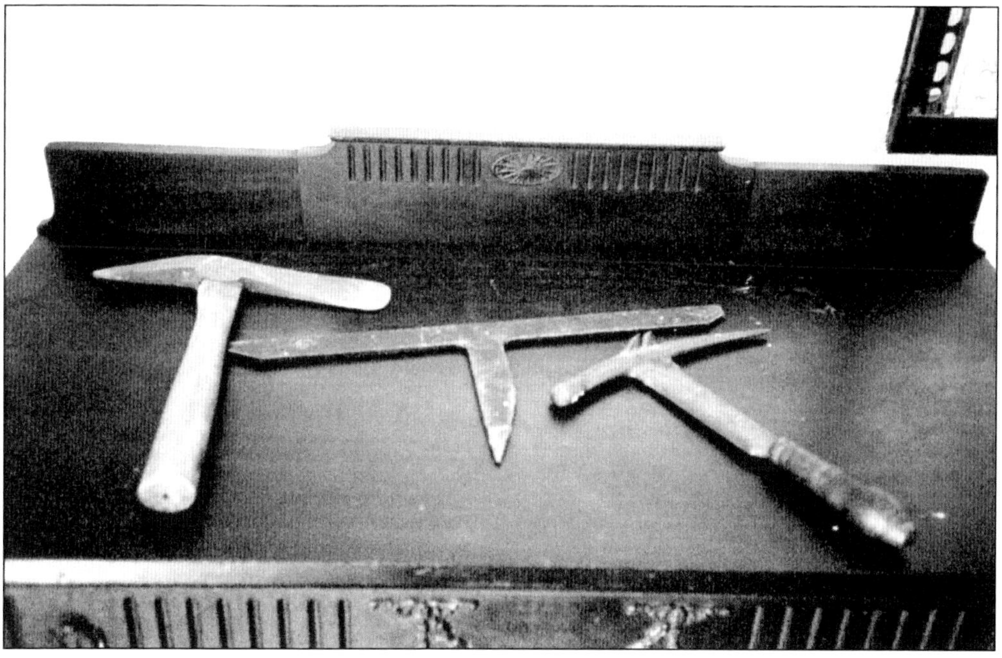

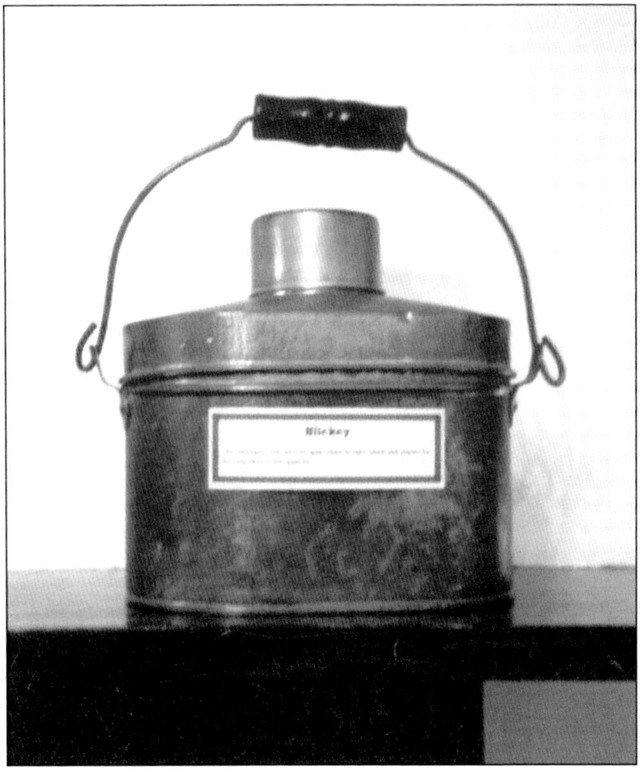

A blickey, or quarryman's lunch pail, could either be small or large. Sandwiches were standard lunch fare, as was hot coffee. The cup on top of the blickey was used for that purpose, and the coffee was heated on small stoves in the shanties. Meat, such as pork or chicken, was a special treat, as were sweets like pie. (Courtesy SBHC.)

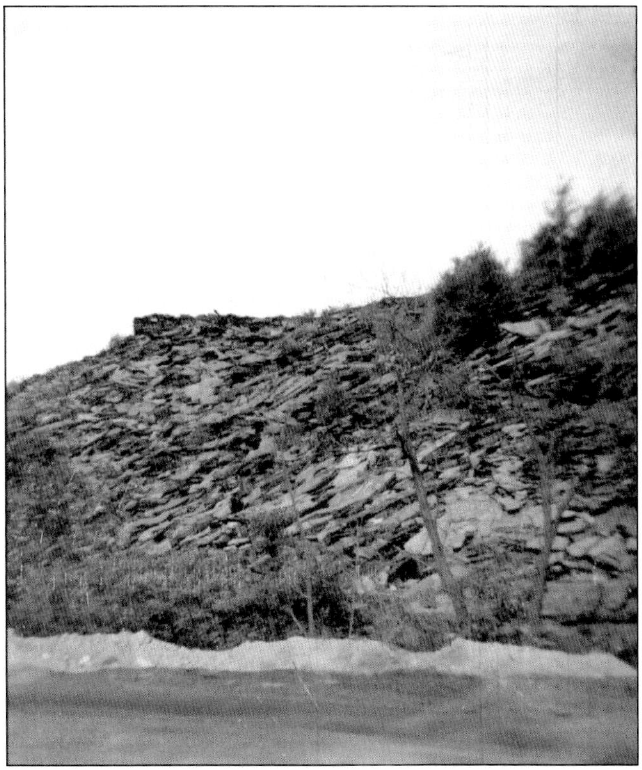

Waste piles like the one shown here can still be found throughout the Slate Belt, particularly along North Main Street in Bangor, where significant piles of slate can still be seen from the North Bangor Quarry. The heaps of waste have finally found some usefulness. Animals such as fox and rabbits now call them home, and, of course, they stand as a monument to the industry that built Bangor and the Slate Belt. (Courtesy BPL.)

Three

BANGOR

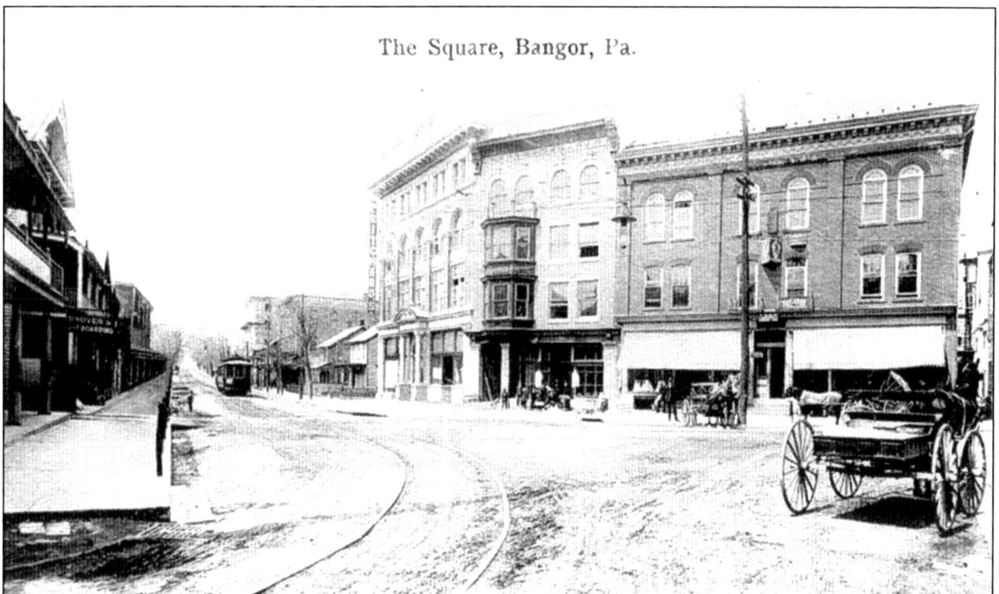

This is a view of the square on Broadway in Bangor. The success of the slate industry caused an increase in population, which created a need for more goods and services. Broadway, along with Market, First, and Main Streets became the main area for business and commercial ventures, particularly after 1890. (Courtesy SBHC.)

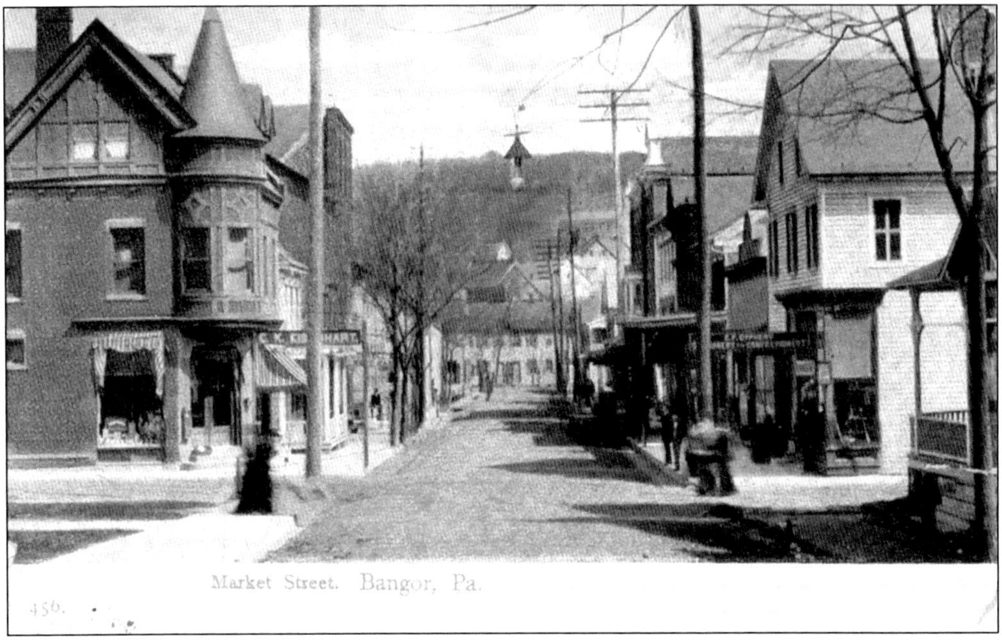

Market and First Streets are shown here. If one were to walk around the block, one would find a variety of businesses, including pharmacies, jewelers, hotels, and grocery and dry goods stores. Along with the trades and entrepreneurs, professionals, such as doctors, lawyers, and photographers, could also be found. A confectionary store, E. F. Cyphers, can be seen on the right on Market Street and the E. K. Eisenhart Pharmacy is on the left. Ivor Griffith, a pharmacist who would go on to do pioneering work with quinine, got his start there. First Street, below, which is basically Route 191, leads to towns like Ackermanville and Flicksville. The clock tower of the town hall can be seen at the end of the road on the right. The building on the left is the Peniel Presbyterian Church. (Courtesy SBHC.)

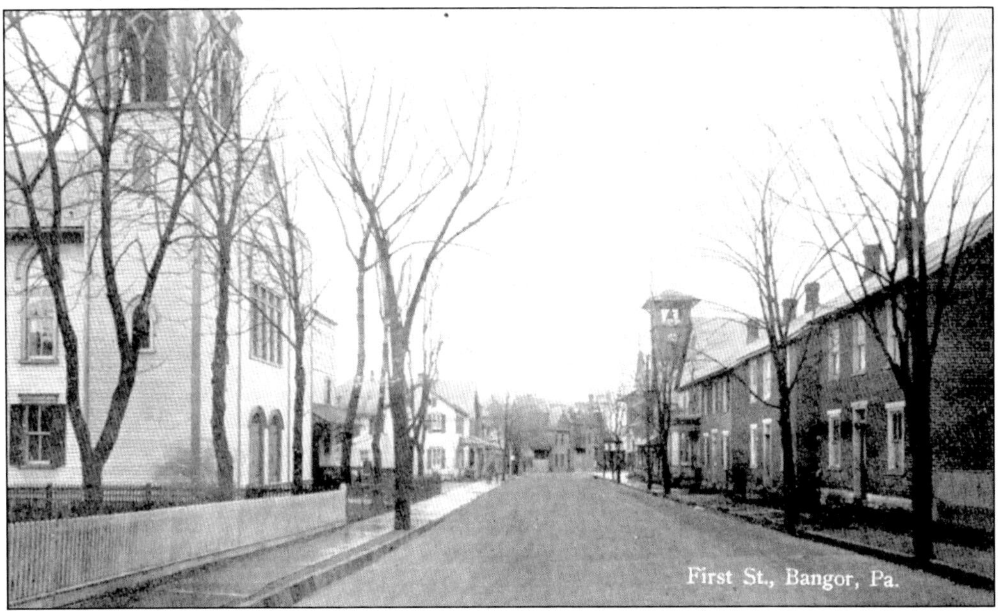

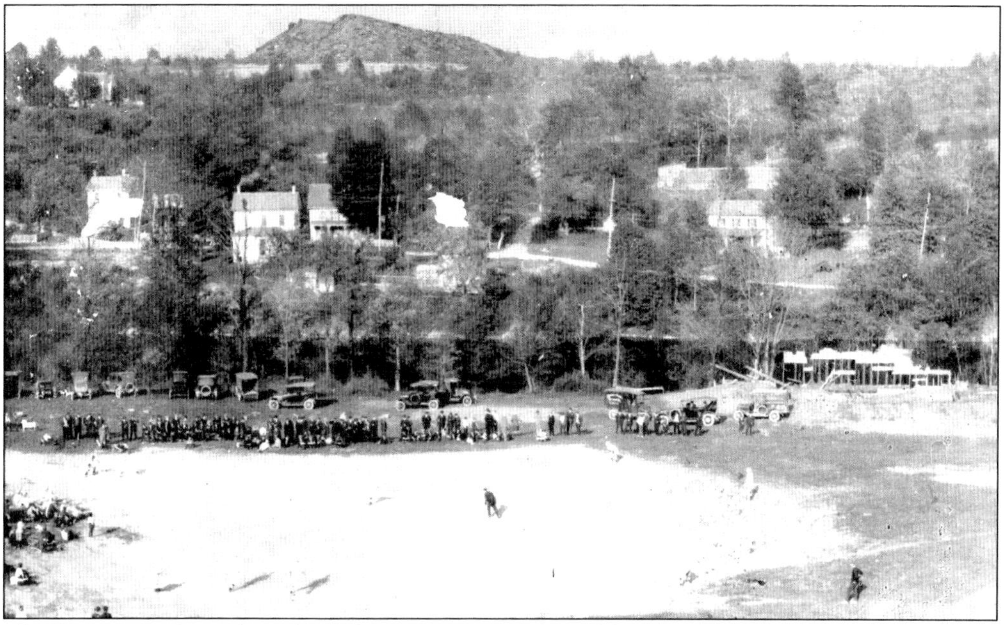

This is a view of North and South Main Streets. Several landmarks can be seen in the North Main Street photograph. In the forefront is Flory's Field, or "Old" Bangor Park, where residents enjoyed one of the area's most popular pastimes, baseball. The creek, part of Martin's Creek that still contains the remnants of Flory's Dam, can be seen between the ball field and the houses on North Main Street and, of course, the always looming slate piles from the quarries, which in this instance is North Bangor Quarry. (Courtesy BPL.)

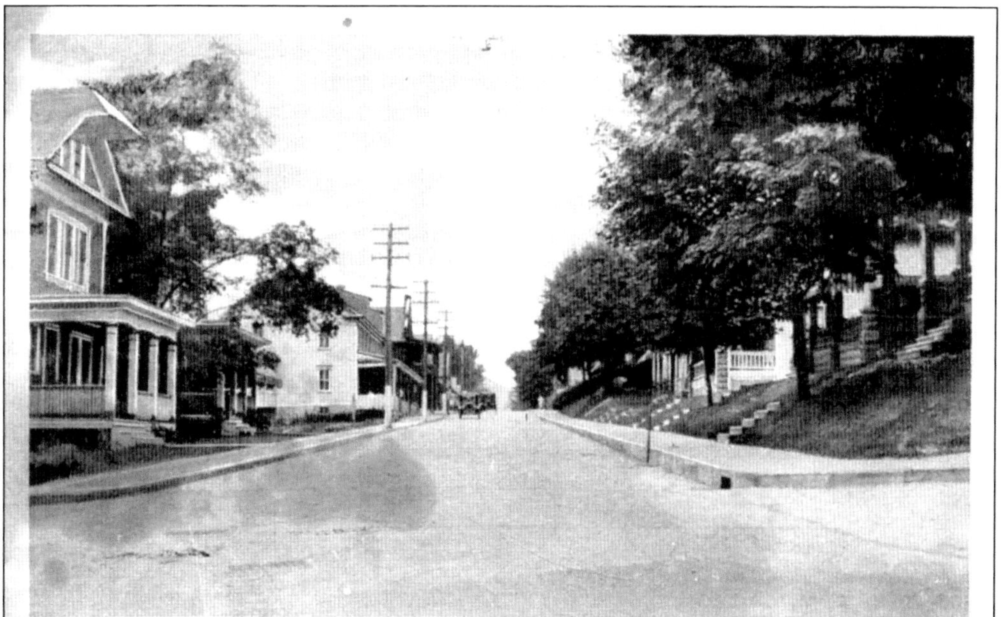

SOUTH MAIN STREET. BANGOR, PA.

South Main Street was and still is primarily residential, but the Bangor Lumber Company was located at South Main and Walnut Streets. The former Salem Evangelical Church building stands at the end of South Main Street. (Courtesy SBHC.)

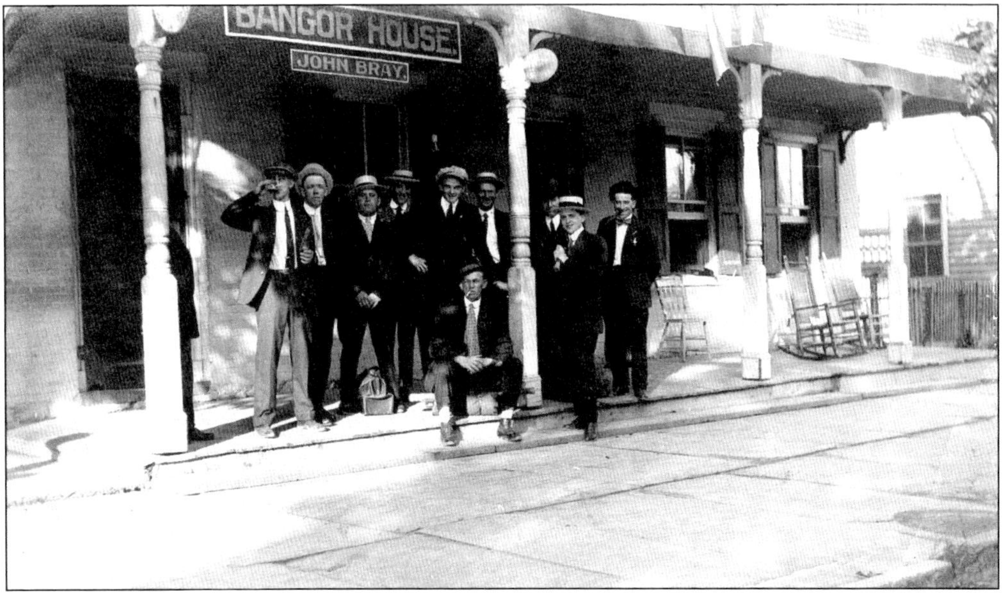

Hotels and boarding houses sprung up due to the influx of quarrymen and others to the area. The Bangor House was located on North Main Street, and John Bray was the proprietor. Shown here around 1910, it was called "The House of Plenty." It was not the town's largest hotel, but it did have an attractive meeting room and was popular with both travelers and local residents because of its good food. (Courtesy SBHC.)

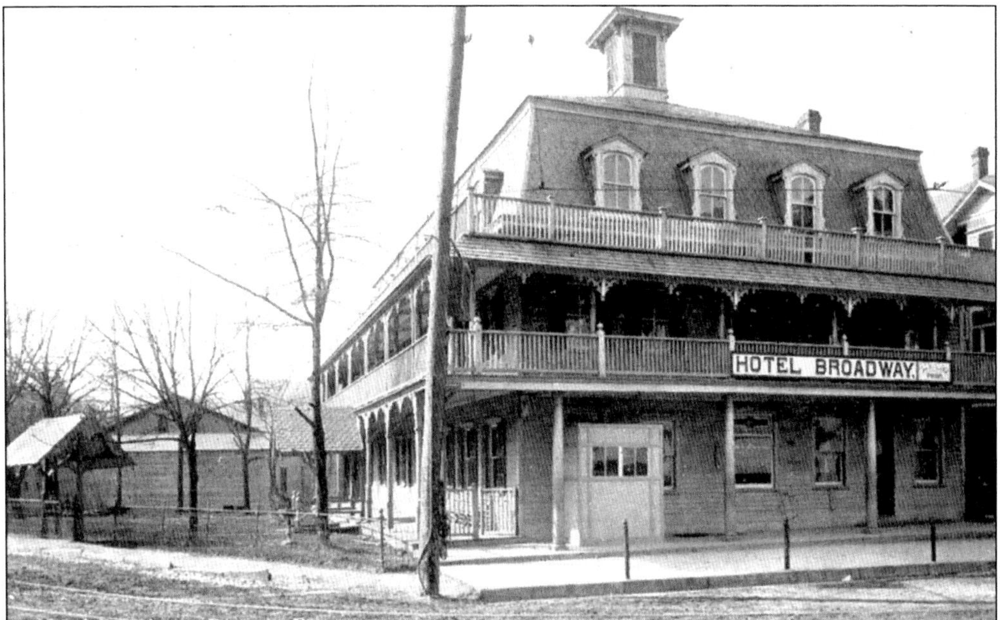

The Hotel Broadway was located on Broadway and Main Street, with H. F. Finkbeiner as the proprietor. Early in the 20th century, it was known as "the Traveling Man's House." The three-story frame building was built in 1877 by W. H. and Christian Speer and operated until 1970, when it was torn down and replaced by a service station. (Courtesy SBHC.)

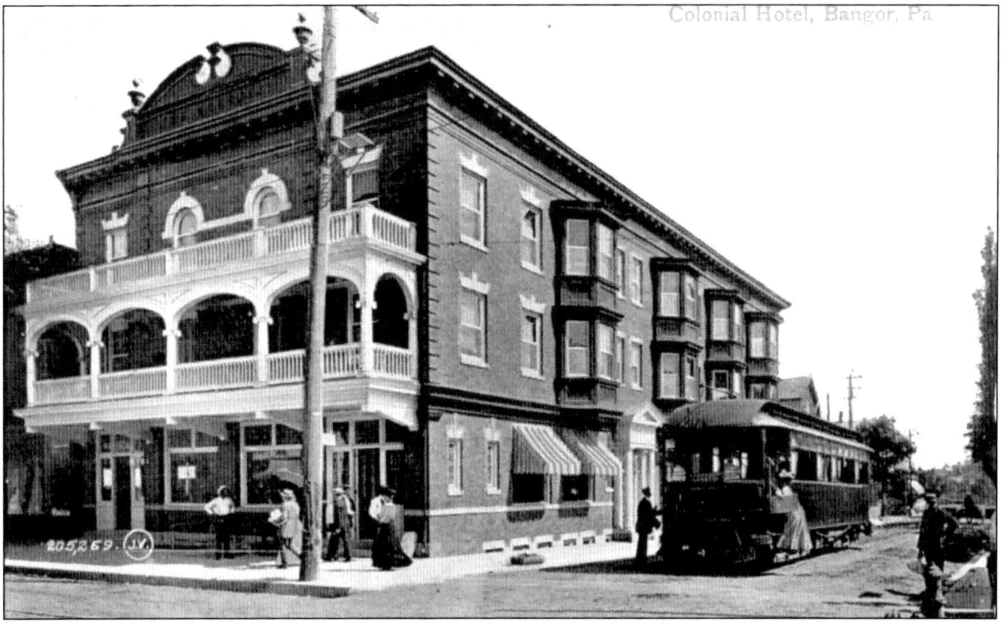

The Mansion House and the Colonial Hotel helped round out the hotels in the area, though there were certainly more than the four mentioned here. The Mansion House was located on Market Street, and in 1877, H. H. Hummel was the proprietor. The Colonial Hotel was a large, brick building that still stands on the corner of Broadway and First Streets. It was built and operated in the 1880s by George Rodenbaugh. It had a bar and large dining room, as well as large rooms and hallways. The hotel was also a trolley stop particularly for the Hay Line trolley. (Courtesy SBHC.)

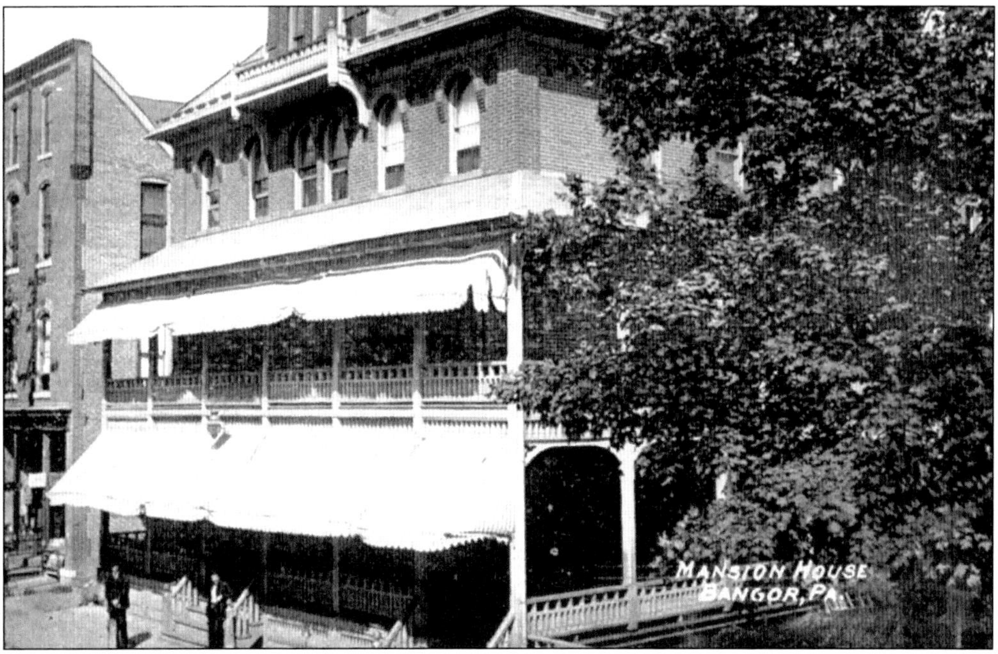

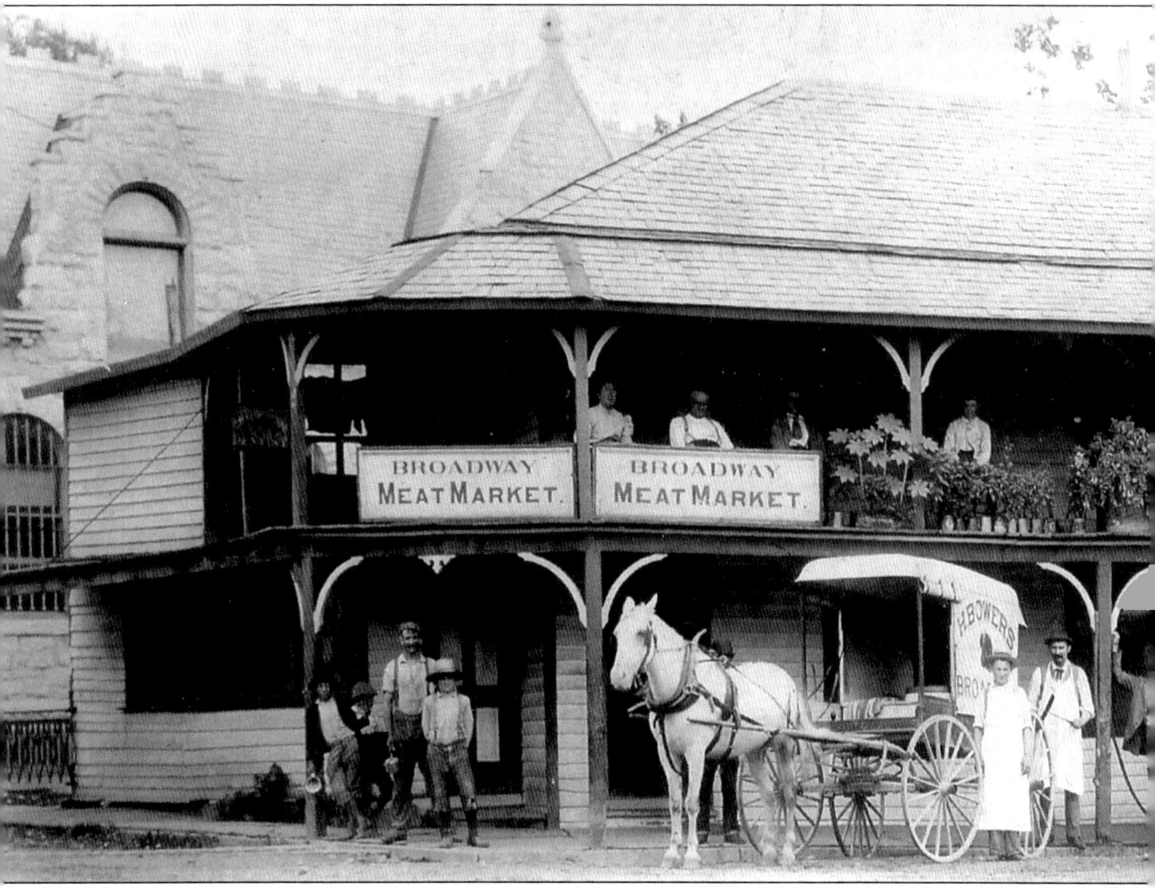

This is the original Bowers Building, which housed a meat market and restaurant. It was located at the foot of Broadway. The Bower brothers, originally from New York City, quickly became the town's most prolific businessmen. In addition to this business,

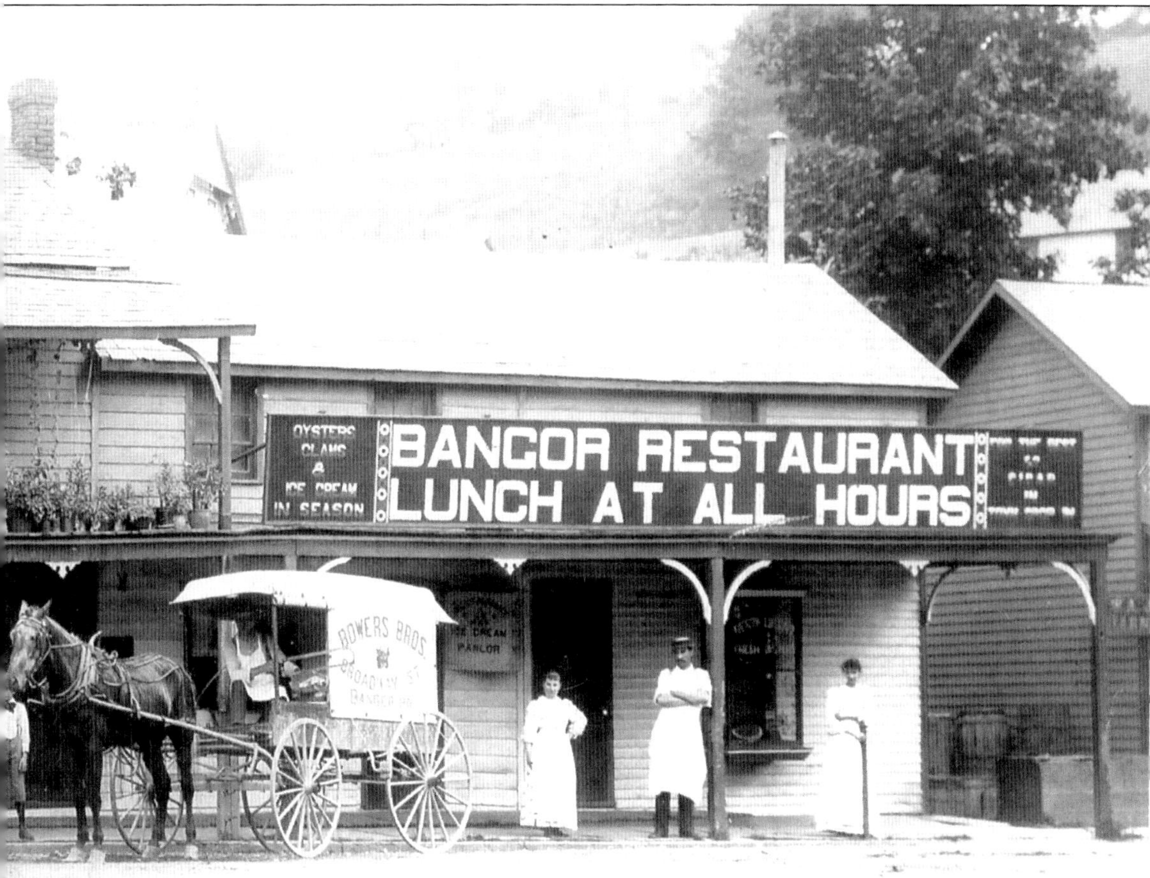

they ran the Majestic Hotel at the end of Broadway and the Bowers Department Store on the corner of Broadway and First Street. (Courtesy SBHC.)

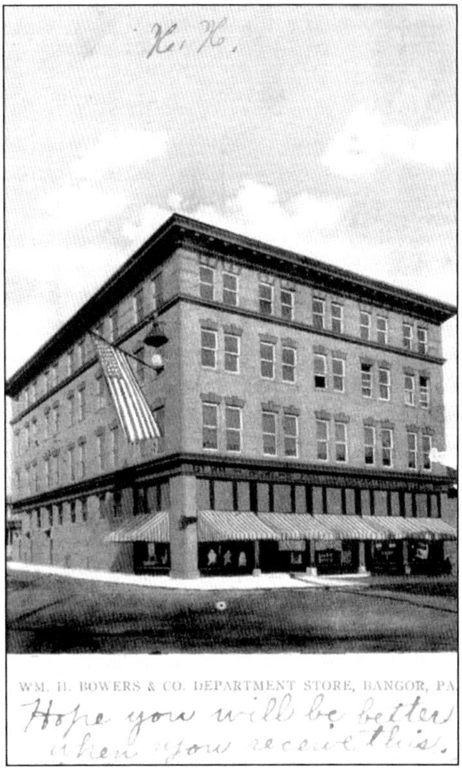

This five-story structure is the Bowers Department Store. Built by the Bowers brothers, it was located on the corner of First and Broadway, where the building still stands. It housed a variety of businesses over the years, including clothing and furniture stores and grocery stores like Acme Markets. (Courtesy SBHC.)

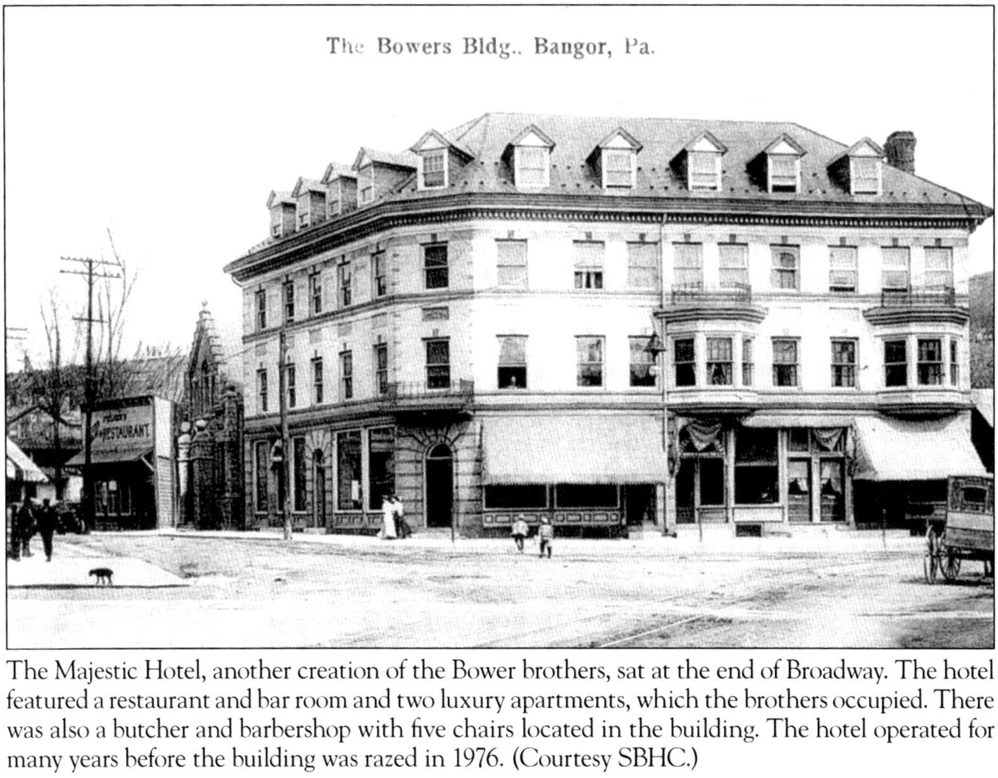

The Majestic Hotel, another creation of the Bower brothers, sat at the end of Broadway. The hotel featured a restaurant and bar room and two luxury apartments, which the brothers occupied. There was also a butcher and barbershop with five chairs located in the building. The hotel operated for many years before the building was razed in 1976. (Courtesy SBHC.)

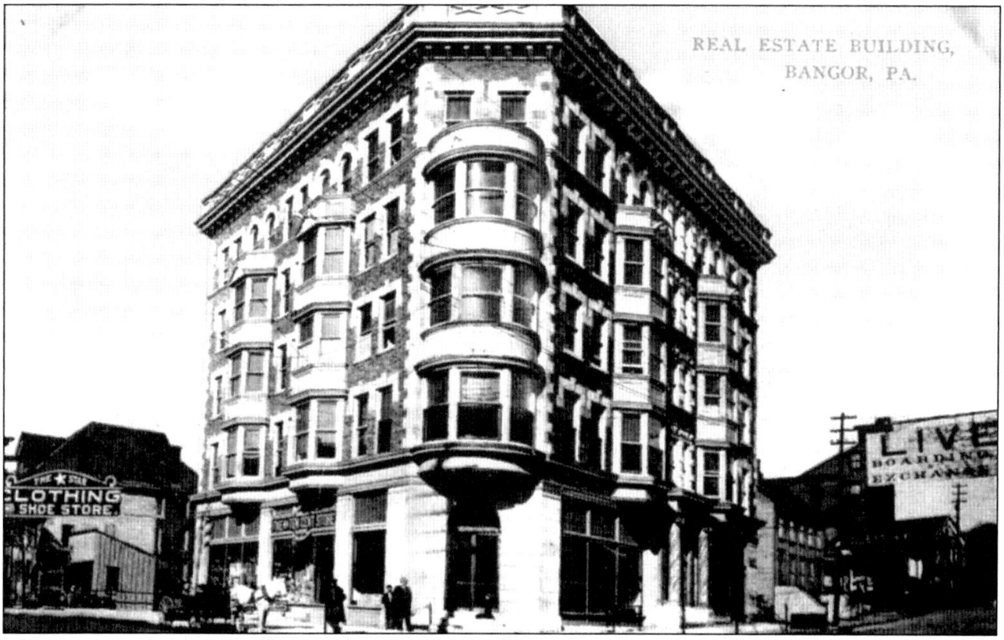

The Real Estate Building, built in 1907, ushered in a new concept of housing in Bangor, namely, that of the high-rise. The building, which still stands on the corner of Main and Market Streets, was reconstructed in 1989 and now goes by the name of the Century House. It is listed in the National Register of Historic Places. (Courtesy SBHC.)

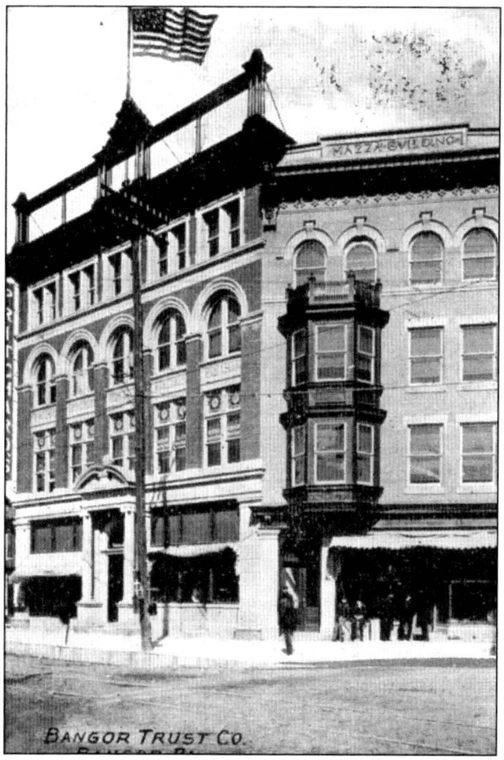

The Bangor Trust Building is shown on the left, and the Mazza Building is on the right. Businessmen erected Bangor Trust, intending to house the Bangor Trust Bank, a post office, and residences for the community there. It was one of the tallest buildings in the area. The Mazza family also built an apartment building that housed a tobacco and candy store. The sign for Pritchard's Clothing Store can also be seen. (Courtesy SBHC.)

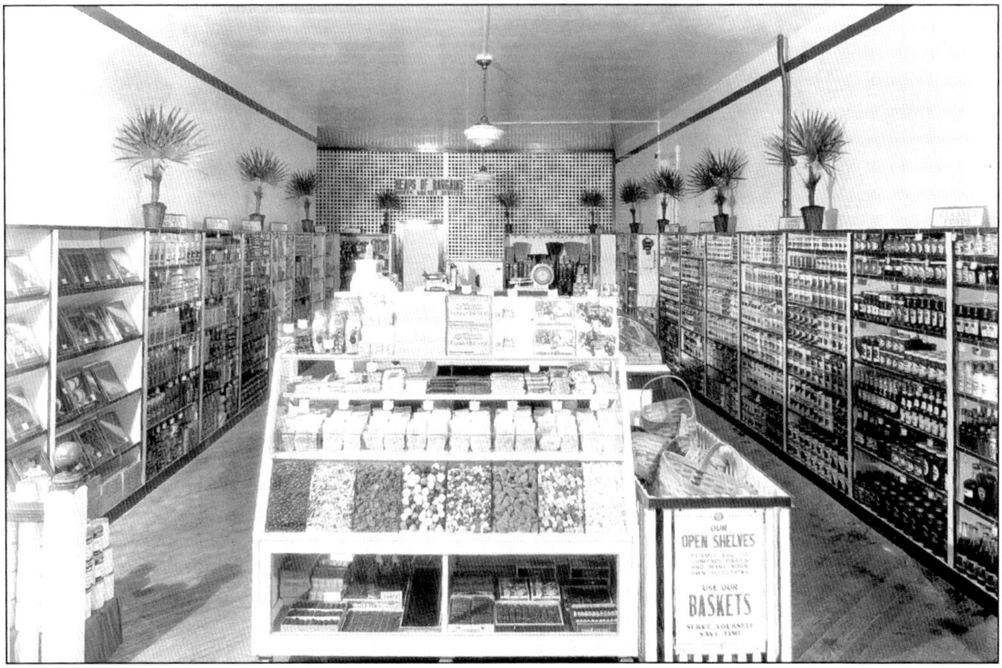

This is one of several grocery stores that operated in the area, and it may have been the forerunner to the self-service store. The store features candy, coffee and teas, canned fruits, and baking supplies, among other items. The sign at the right boasts that the open shelves allow customers to compare prices and make their own selections. (Courtesy BPL.)

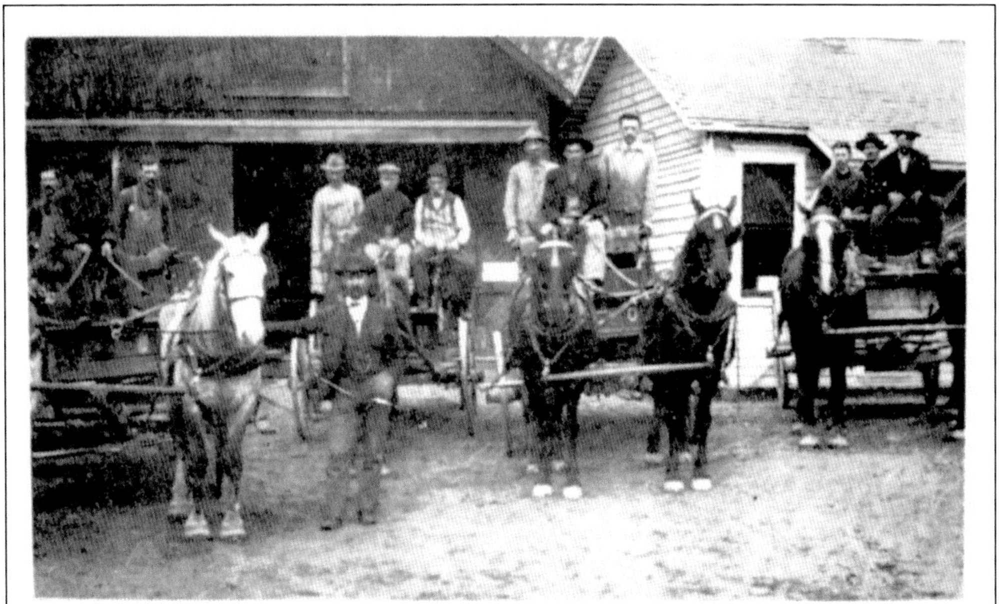

The Bangor Lumber Company, along with F. S. Wise Lumber, helped supply the building needs of the community. Founded in 1895, it was located on South Main Street and was originally the site of a tannery owned by John Albert. During the early 20th century, it supplied pine and hemlock lumber, coal, and wood and continued to operate through the 1980s. (Courtesy SBHC.)

The W. O. Houck Hardware building was located on Main Street, where the building can still be seen. Together with Dutt Brothers Hardware, they installed coal furnaces and provided oil burners to businesses. Houck was also a tinsmith who was said to have made thousands of pails for his customers. (Courtesy PSA.)

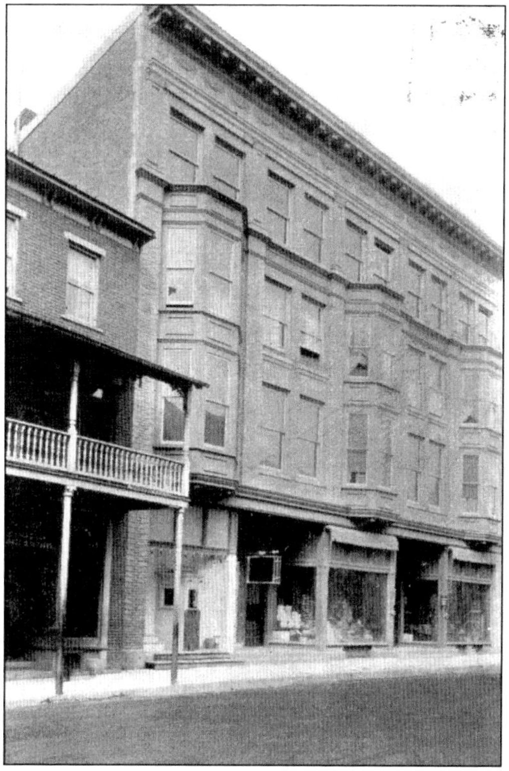

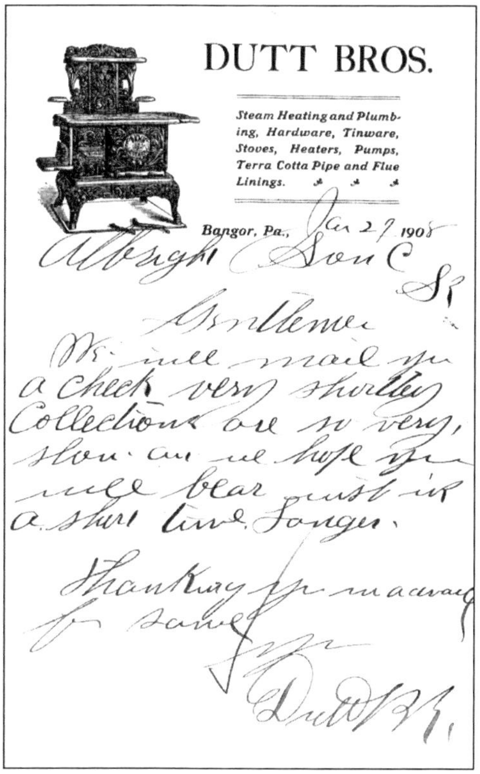

DUTT BROS.

Steam Heating and Plumbing, Hardware, Tinware, Stoves, Heaters, Pumps, Terra Cotta Pipe and Flue Linings.

Bangor, Pa., Jan 27 1908

Albright & Son Co.

Gentlemen

We will mail you a check very shortly. Collections are so very slow and we hope you will bear with us a short time longer.

Thanking you in advance for same

Yours

Dutt Bros.

This is an original invoice from Dutt Brothers Hardware, dated 1908. Dutt Brothers was established in 1899. In addition to supplying furnaces to the business community, they supplied tinware, hardware, stoves, heaters, pumps, and piping, as the invoice indicates. (Author's collection.)

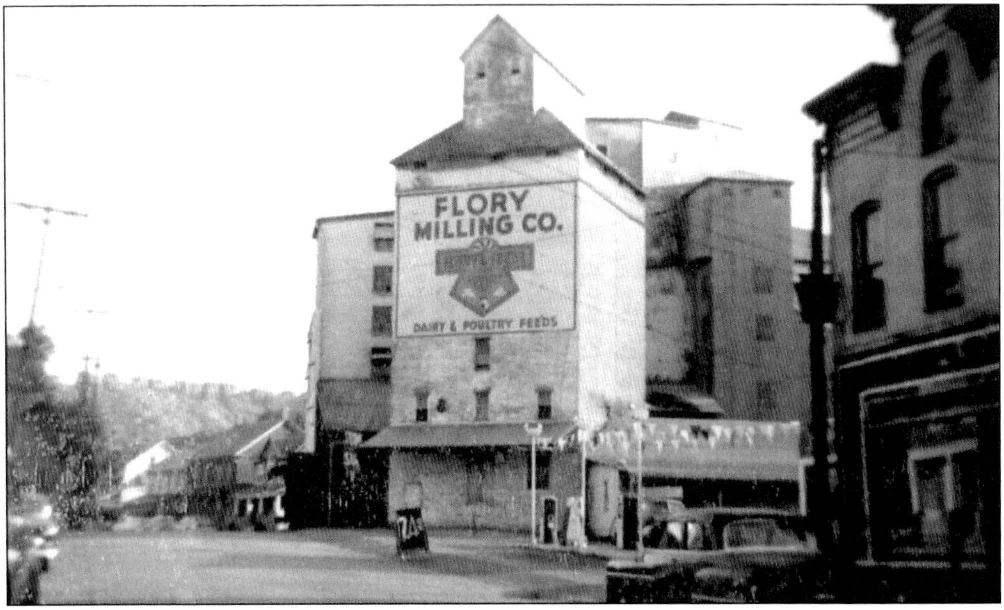

The Flory Milling Company (above) was located on North Main Street. The large complex was started by Solomon Flory, grandson of German immigrant Johannes Florhi, and Solomon's son Samuel. The company started out as the S. Flory Manufacturing Company and supplied hoisting equipment to the world. Solomon, a miller and businessman, eventually turned the operation into a flour mill, which made Globe Flour its trademark. Solomon eventually handed the business over to his son Milton, who expanded it to include feed for animals. Flory Milling Company was one of the area's largest employers, at times employing over 500 workers. The flamboyant Milton was said to own one of the first cars in the borough. The Milton Flory residence is shown below. It had a garage to house the car. (Above, courtesy BPL; below, author's collection.)

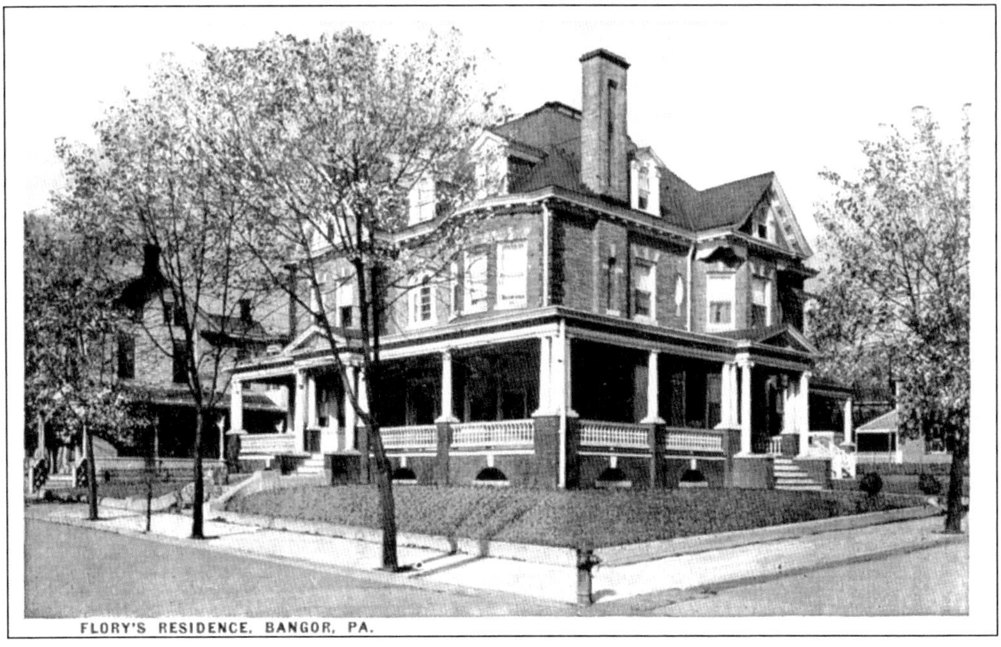

FLORY'S RESIDENCE, BANGOR, PA.

A horse and buggy stand outside the First National Bank around 1910. The bank was incorporated in 1882 and, together with the Merchant's National Bank and Bangor Trust, served the financial needs of the community for many decades. The building still stands at the corner of Main Street and the East Bangor Highway (Route 512), where it still houses financial institutions. (Author's collection.)

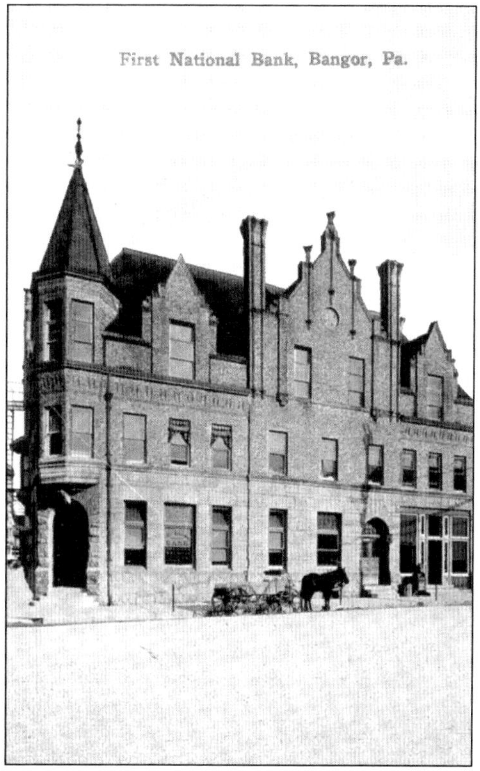

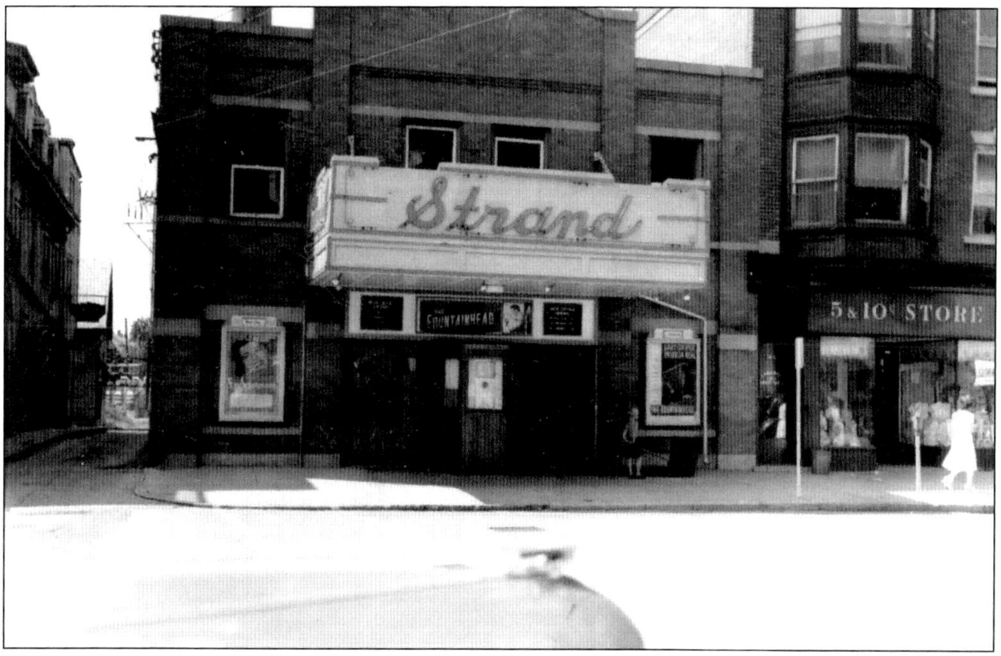

The Strand Theatre was located at the corner of Broadway. It was the area's only theater for many years, closing for good in the late 1970s. Townspeople recall seeing many first-run movies there, including nearly continuous showings of *The Godfather* when the movie was released in 1972. (Courtesy NCHGS.)

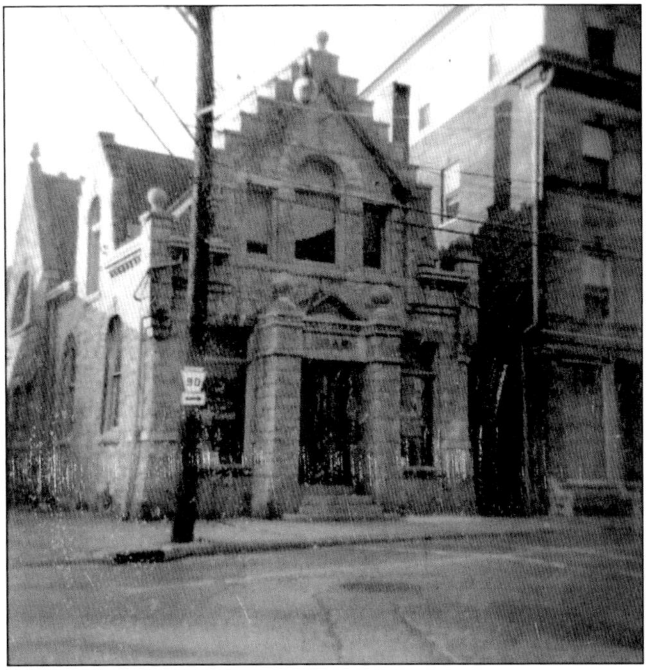

The Bangor Public Library was opened in 1921 and incorporated on May 29, 1922, thanks to years of work and fund-raising by the community. Originally a subscription library that people paid a fee to join, the library had several homes before it came to its present location in this stone building at the end of Main Street, which once housed the Merchant's National Bank. (Courtesy BPL.)

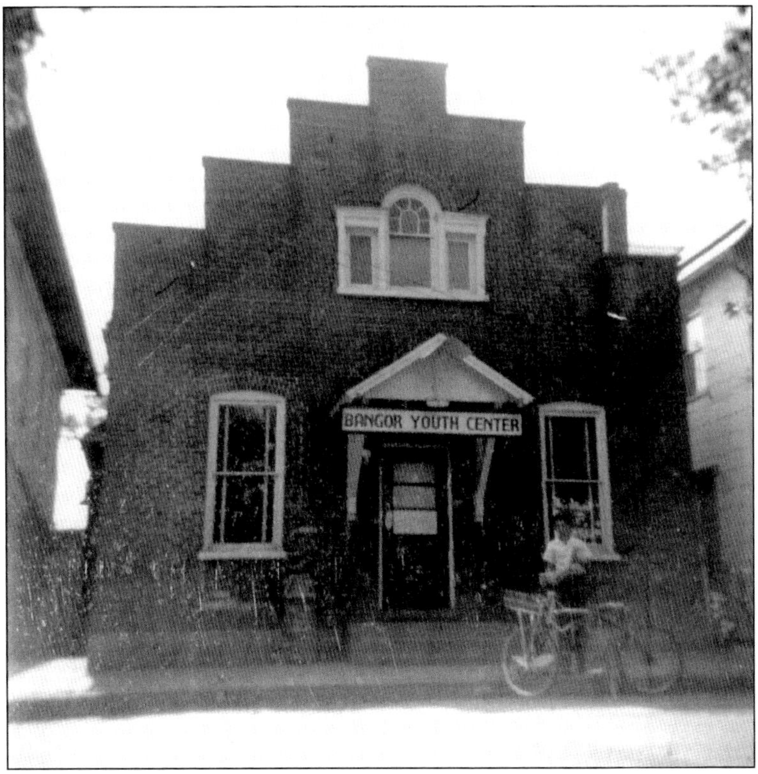

This was Bangor's first youth center. The two-room building was located on North First Street and first served as the library. The town, wanting to provide a place for the youth to go, eventually opened a bigger facility on Pennsylvania Avenue known as the Beehive, where teenagers could dance and play ping-pong, shuffleboard, and quoits. (Courtesy BPL.)

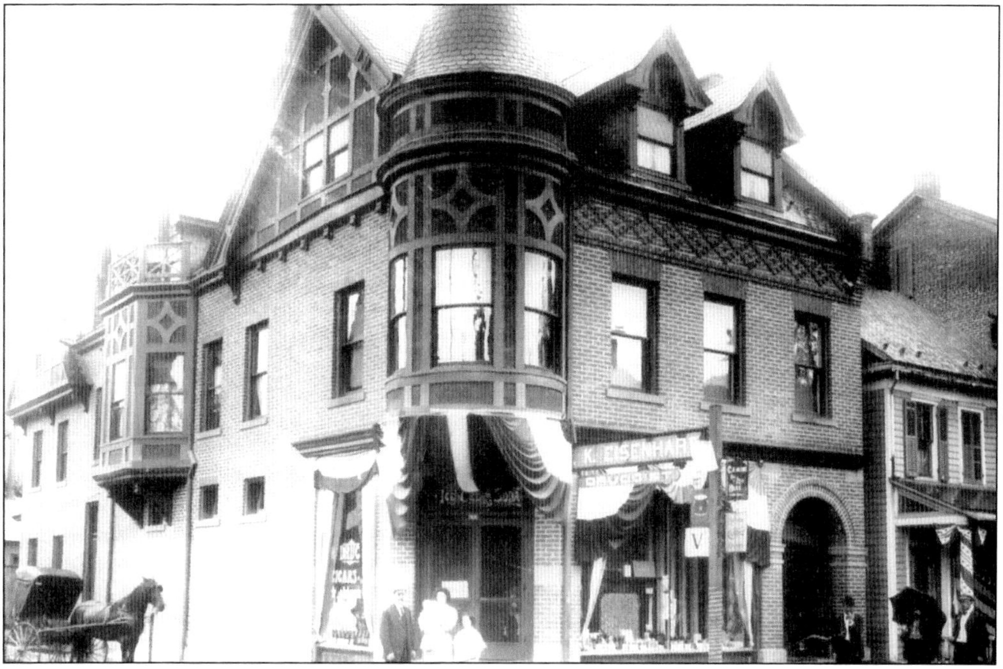

E. K. Eisenhart, his wife, Anna, and their children are shown in 1909 outside their drugstore on First and Market Streets. Eisenhart, a graduate of Philadelphia College of Pharmacy and Science, came to Bangor in 1890 and, in 1899, built the drugstore to resemble buildings found in Germany. Note the scalloped slate on the building's cupola. (Courtesy NCHGS.)

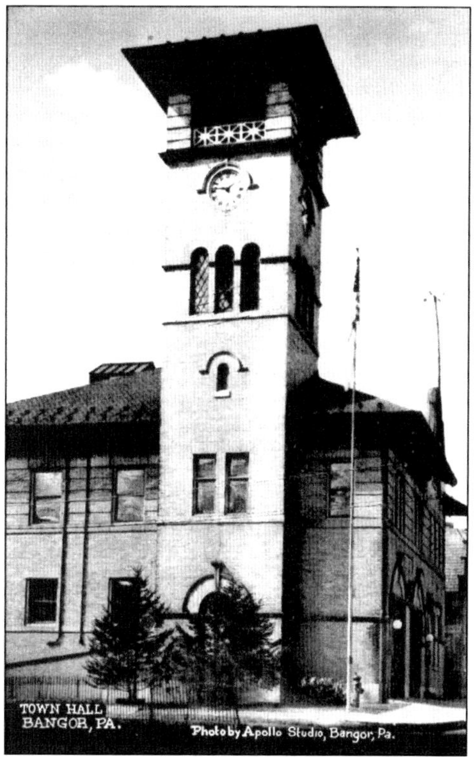

This is a picture of Bangor Town Hall. The building was constructed in 1905 and, for many years, housed the council chamber and fire department. The four-faced clock was manufactured by the E. Howard Clock Company of Boston, Massachusetts. It chimed a coded ring to alert the fire department to fire locations. Today it is the home of the Slate Belt Heritage Center and the Bangor Police Department. (Courtesy SBHC.)

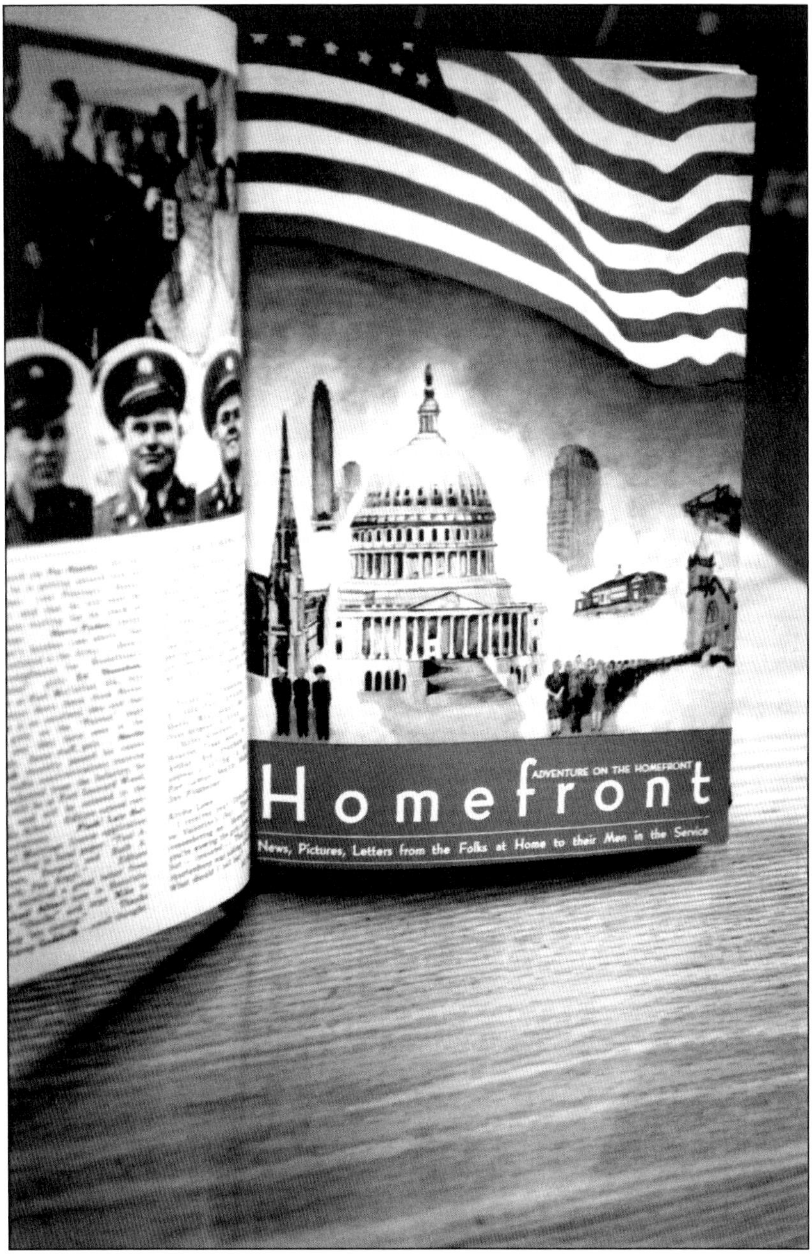

Bangor was the home of a unique magazine, *The Homefront*. The magazine was started in the Pennsylvania Avenue home of husband and wife team J. Horace and Mona Strunk and was distributed monthly to area veterans serving overseas during World War II. Church members and volunteers helped produce the magazine, which featured news from back home and messages of inspiration and encouragement. Published before the days of sexual harassment, the magazine also contained the "Fairest of the Month," which featured pictures and news of local, single women. The magazine is recognized as the only official wartime publication of its kind and can be found in several museums and libraries, including the Pennsylvania State Museum. The Library of Congress also featured it in their book *I'll Be Home For Christmas*. (Author's collection.)

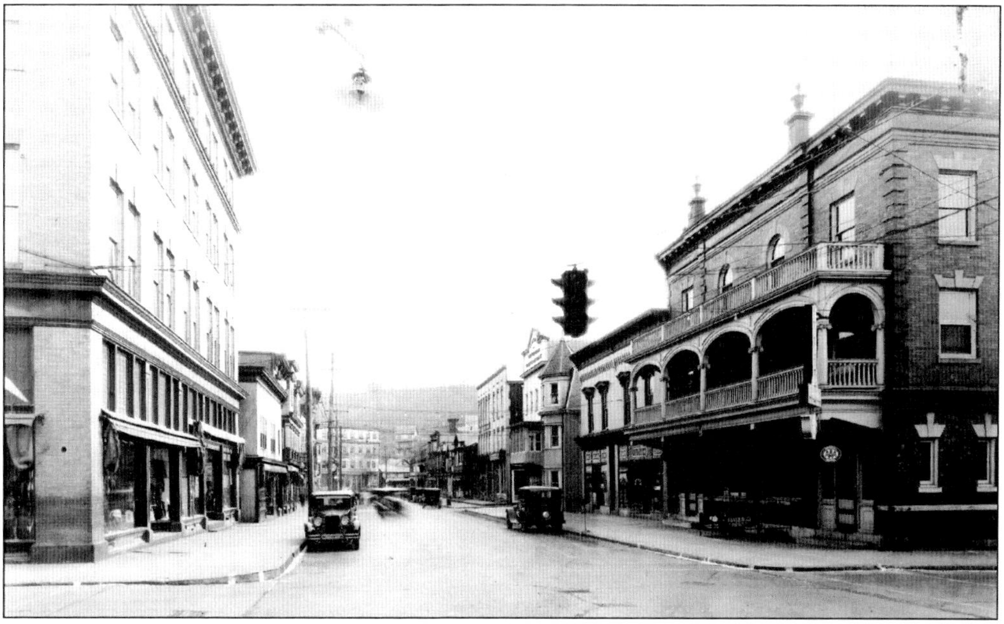

Two different views of Broadway can be seen during the summer (above) and around Christmas (below). The five-story building on the left is the Bower Brothers Department Store. The Colonial Hotel is on the right. Both buildings are still standing. Another Bowers brothers building, the Majestic Hotel, can be seen at the end of the road, just past the speeding car. The hotel was razed in 1976, and Founder's Park occupies the site today. The Christmas scene shows the Bowers Building when it housed Acme Markets. The Christmas tree standing in front of the Majestic Hotel was erected every year in front of a concrete pillar called a dummy, and drivers had to go around to the right of the tree in order to go up and down Broadway. (Courtesy BPL.)

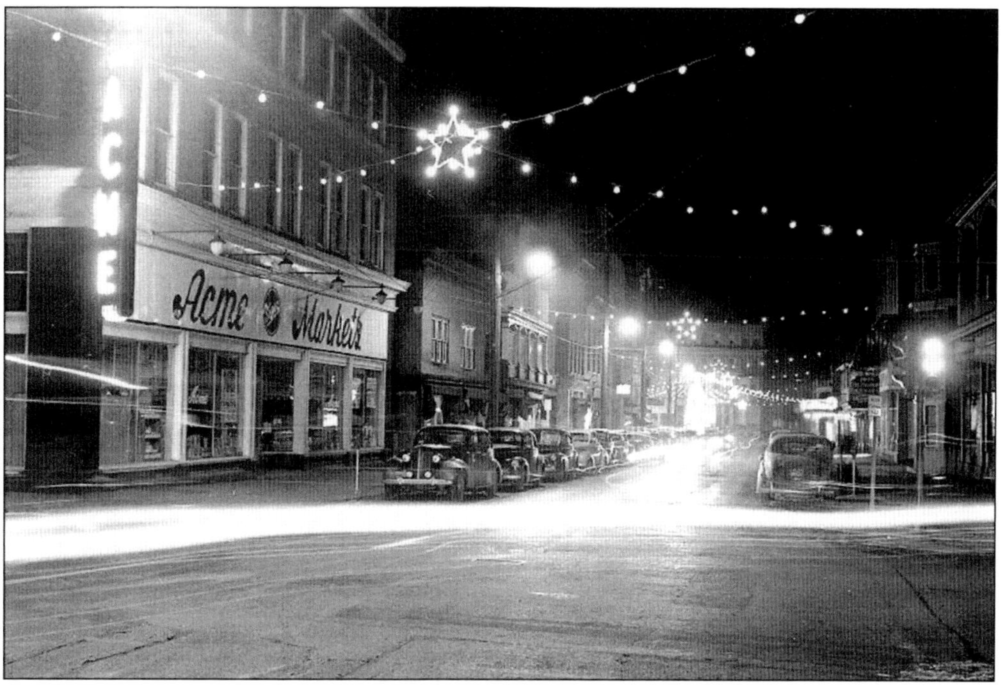

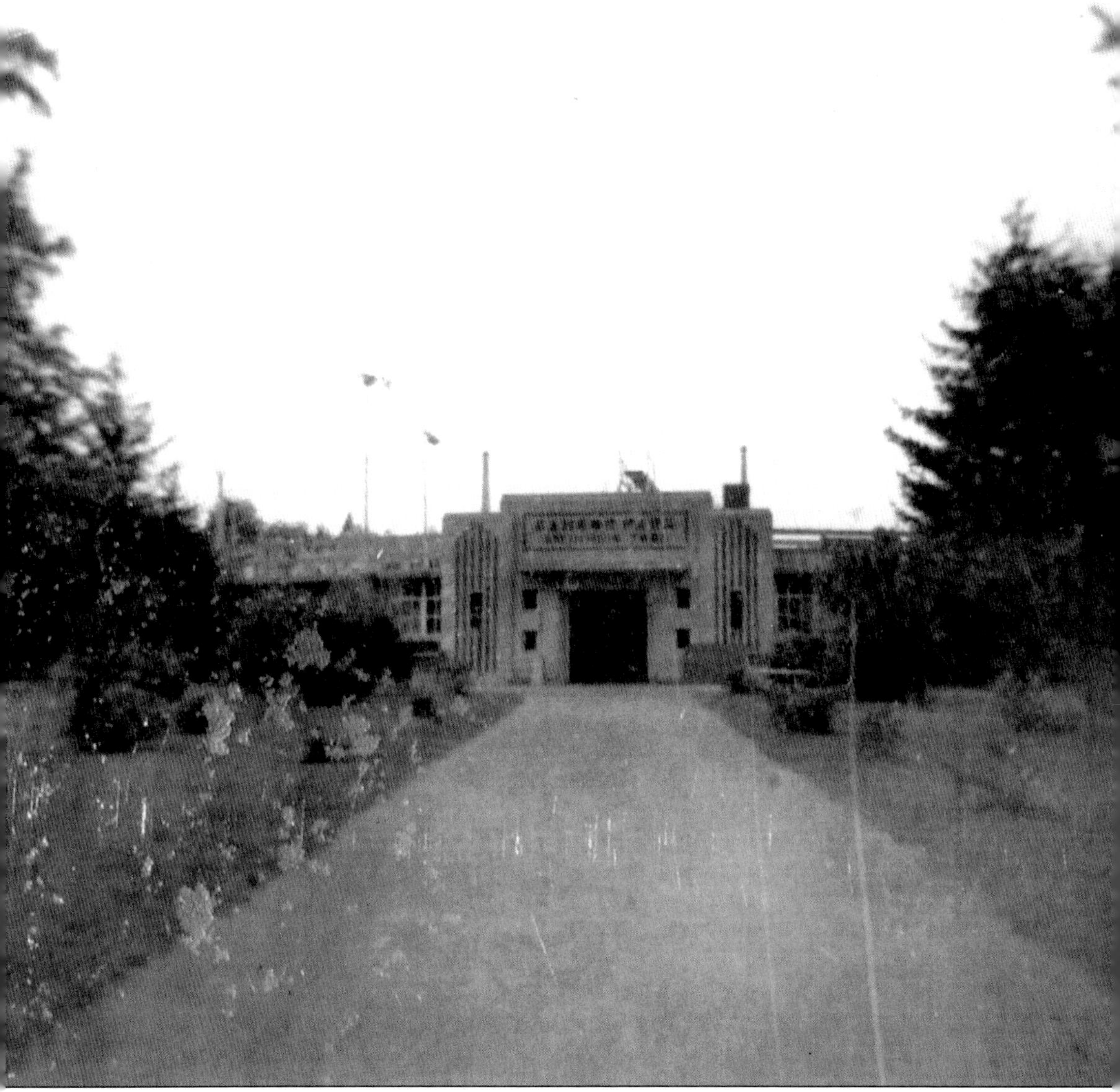

The art deco entrance to the pool at Bangor Park is shown here from a distance. The park was constructed in 1938 as part of a project to develop an 18-acre park for the town. The large, oval pool was opened on May 27, 1939, and was actually located on the second floor. A locker room with showers and a footbath were located on the first floor, which, because of its construction, was usually cool. Over the years, the park consisted of an athletic field and a concrete surface for dancing. It had a concession stand, swings, slides, and a small train for rides. (Courtesy BPL.)

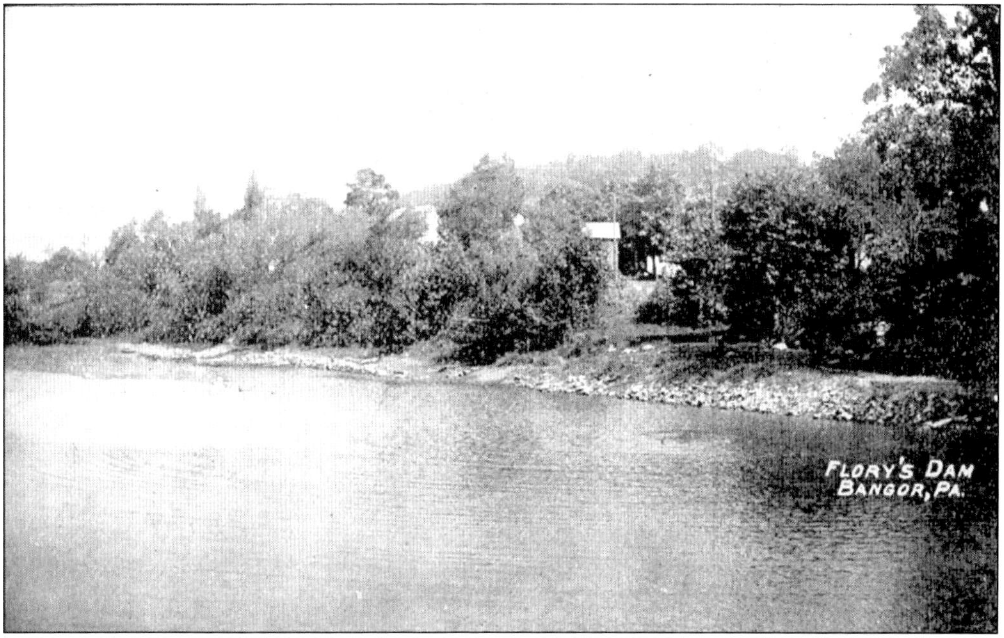

Flory's Dam (above) was located on North Main Street and Rutt's Dam (below) was on First Street. Local youths and residents used the dams for recreation, swimming in the summer, and ice-skating and hockey during the winter, although the real purpose for Flory's Dam was to power the Flory Manufacturing complex. (Courtesy SBHC.)

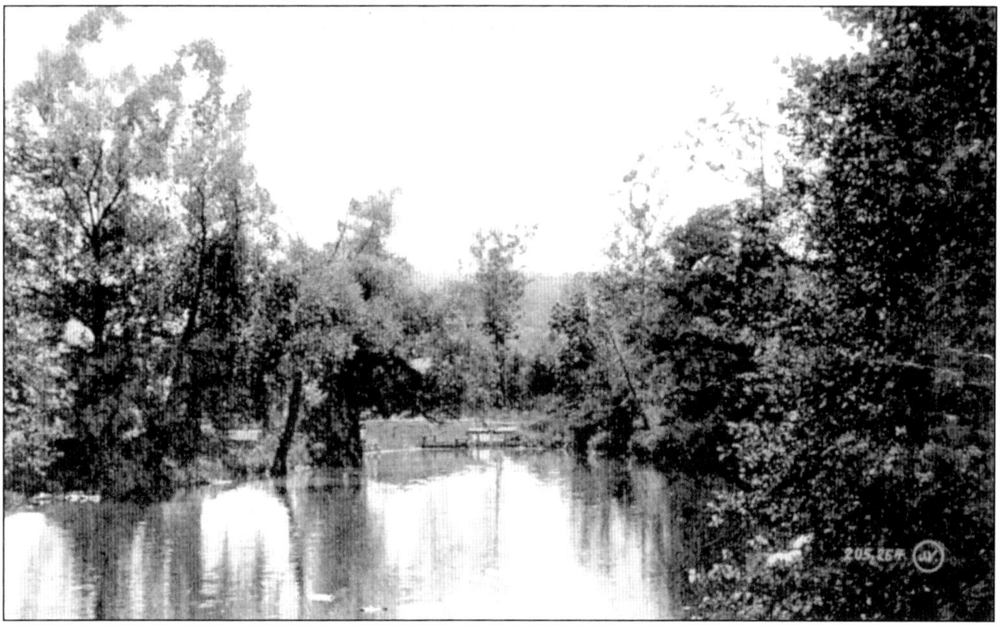

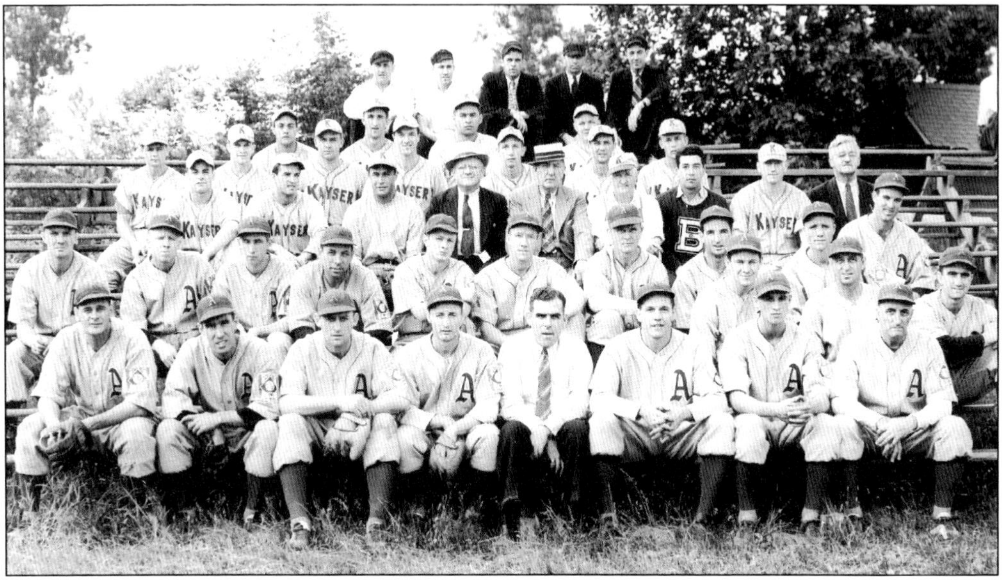

This photograph from 1939 shows the Kayser Athletic Association of Bangor and the Philadelphia Athletics. The Kaysers, supported by the Kayser Silk Mill, were part of the second Bi-State League formed in 1935. The original league lasted from 1926 to 1929 before the Great Depression helped bring about its demise. The members of the various teams were said to be so good that Philadelphia Athletics owner Connie Mack offered many of them professional contracts. (Courtesy BPL.)

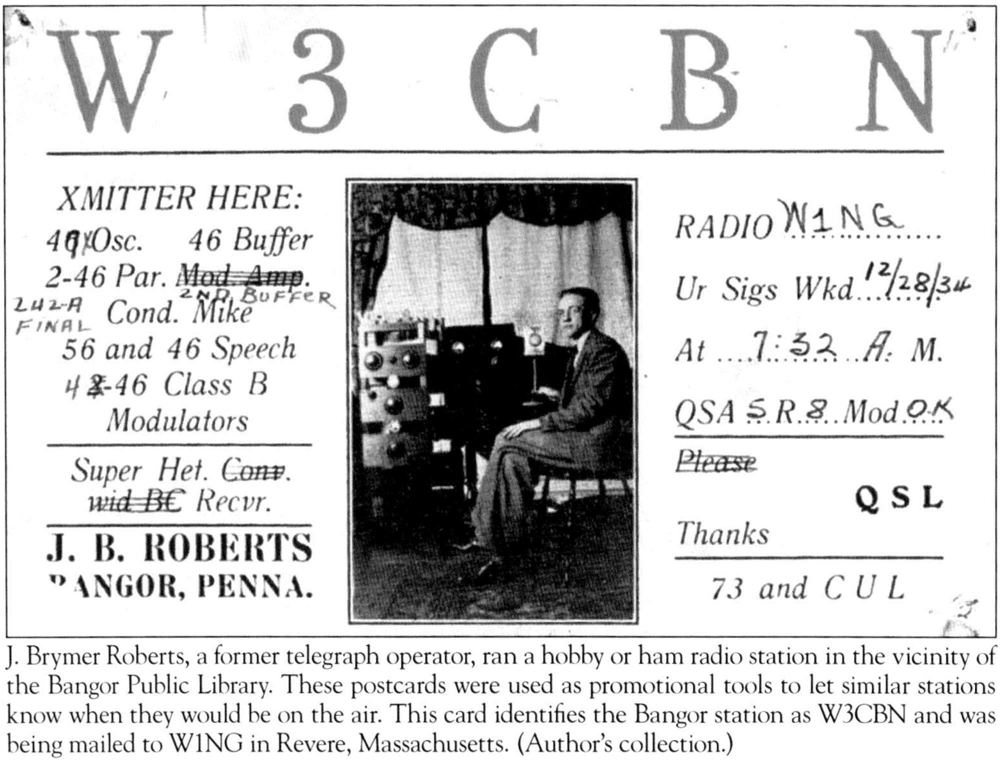

J. Brymer Roberts, a former telegraph operator, ran a hobby or ham radio station in the vicinity of the Bangor Public Library. These postcards were used as promotional tools to let similar stations know when they would be on the air. This card identifies the Bangor station as W3CBN and was being mailed to W1NG in Revere, Massachusetts. (Author's collection.)

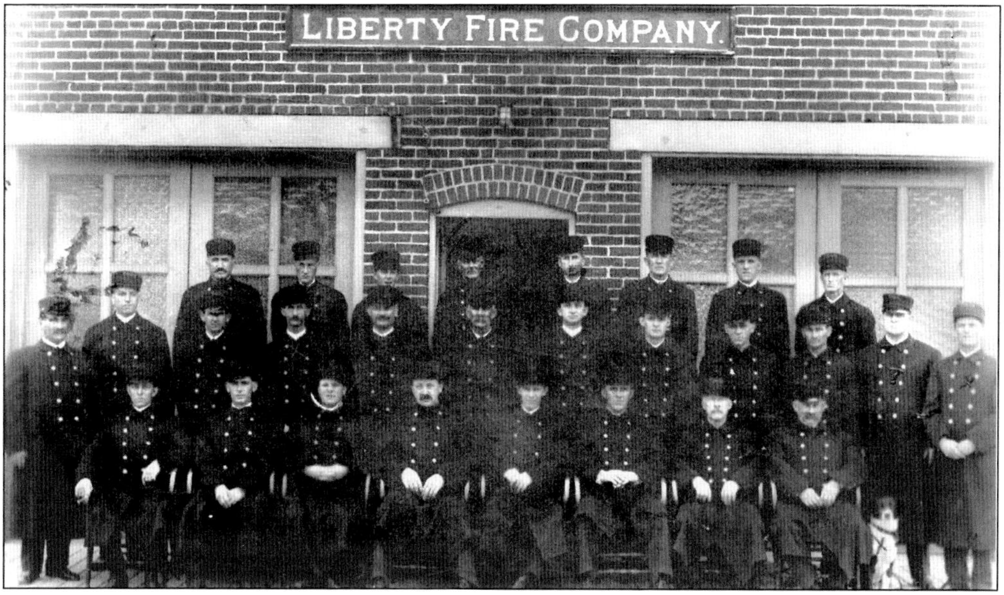

The Liberty Fire Company began on July 4, 1908, when about 30 men met to determine how to offer fire protection to the wards of Bangor. Liberty, which protected the fourth ward, was granted a charter for "Company No. 2" on October 26, 1908, and building construction was completed on February 6, 1811. Today Liberty still operates with about 40 members on North Eighth Street. (Courtesy SBHC.)

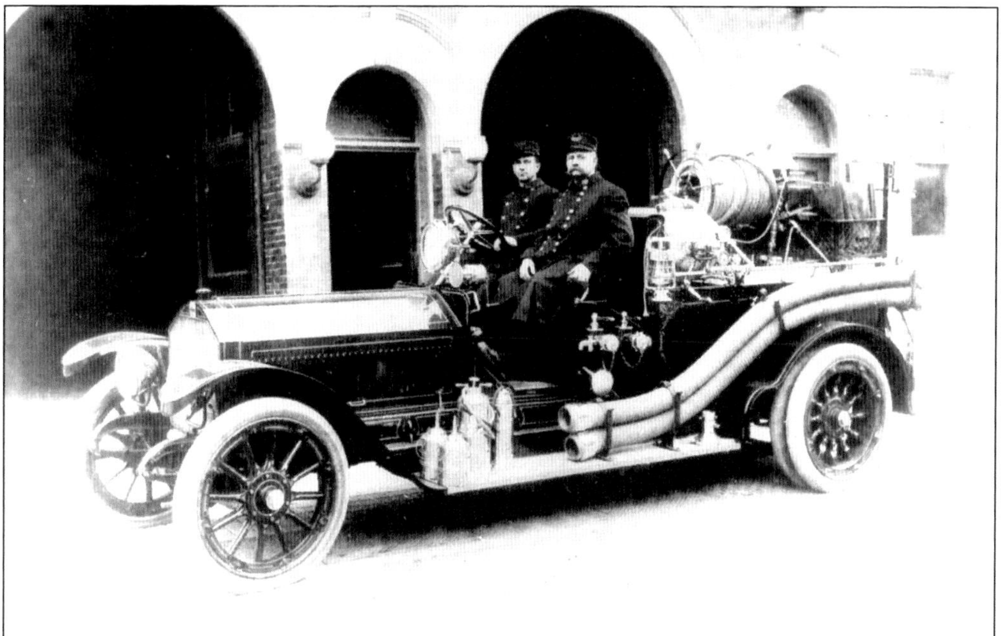

Edward Werkeiser and Elmer Ackerman are seen here aboard an early fire engine from Rescue Company No. 1. The company was organized on August 21, 1886, when it went by the name of the Rescue Hose Company No. 1. It was one of the oldest fire companies in the Slate Belt area. (Courtesy NCHGS.)

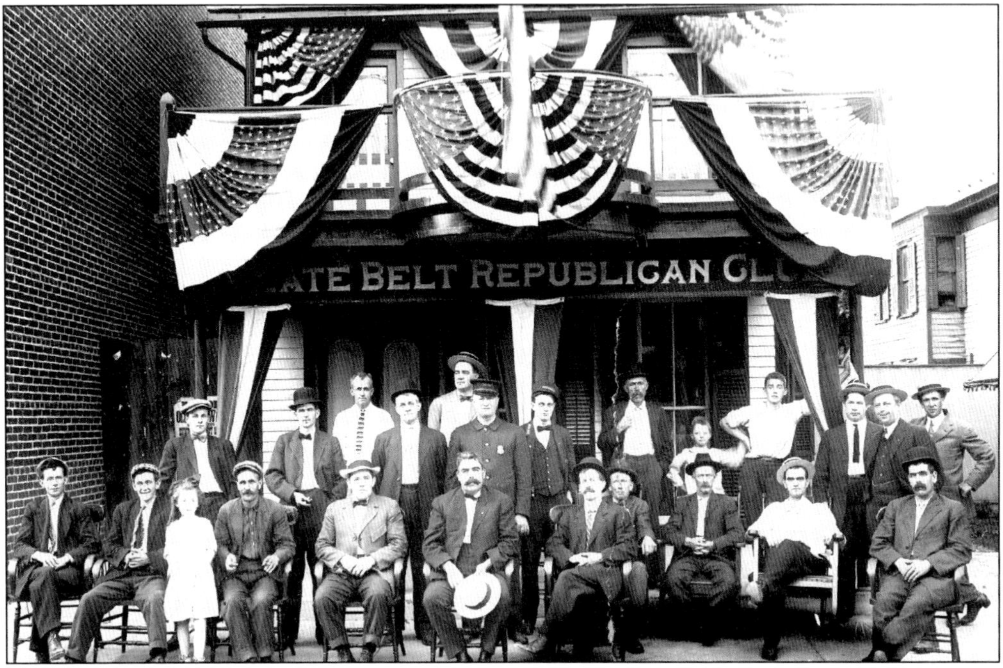

The Slate Belt Republican Club had numerous homes, including 25 Broadway which is possibly shown here. The Republican Party in Pennsylvania was founded on November 27, 1854, in the Towanda, Pennsylvania, home of David Wilmot. Wilmot asked his friends, many of whom were governors and congressman, to form local Republican clubs in their home counties. The members here are unidentified. (Courtesy SBHC.)

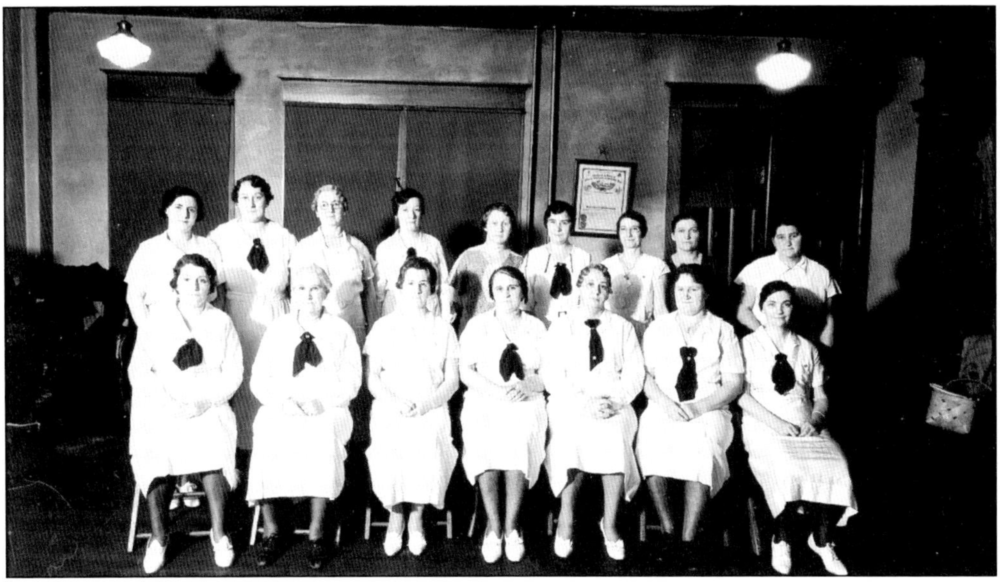

Bangor was not without its share of social and charitable organizations, which included the Elks, Moose, Knights of Columbus, Foresters, and Order of the Redman, to name a few. It also had several business, professional, and women's clubs, including the Auxillary of the Sons of Union Veterans of the Civil War, shown here, which started out as a military organization. (Courtesy BPL.)

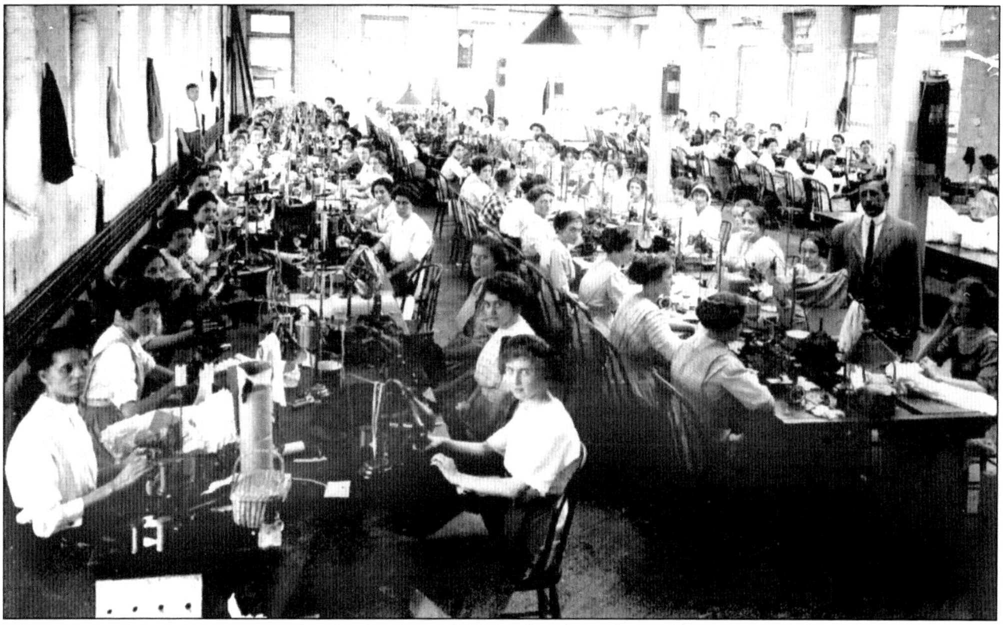

Women workers are seen inside the Sterling Silk Mill. The silk, and later apparel, industry provided work to the area as the slate industry began to decline. Sterling was opened in 1907 by Wilson R. Jordan. It was known for its beautiful gloves and jersey cloth, and many in the community regarded the mill as worthy of being called "sterling." Salaries of $125 a week were also considered worthwhile. (Courtesy SBM.)

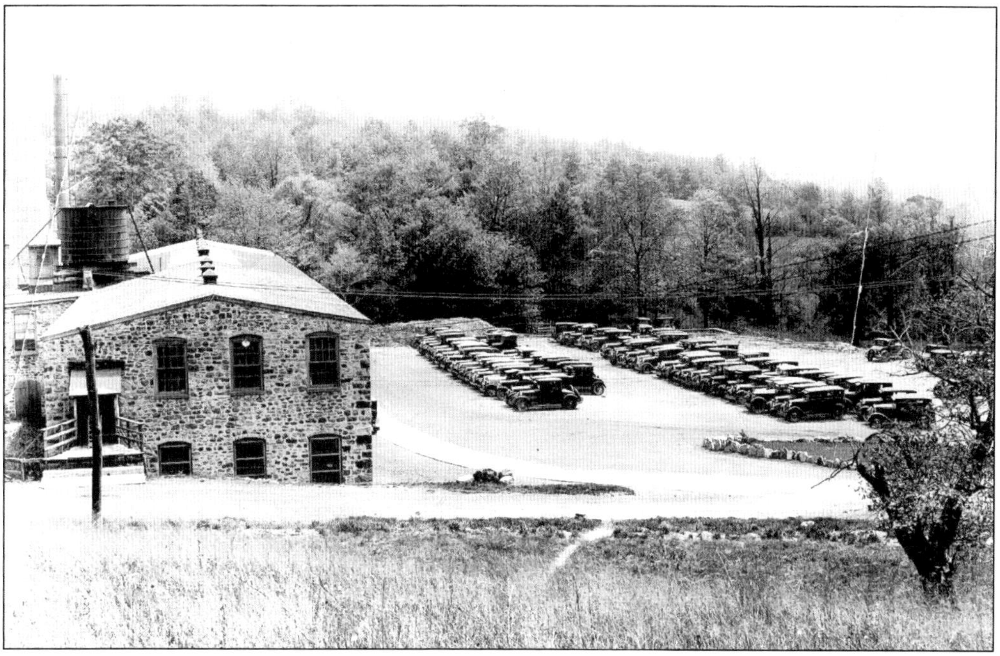

In 1919, the Crown Silk Mill was purchased by Julius Kayser and Company, which also purchased Sterling Silk around the same time. Located in South Bangor, it produced hosiery, gloves, underwear, and the area's first Milanese cloth. By 1936, it was one of the largest textile mills in the United States, with a worker's payroll of more than $1.5 million. (Courtesy BPL.)

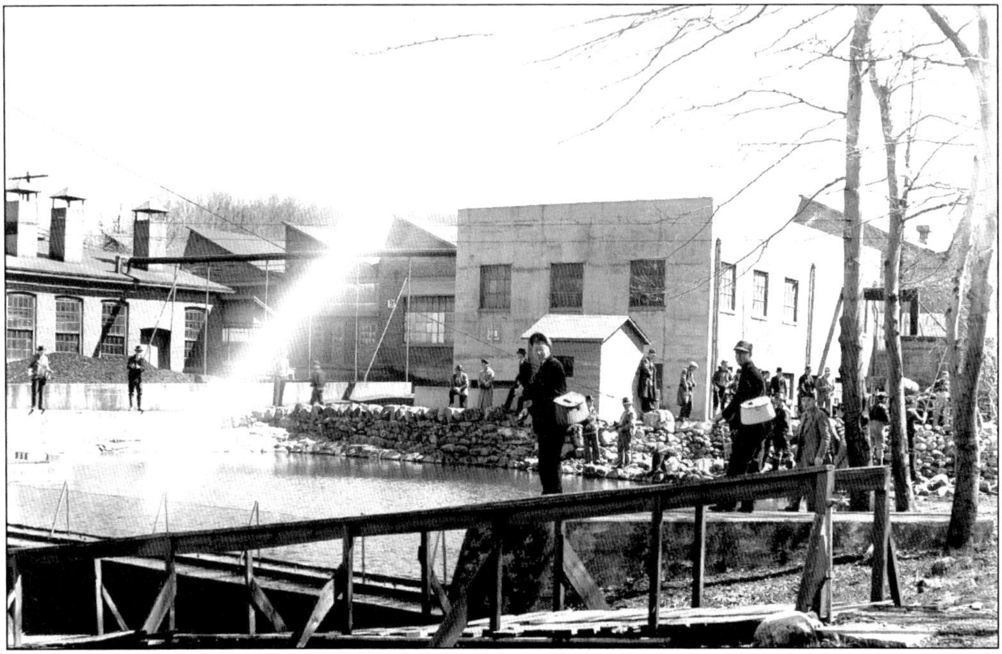

Both the Sterling and Crown mills were involved with their workers and the community, providing social reinforcement and even sick, accident, and death benefits. Sports were a part of their programs, like baseball and basketball teams and the fishing tournament seen here at the pond at Crown Silk Mill. (Courtesy BPL.)

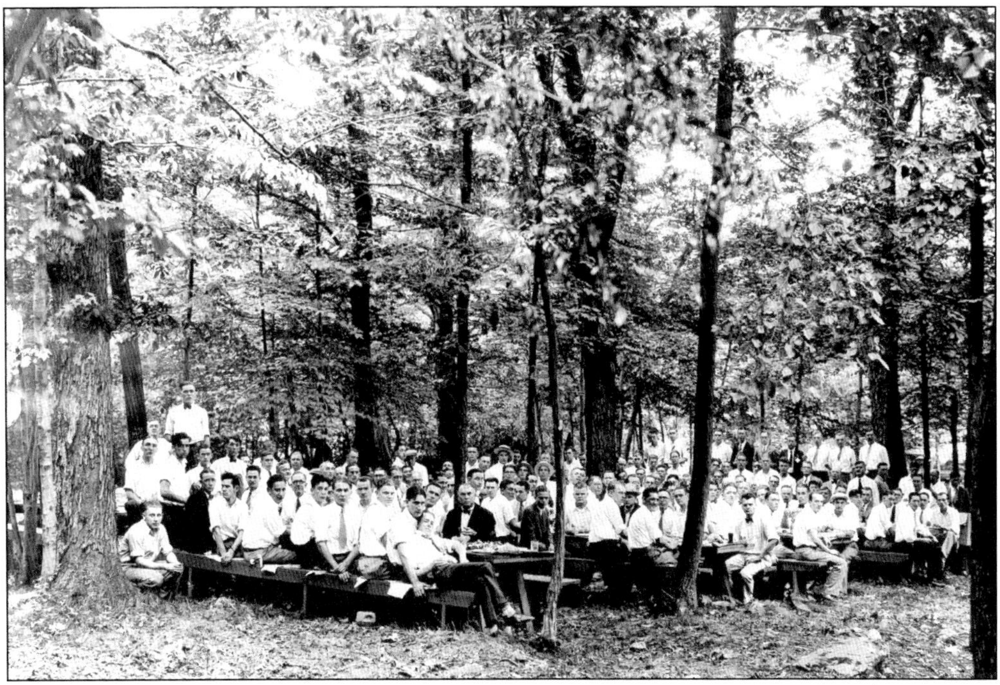

Sports were not the only social and recreational activities provided by the mills. This group of gentlemen, hosiery knitters from the Crown Silk Mill, is attending a clambake on August 10, 1929. (Courtesy BPL.)

Four

THE TOWNS

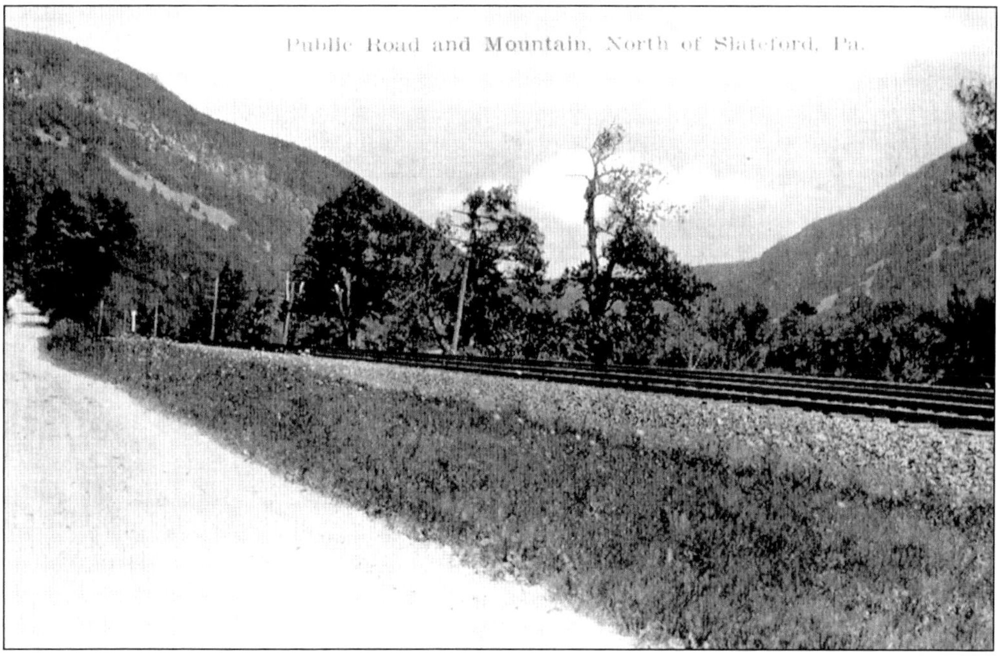

This is an early view of a public road (Route 611) just north of Slateford. The Delaware Water Gap can be seen in the background, behind the trees. If one continued to travel north, he would reach the Pocono Mountains. Traveling south would take you to Portland. Slateford was the town where the slate industry all began, when Samuel Taylor and James Porter discovered slate there in 1836. (Courtesy PSA.)

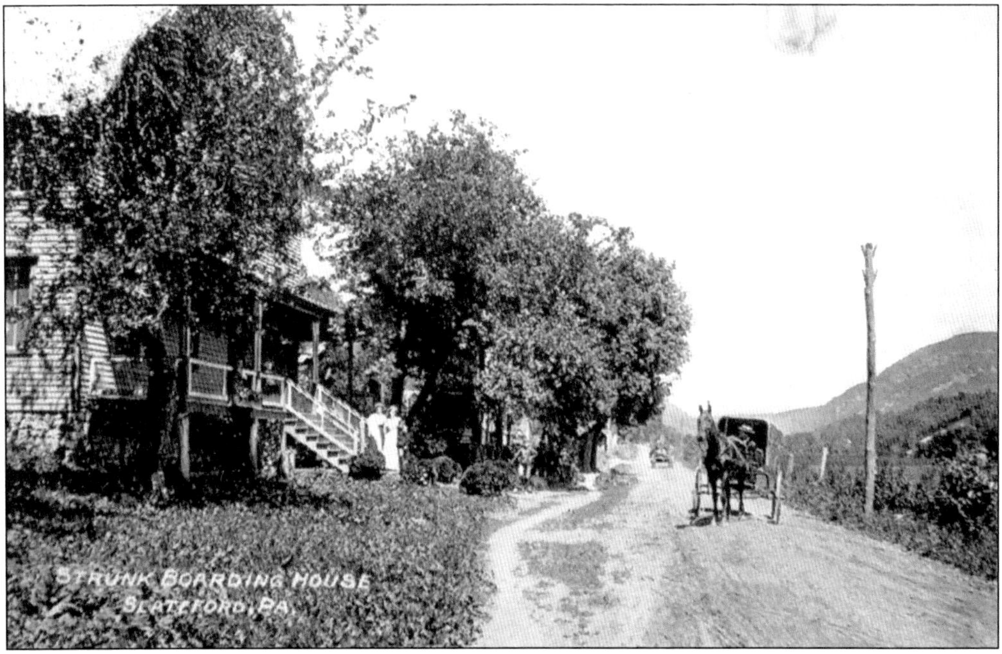

Strunk Boarding House in Slateford is shown here. Hotels and boarding houses like this one were not as common in other areas of the Slate Belt as they were in Bangor, which had quite a few such establishments. In addition to Strunk's, the Maple Dell in Slateboard provided accommodations. (Courtesy SBM.)

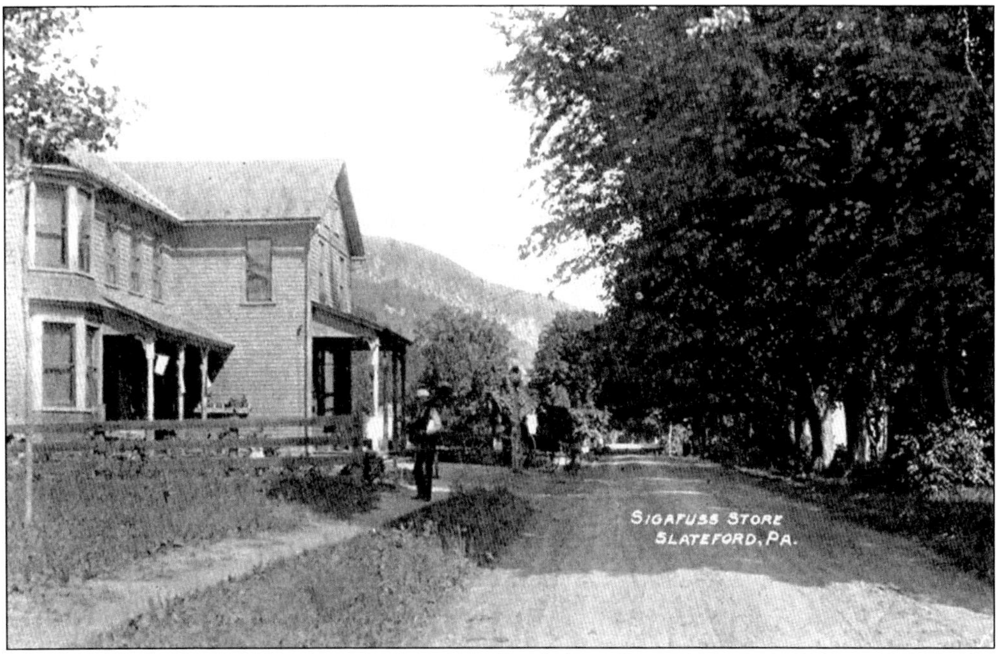

The Sigafuss Store in Slateford was built in 1902 by Phil Sigafuss, who operated the store until the start of World War II. A little bit of everything was sold here. Food items and material were sold on the first floor, while shoes, boots, clothing, nails, bedding, and stovepipes were sold on the second floor. A post office was also located in the building at one time. (Author's collection.)

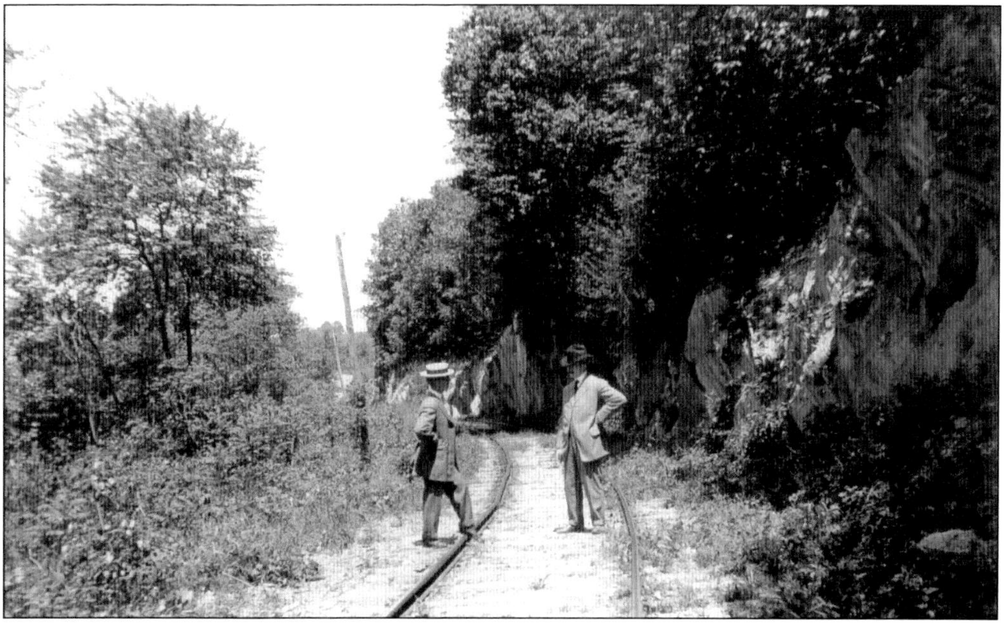

Two gentleman converse along the railroad tracks just below Portland. The railroads played an important role in the area. They came to the area as a result of the booming population and, together with the trolleys, allowed residents to leave the area for work and business. The railroads also greatly helped in transporting slate from the quarries to their markets. (Courtesy PSA.)

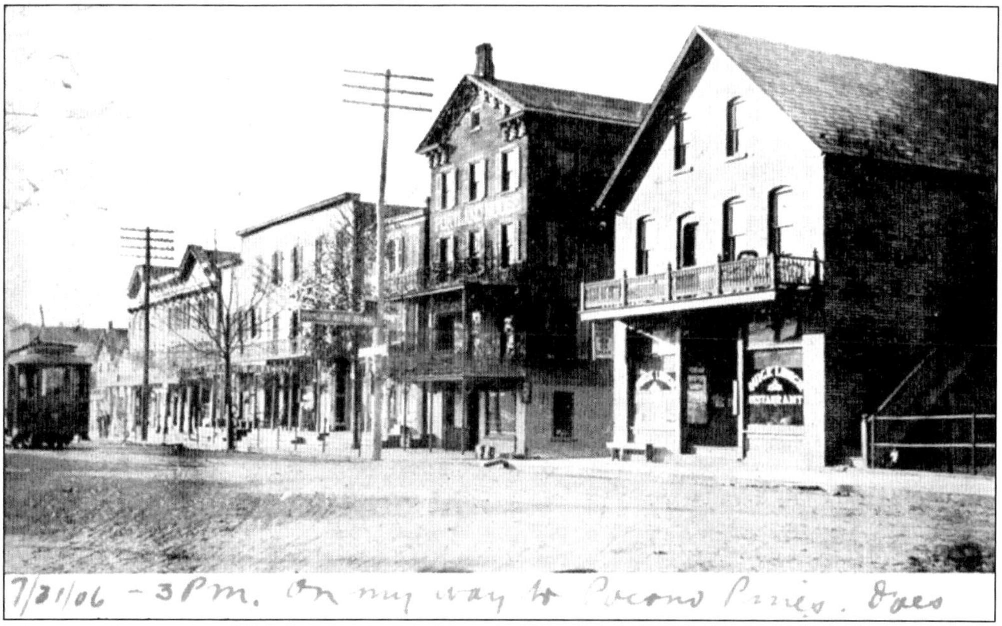

This was the main road through Portland around 1906. Portland was incorporated in 1876 and prior to that went by a variety of names. In the 18th century, it was called Dill's Ferry and later in 1851, New Market. When the railroad came through, it was known as Columbia Station. No one knows for certain why the name Portland was chosen, but many say it was named for Portland, Maine. (Author's collection.)

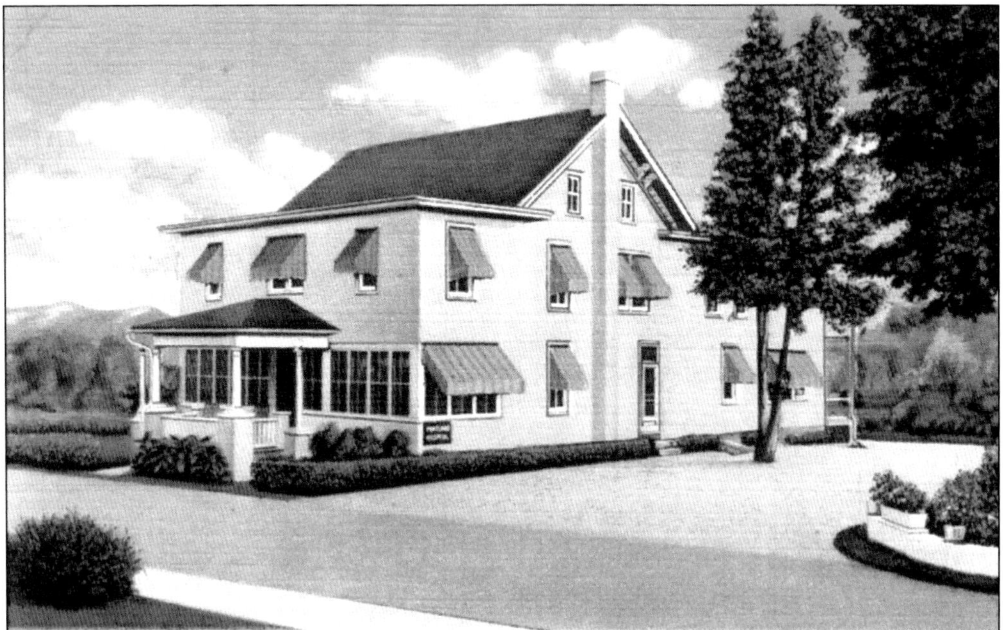

PORTLAND HOSPITAL — PORTLAND, PA. 2A-H935

Portland, along with Pen Argyl, was fortunate enough to have its own hospital. It was only three miles from the Delaware River and had a spacious lawn and flower garden, shown below. Hospital literature stated that "any person" could come for medical and surgical treatment and have their personal surgeon or physician attend to them. The hospital had an x-ray machine and "all kinds" of electrical treatments were given. Literature also stated that a "colonic Irrigation Table" was available for different treatments, and free booklets and information were furnished upon request.

SCENIC GEM OF THE BEAUTIFUL DELAWARE VALLEY AS SEEN FROM REAR WINDOWS OF "SUN PARLOR"

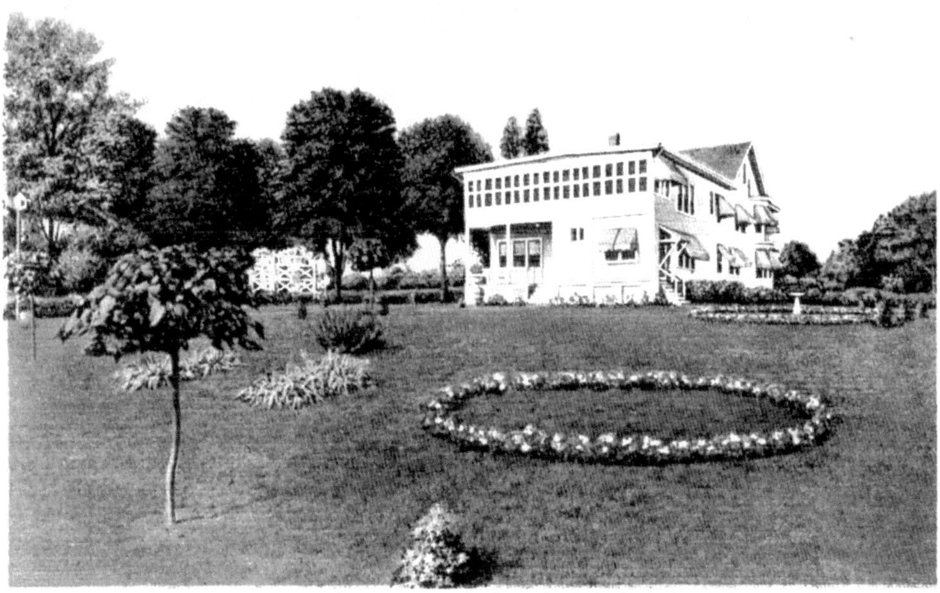

PORTLAND HOSPITAL — PORTLAND, PA. 2A-H934

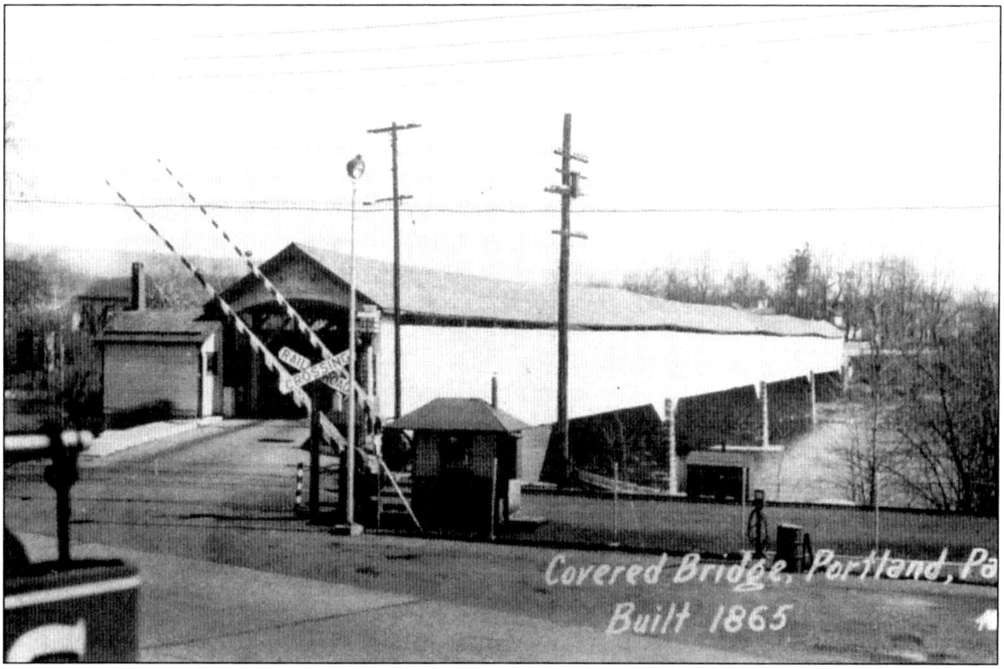

Two views of the Portland-Columbia Covered Bridge are shown here. The bridge was made entirely of wood and was 796 feet long and 18 feet wide. It was incorporated in 1816 by the legislatures of Pennsylvania and New Jersey, the two areas that the bridge connected, but a variety of problems delayed actual construction until 1839. It cost $40,000 to build, but by 1954, it was closed to all but pedestrian traffic. On August 19, 1955, Hurricane Diane hit Northampton and nearby counties, destroying the bridge, which, at that time, was the longest covered bridge in the United States. Today a walking bridge and new steel span the Delaware River. (Author's collection.)

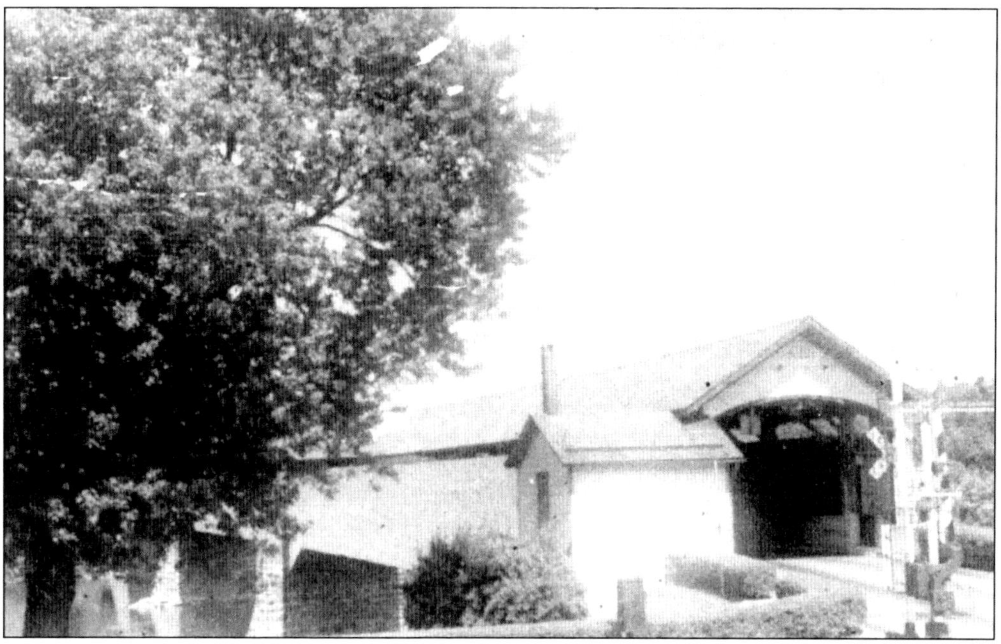

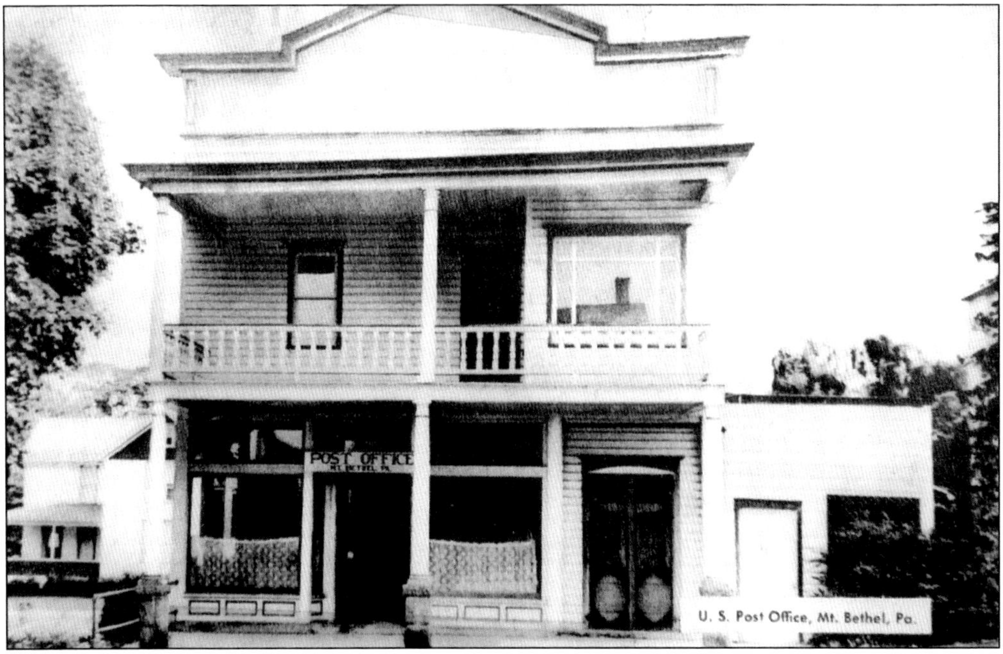

Post offices became commonplace in the 19th century as the population of the Slate Belt grew. The Mount Bethel Post Office is shown here, but this was just one of many buildings that housed the post office. It was established on June 23, 1829, when the town was still known as Williamsburg. (Courtesy SBM.)

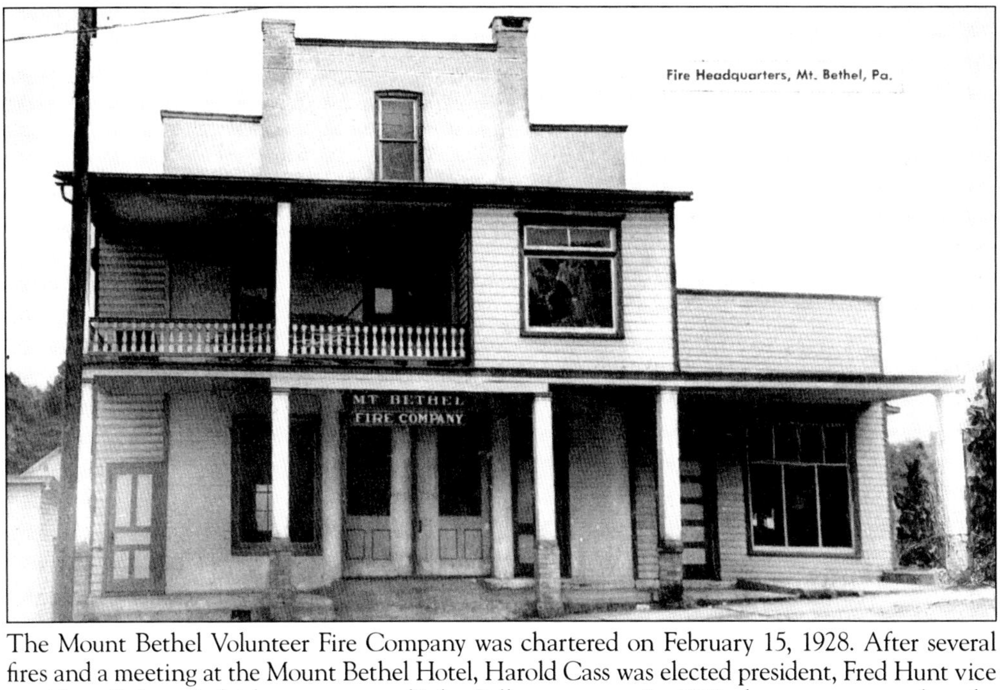

The Mount Bethel Volunteer Fire Company was chartered on February 15, 1928. After several fires and a meeting at the Mount Bethel Hotel, Harold Cass was elected president, Fred Hunt vice president, Robert Farleigh secretary, and John Felker treasurer. In 1928, the company purchased a 1917 Model-T Ford fire truck, which had two 50-gallon tanks and 100 feet of hose. Water pressure was supplied by acid and soda. (Courtesy SBM.)

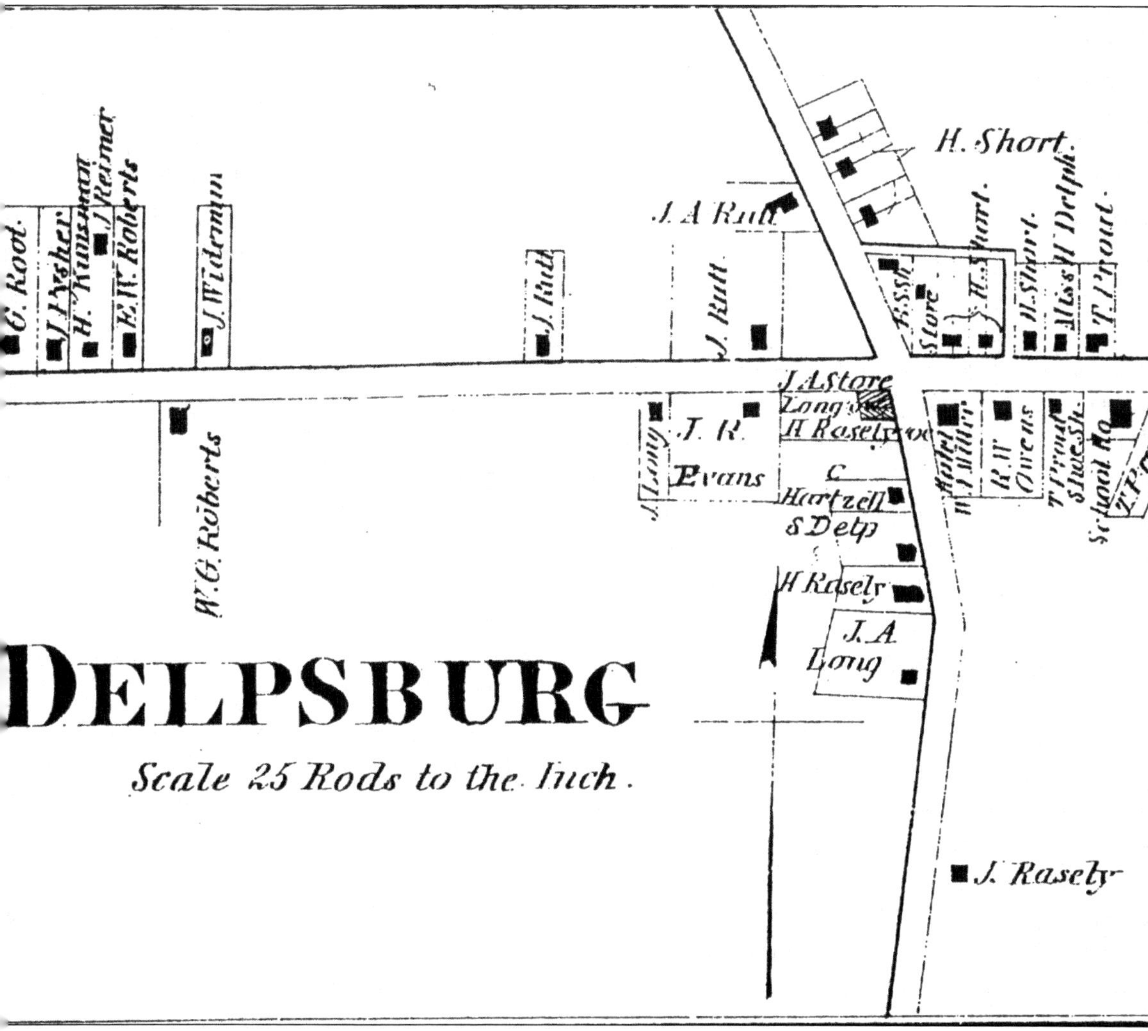

This 1874 map shows the tiny town of East Bangor. The town, which comprises about a half square mile, was originally called Delpsburg after Andrew Delp, who owned most of the land. The name change seems to have occurred over several years, but by 1875, Delpsburg was called East Bangor, probably to capitalize on its proximity to Bangor, which was then internationally known for its slate. (Author's collection.)

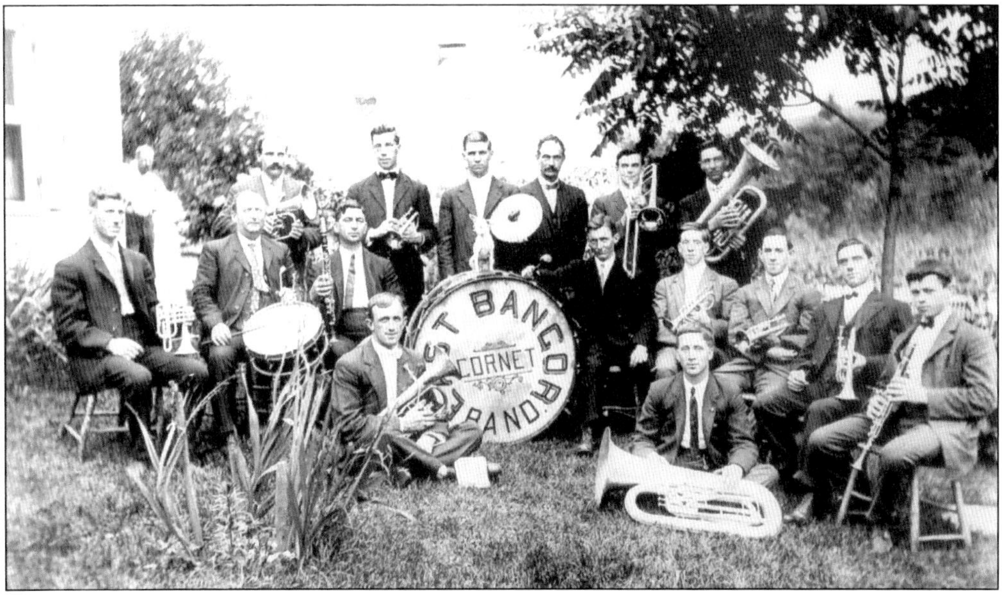

The pride of East Bangor, the East Bangor Cornet Band, was formed in 1885 and was quite popular. Shown here are the following: (seated) Thomas Lobb, Doc Trewin, John Lobb, Evan Ewing, Clifford Lobb, Herbert Amy, John Richard, Harrison Jones, Jim Parsons, and Elijah Lobb; (standing) Malon Lohman, Richard Heard, Marvin Lobb, Al Warrick, Frank Stenlake, and Heper Tucker. (Courtesy SBM.)

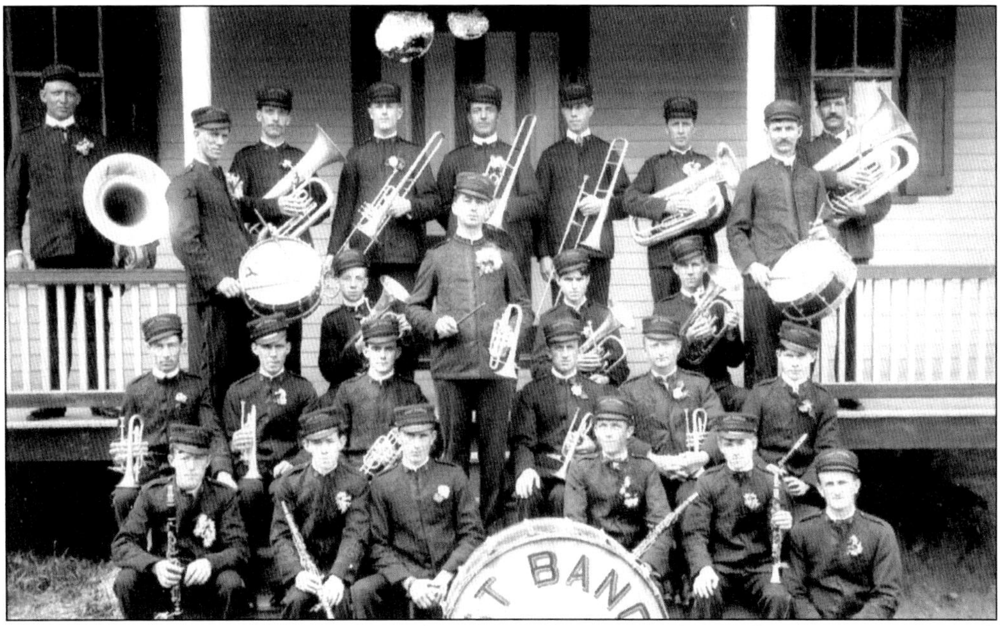

The East Bangor Cornet Band is shown here around 1905. Included in this photograph are Jack Hockins, John Richards, Sam Baker, Clyde Lobb, John P. Lobb (band leader), Clarence Rowe, Tommy Lobb, Frank Trewin, Dick Heard, Elias Robert, Cliff Lobb, Marvin Lobb, Herbert Brittion, Heper Tucker, Ernest Lobb, Frank Stinlake, James Parson, Morrie Trewin, John Norton, Ed Amy, Herb Amy, Windy Hamm, Ted Hill, and Garnet Rowe. (Courtesy SBM.)

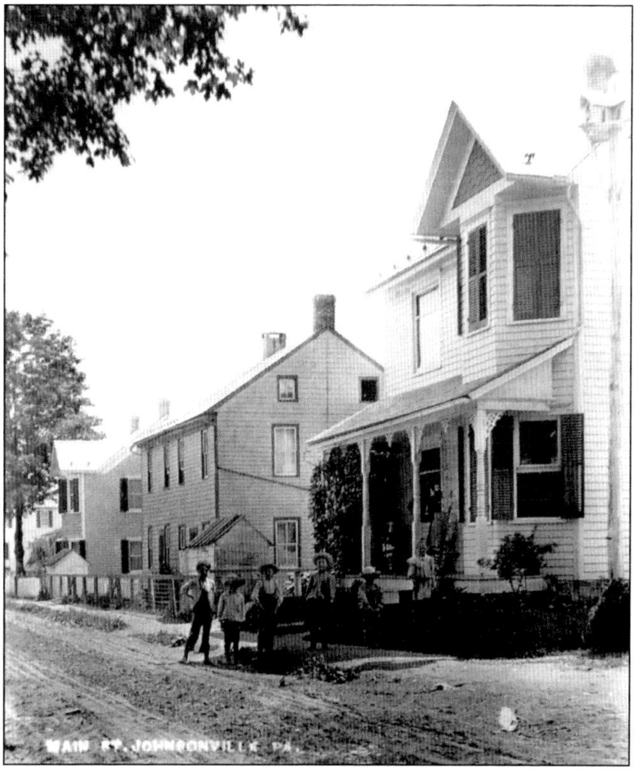

The homes and children of Johnsonville are seen here on Main Street. The tiny town was originally called Roxburg, and in the 1860s, had approximately 20 dwellings. Like many areas it had a church, post office, hotel, stagecoach, and a few businesses, but was best known for its beautiful redware pottery that was produced from local clay by potters like the Kellers and the Jacob Stiers family. (Courtesy SBM.)

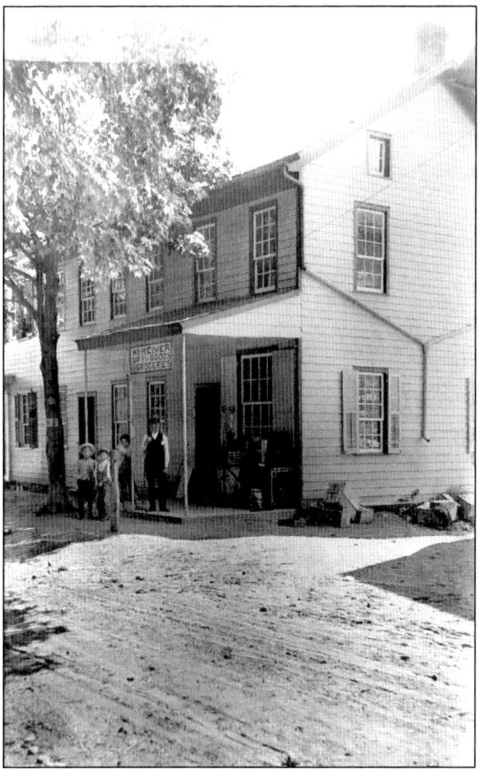

Children gather outside the William Reimer Grocery Store in Johnsonville. The store, which was located on Main Street, was the only grocery store in the area. It was formerly owned by William Apple. In addition to groceries, shoes, boots, kerosene, and other family staples were sold. (Courtesy SBM.)

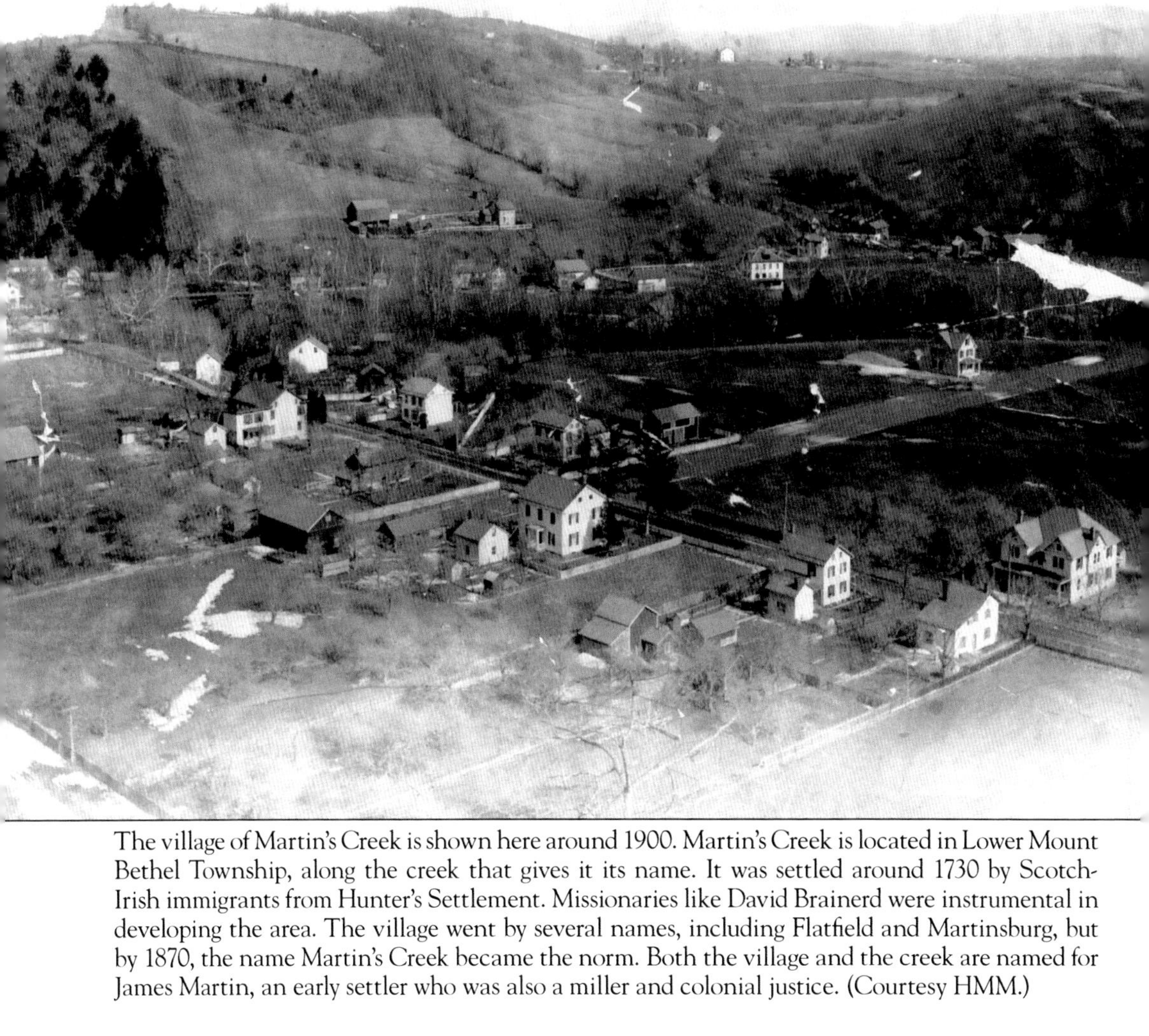

The village of Martin's Creek is shown here around 1900. Martin's Creek is located in Lower Mount Bethel Township, along the creek that gives it its name. It was settled around 1730 by Scotch-Irish immigrants from Hunter's Settlement. Missionaries like David Brainerd were instrumental in developing the area. The village went by several names, including Flatfield and Martinsburg, but by 1870, the name Martin's Creek became the norm. Both the village and the creek are named for James Martin, an early settler who was also a miller and colonial justice. (Courtesy HMM.)

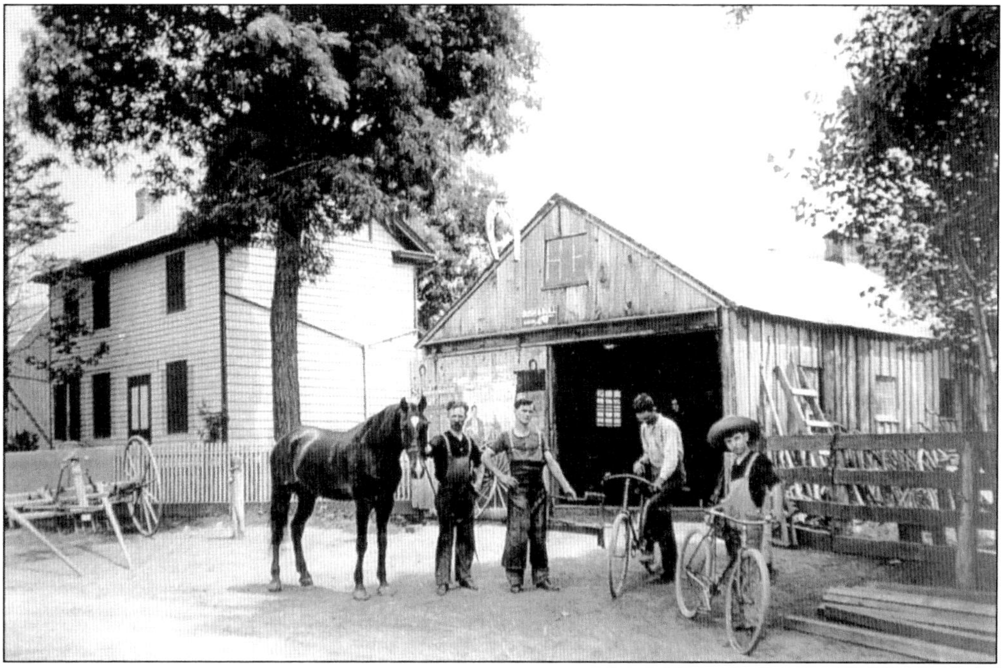

Men and boys are seen above at a blacksmith shop in Martin's Creek. Blacksmith shops not only provided for residents of the community but also were important to the quarries, which needed specialized tools. Several quarries had blacksmith shops on the premises. The Martin's Creek Post Office (right) was opened on October 13, 1810. A. Whitesell was the postmaster. William McIlhaney was postmaster in 1832. (Courtesy HMM.)

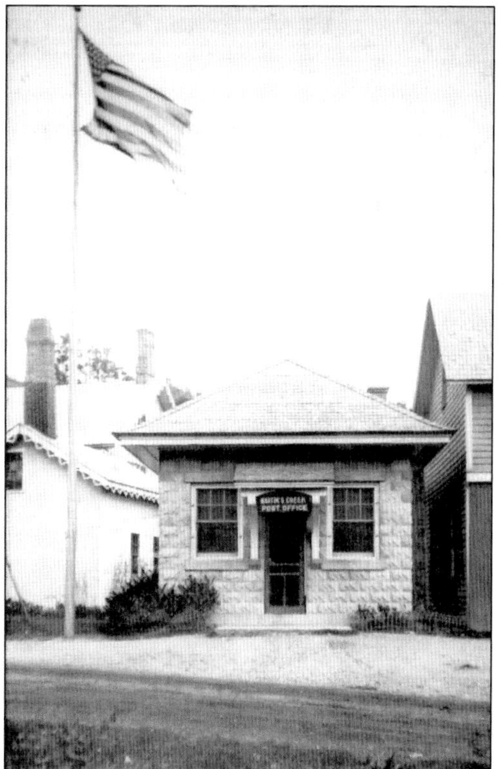

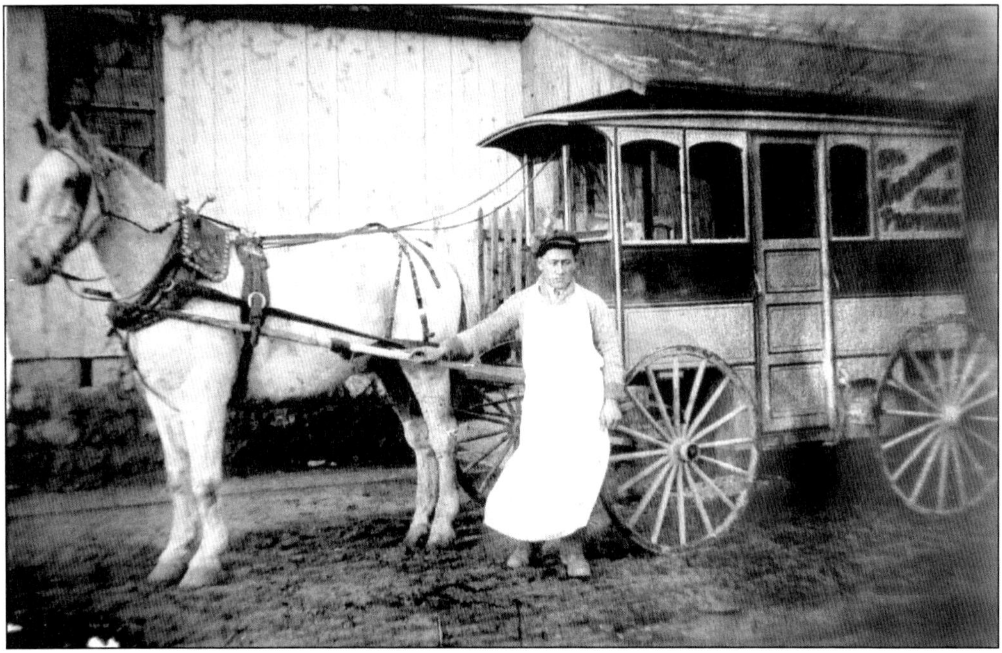

Angelo Pitoni is shown here with his butcher wagon around 1912. The business was actually owned by Julius Karabinus, but Pitoni made weekly deliveries of meat, protected by blocks of ice, to Martin's Creek and Easton residents. The horse, Paul, was said to have known the route by heart. (Courtesy HMM.)

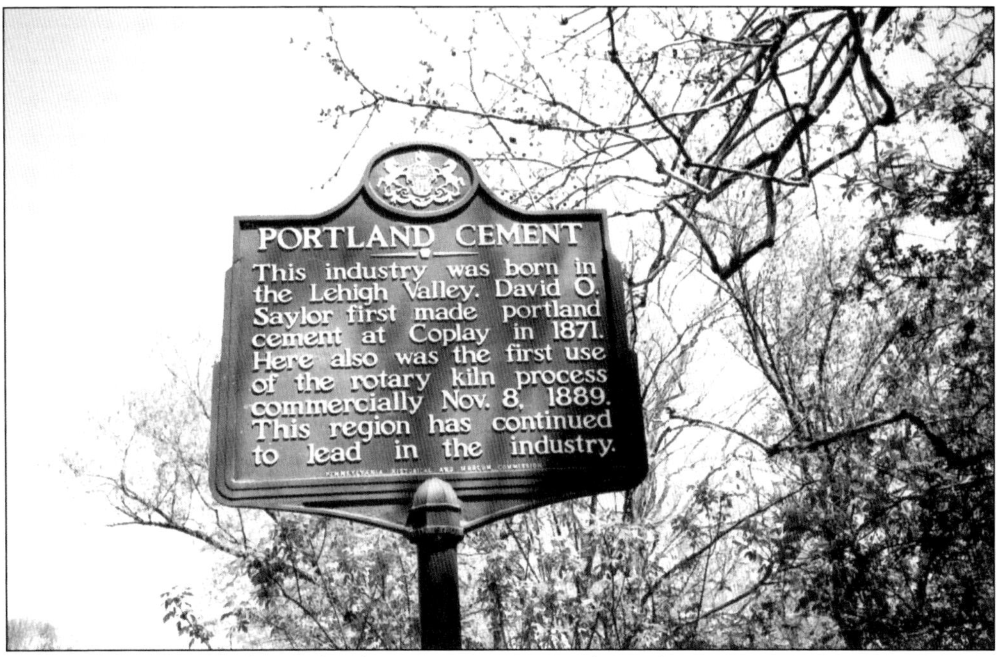

This historical sign for the Portland Cement Company is located on Route 611, near Easton. In 1871, David O. Saylor developed a process for making Portland Cement in Coplay, Pennsylvania. Before that, the cement, which was needed in the area for the canals, was imported at considerable cost from Portland, England. (Author's collection.)

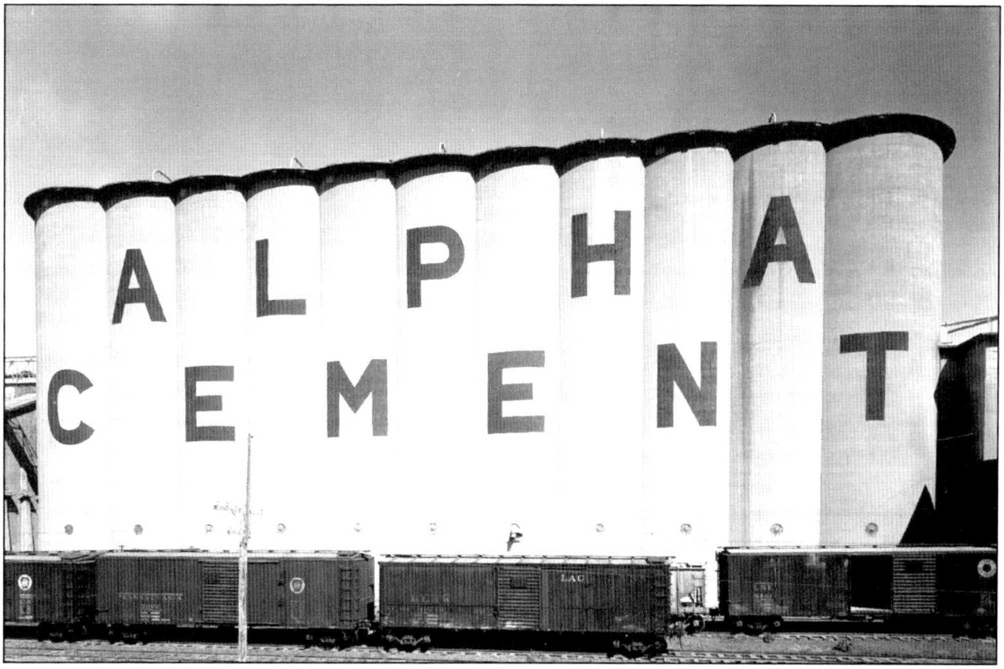

The Alpha Portland Cement Company silos, shown here, are still standing. The company was originally started in Alpha, New Jersey, in 1895 but changed its incorporation from New Jersey to Pennsylvania in 1902. The silos were located in plant No. 4, which began operations just south of Martin's Creek in 1908. Together with plant No. 3, it produced about 8,000 barrels of concrete daily. The company was big enough to have its own trains (below) for transporting its product. Plant No. 4 was closed in 1964, ending 74 years of cement manufacturing along the Delaware River. (Courtesy David Drinkhouse.)

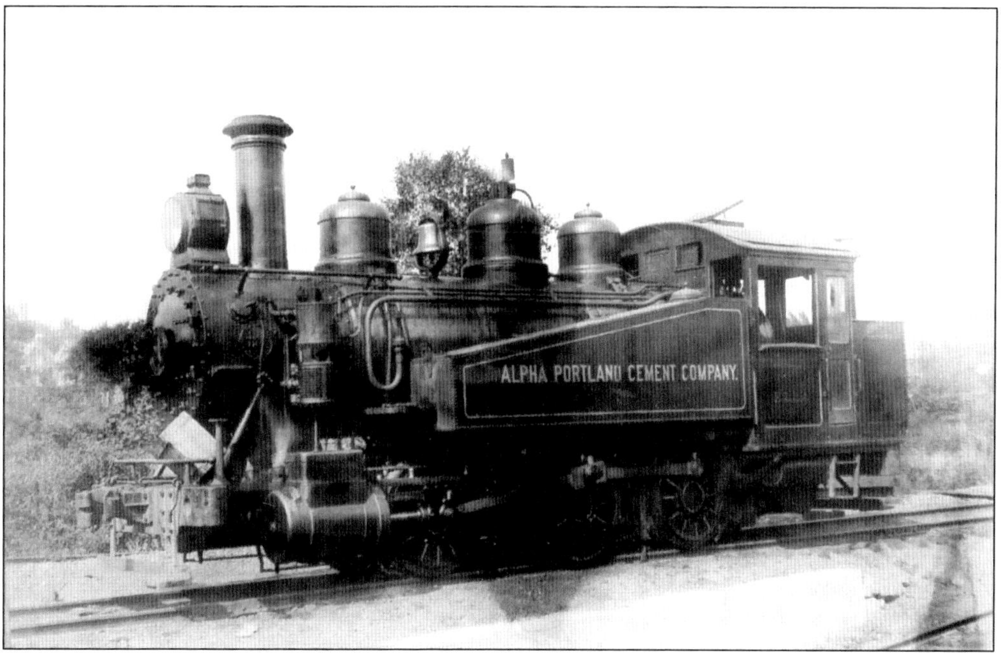

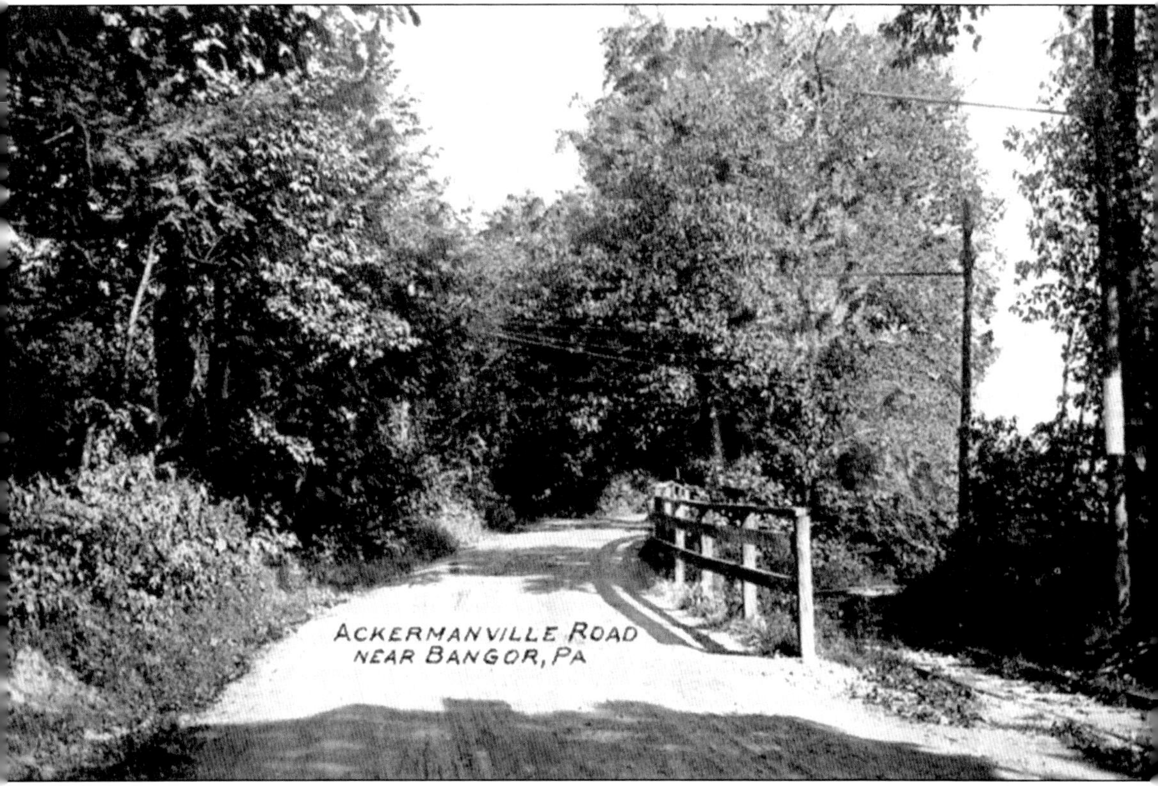

Ackermanville is a village southwest of Bangor that is named after one of its first residents, John Ackerman. According to the Ackerman genealogy by Claire Ackerman Vliet, John Ackerman and his family arrived in the community in the later part of the 18th century from Bucks County. It is said that he and his wife walked all the way with their young children in tow. Ackermanville was a small farming community and a village of gristmills. The first gristmill was built in 1792, with a second one built in 1822. The second gristmill was destroyed by fire in 1927. (Courtesy SBHC.)

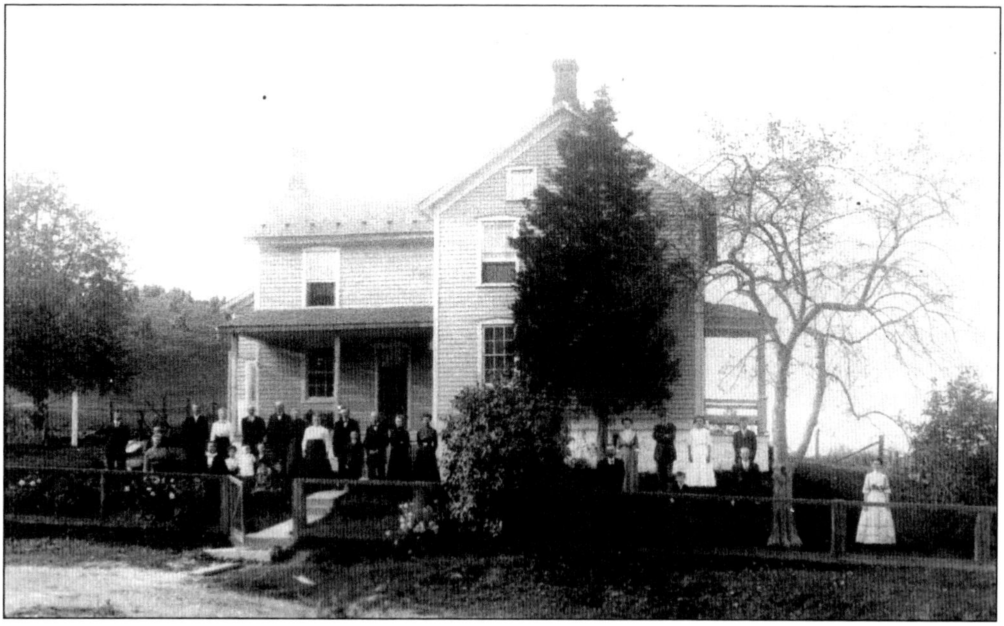

The Ruch family of Flicksville is seen here at their homestead in 1911. Flicksville, like Ackermanville, was named for one of its first prominent residents, John Caspar Flick, who arrived in the early 19th century. The Ruch family arrived later but was so large and had several business interests that many people wonder why the area was not called Ruchville. (Courtesy FHS.)

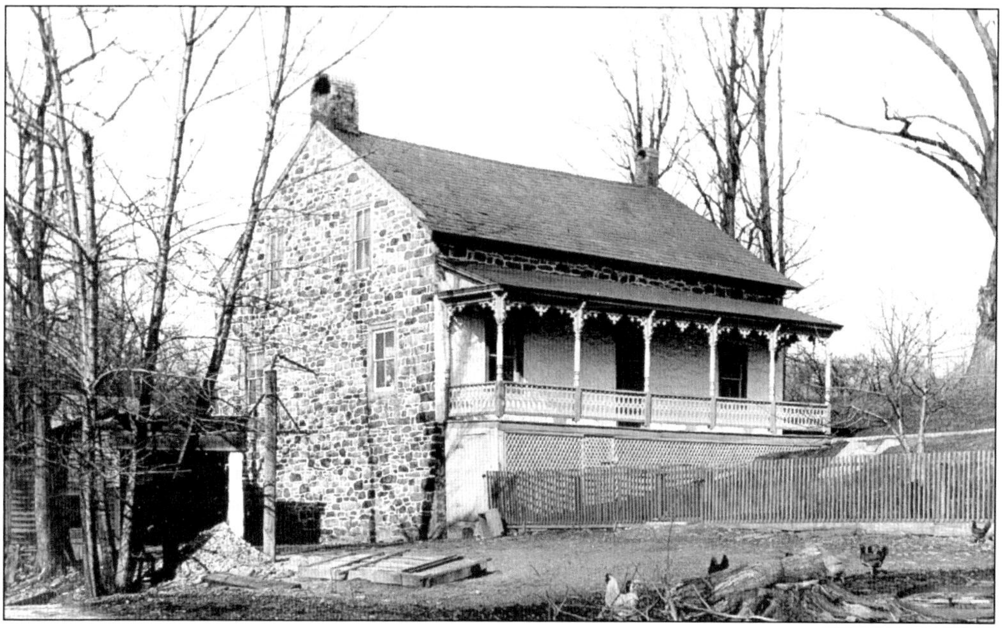

Flicksville, like Ackermanville, was a sleepy farming community whose expansion revolved around the operation of several gristmills. Samuel and Henry Rothrock built the first mill in 1791 along Smalley's Creek, now Martin's Creek. A millhouse, shown here, stood just north of the mill. It was a lovely stone structure, built to resemble Swiss-style homes. (Courtesy FHS.)

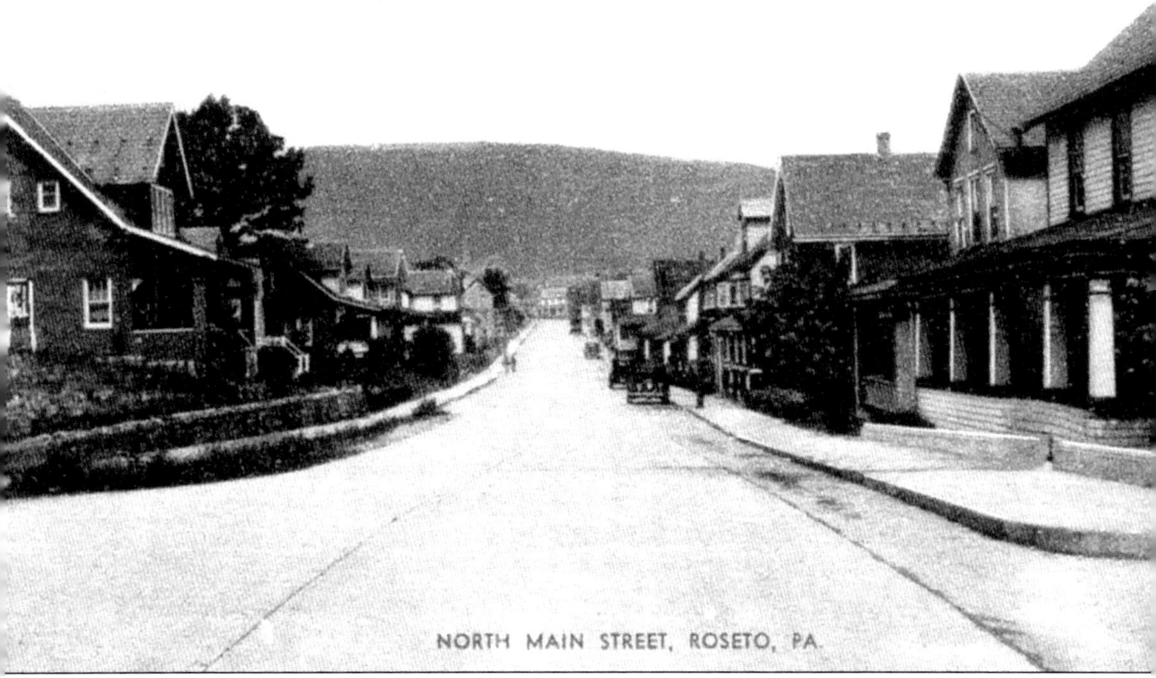

The town of Roseto was settled by Italian immigrants from a similar village in the Foggia province of Italy, along the Adriatic coast. Extreme poverty caused immigration to America after a Jesuit priest, Father Luigi Sabetti, became the town's first citizen to come to America. In 1882, several immigrants arrived and helped settle the "New Italy" area, with names like Cascioli, D'Iorio, Finelli, Policelli, Albanese, and Luisi. In 1879, Father Pasquale DeNisco arrived from London, England, and was instrumental in helping the town progress. Around this time, Nicola Rosato built the first house, and the area was incorporated as a borough in 1911. Roseto gained national attention in the 1960s when Dr. Stewart Wolf and Dr. John Bruhn published a study on the absence of heart disease in the town, which was attributed to close family and community ties. (Author's collection.)

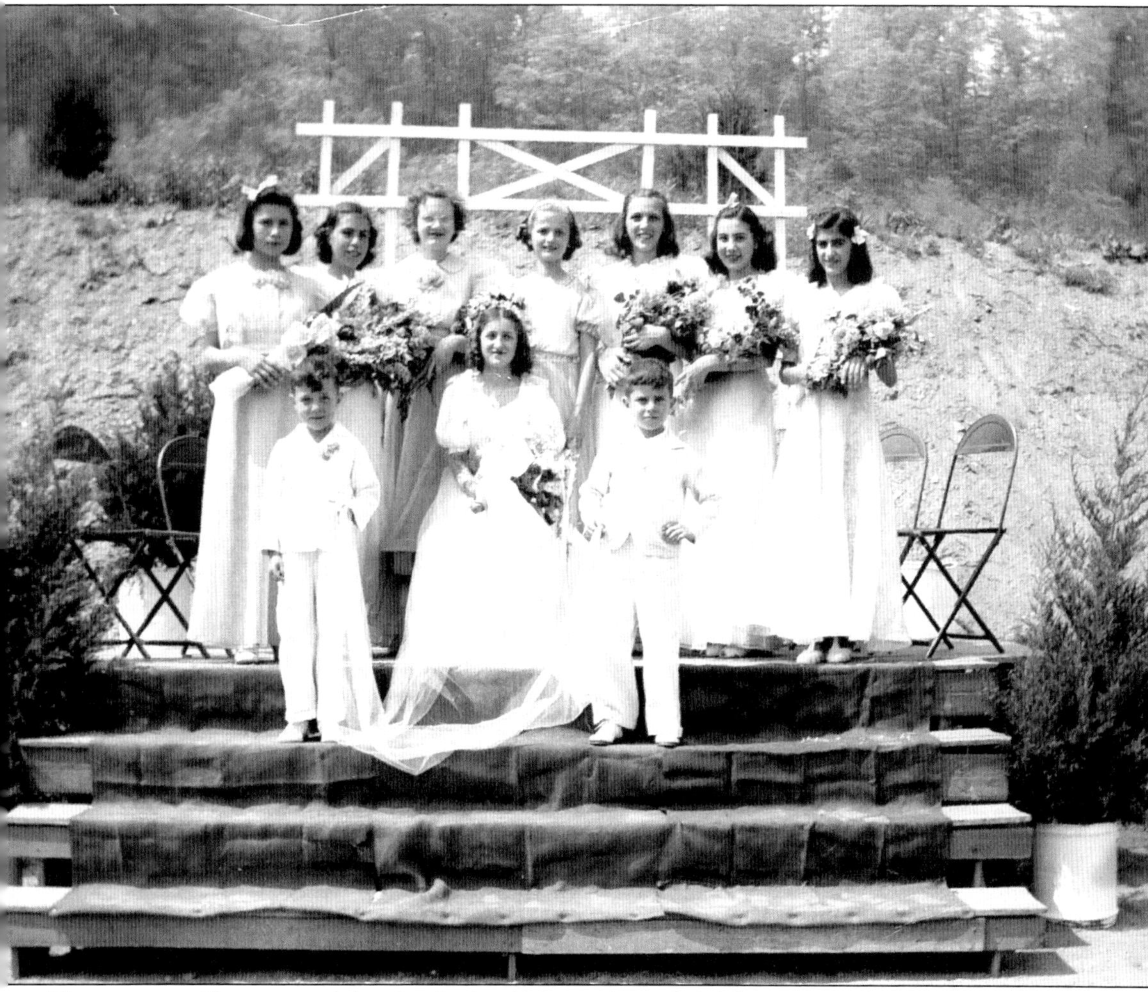

The queen and her court of the Our Lady of Mount Carmel Celebration are shown here. More popularly known as the "Roseto Big Time," the carnival is both a religious and civic event that is held the last week in July. It was a tradition that was started in Roseto, Italy, and continues to this day. In the early days of the event, thousands of people came from all around to a big field, where they could socialize with friends and neighbors and enjoy rides, games, and good food, including a Italian specialty known as pizza fritta, which is a tasty dough fried in oil. (Courtesy BPL.)

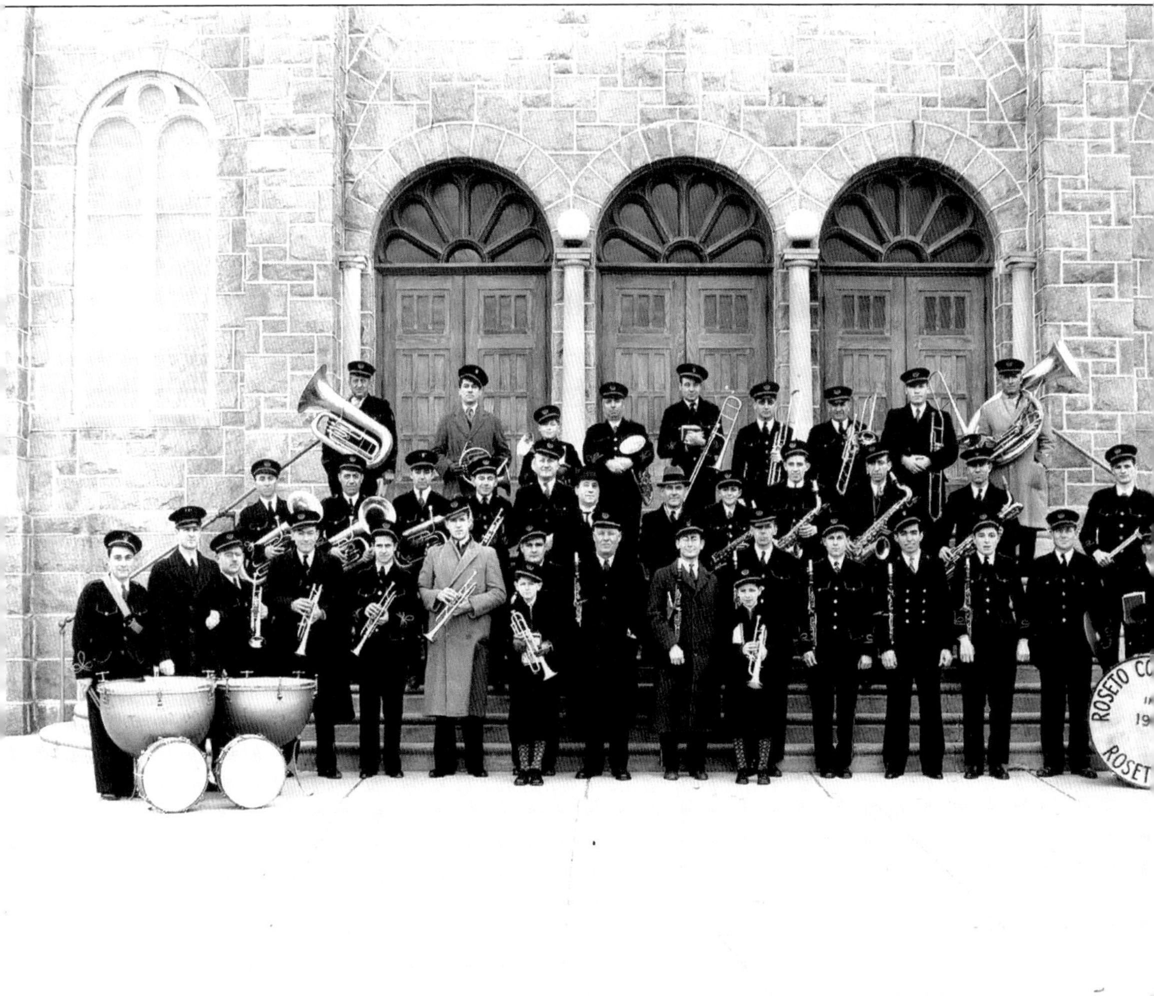

The Roseto Cornet Band was formed in 1889 at the Our Lady of Mount Carmel Celebration and was incorporated in 1907. It is shown here around 1960. The first members were former members of the Brass Band of Roseto Valfortore. The band, which only played a few dance pieces in the beginning, later expanded its program to include the music of classical masters like Verdi, Rossini, and Puccini and became well known enough to play in venues like Newark, New York, Washington, D. C., and Atlantic City. It was guided by maestros such as Michelangelo Donatelli, Nicole D'Italia, and Arturo Ungaro. Louis Angelini guided the musical direction of the band in later years. (Courtesy BPL.)

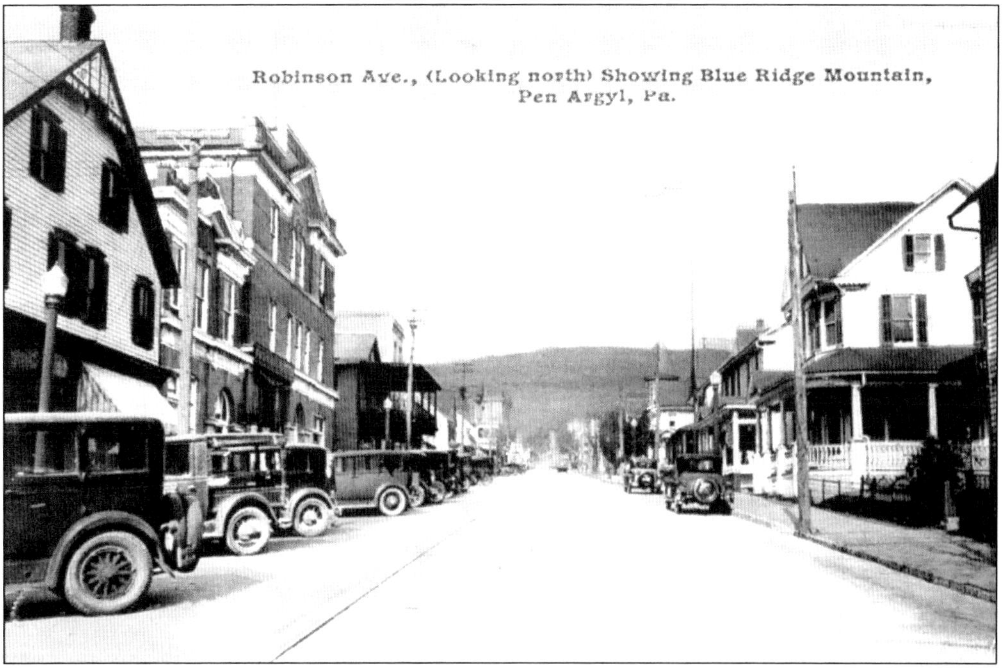

Seen here are views of Robinson Avenue (above) and Jackson Avenue (below) in Pen Argyl. Most of the streets in Pen Argyl were named for real estate people. In 1882, real estate man Hiram Westbrook of Milford, Pennsylvania, visited the area and became convinced that the small town nestled in the Blue Ridge Mountains had great real estate potential. He bought the land around Robinson Avenue and Main Street for $7,000 and negotiated to sell lots to local customers. At a subsequent sales event, lots were said to be sold as people walked. The area itself was founded by Cornish immigrants. "Pen" is Celtic for mountain and "Argyl" is Greek for slate. In Welsh, Pen Argyl means "chief deposit of clay slate rock." (Author's collection.)

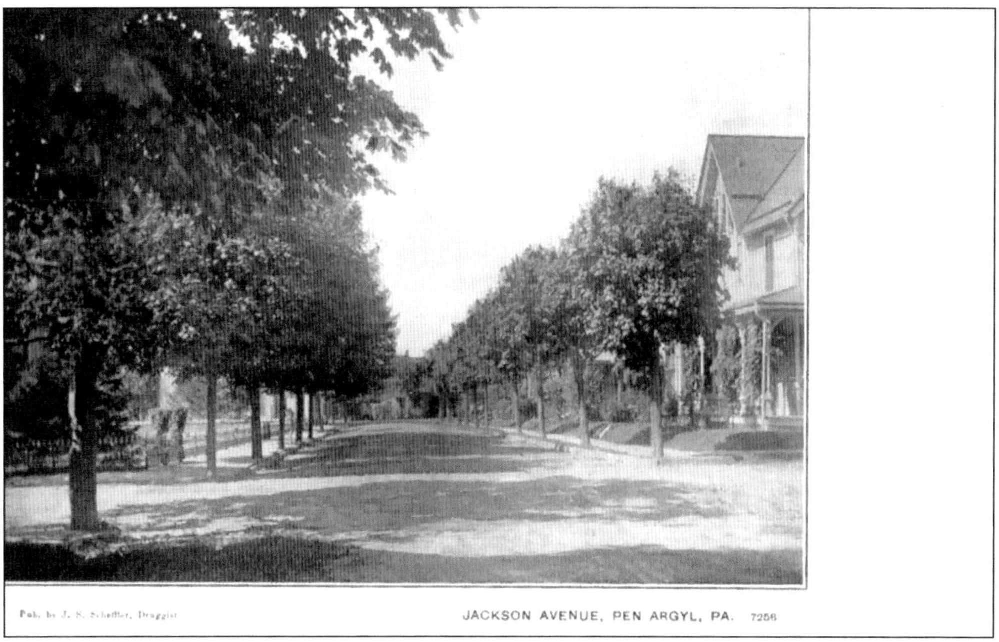

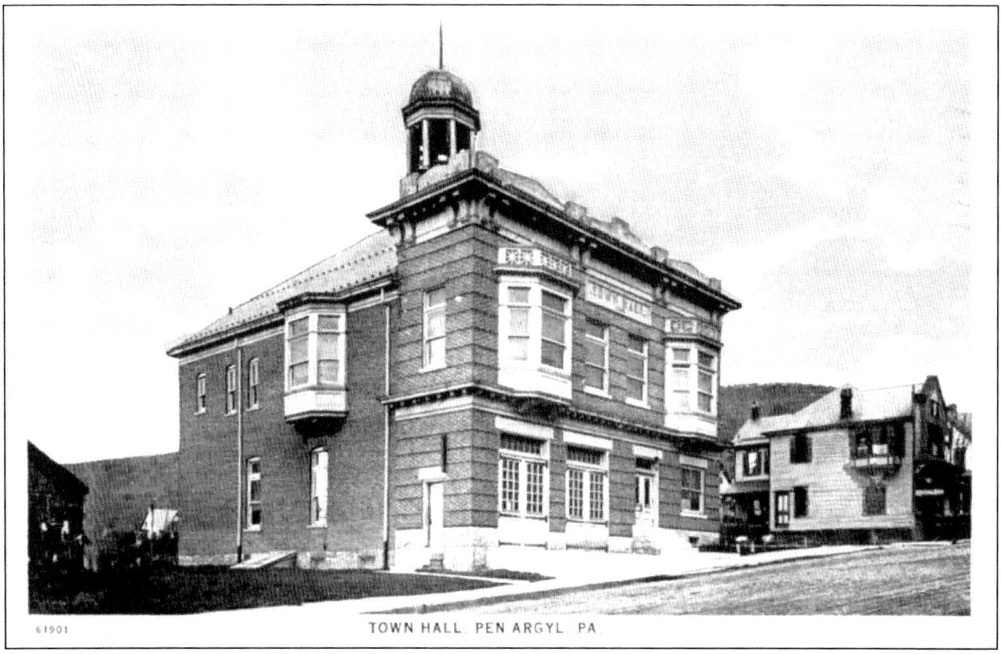

The Pen Argyl Town Hall is seen here in the 1920s. It still stands on Robinson Avenue, although the first town hall was located on George Street. The first town council was organized on April 12, 1882, which is also considered the date of its incorporation. (Author's collection.)

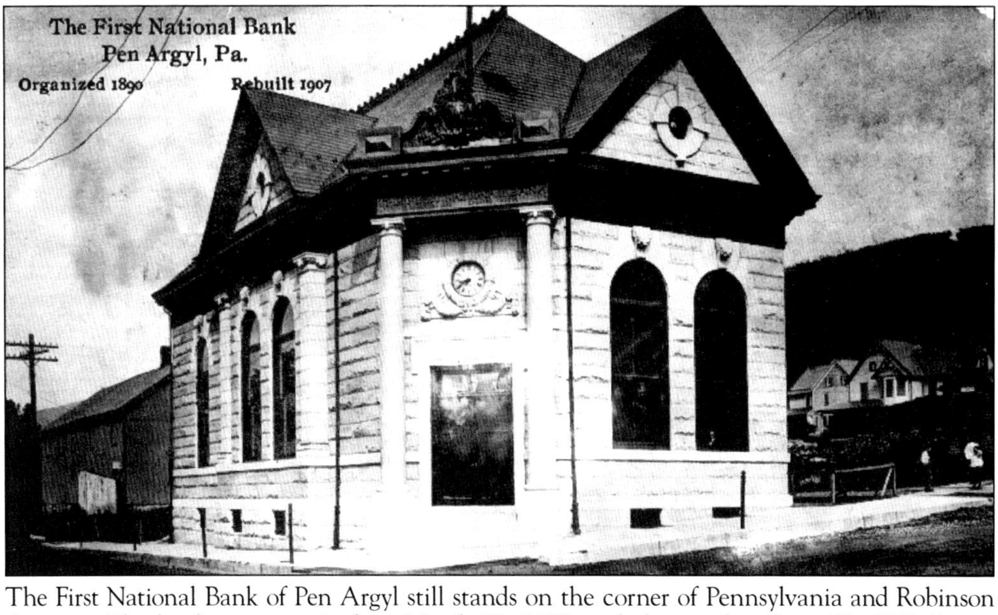

The First National Bank of Pen Argyl still stands on the corner of Pennsylvania and Robinson Avenues. The bank was organized on March 22, 1890, and chartered on June 30, 1890. It was rebuilt in 1907 and reopened for business on March 23, 1908. A new addition was added in 1979–1980. (Courtesy SBHC.)

The Correll Opera House can be seen here on the left. It was owned by Richard Correll, who came to Pen Argyl in 1879 and opened the opera on the third floor of his home in February 1886. One had to enter through the side door to reach the opera house. Plays, concerts, and minstrels were performed, and the town's first phonograph was displayed there in 1890. (Courtesy SBHC.)

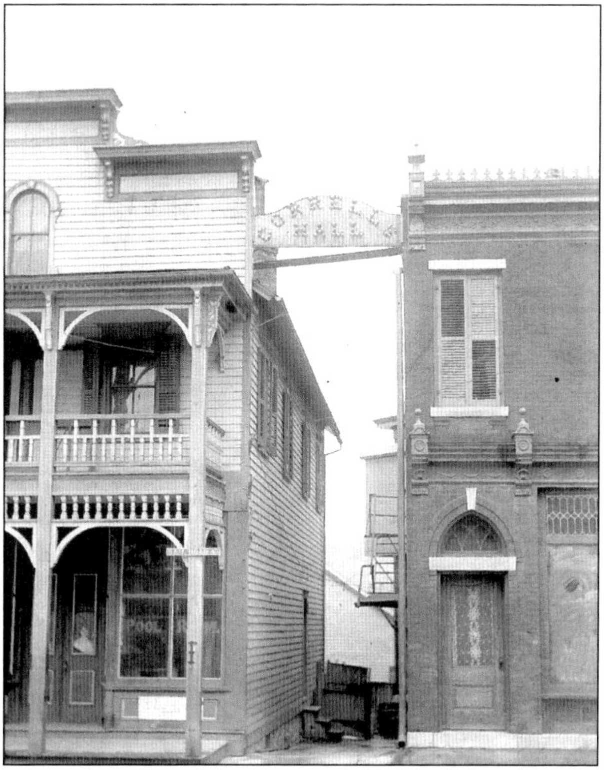

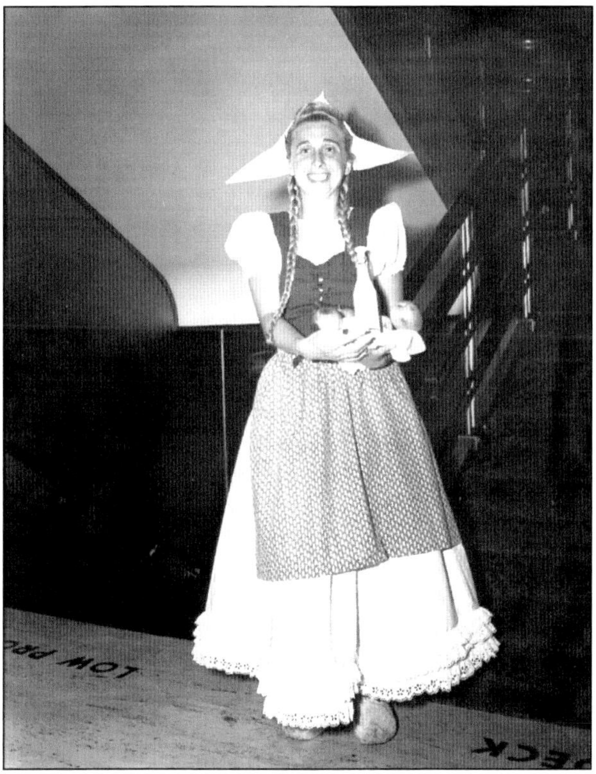

Maryella Correll, granddaughter of Richard Correll, is shown here in costume in the 1950s during a cruise ship contest, of which she won first prize. Maryella lived in Pen Argyl and in the opera house for most of her life. In later years, she gave interviews about the opera house and life in Pen Argyl, stressing the importance of community. (Courtesy SBHC.)

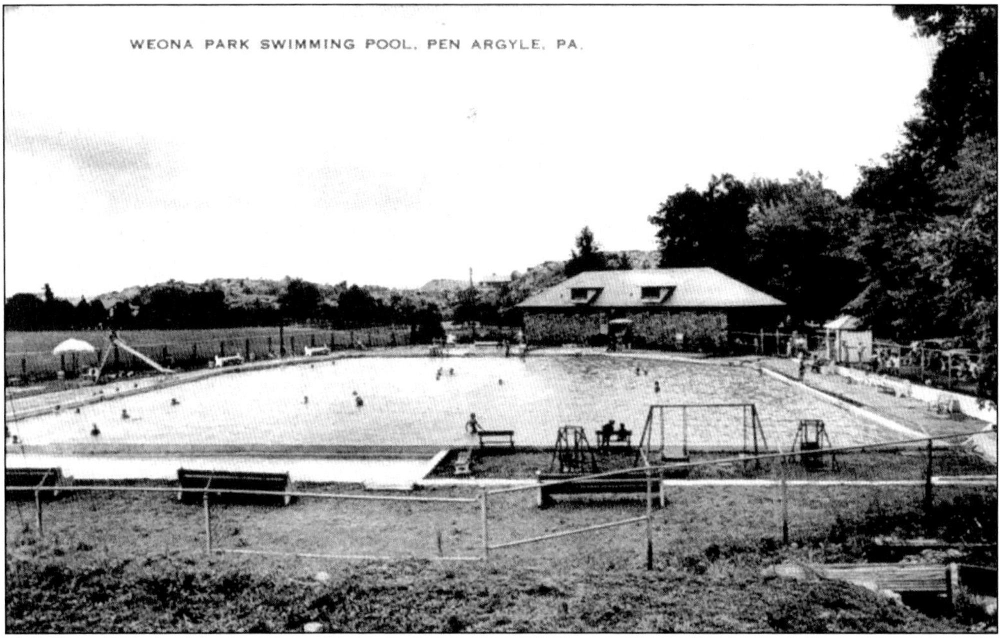

Like Bangor, Pen Argyl officials wanted to provide its youth and residents with a good recreational facility and turned a bog and field into a park in 1920. Unable to decide on a name, the town's board of directors held a contest to name the new park. Corienne Broad won with the name "Weona," a play on the words, "we-own-a-park." (Author's collection.)

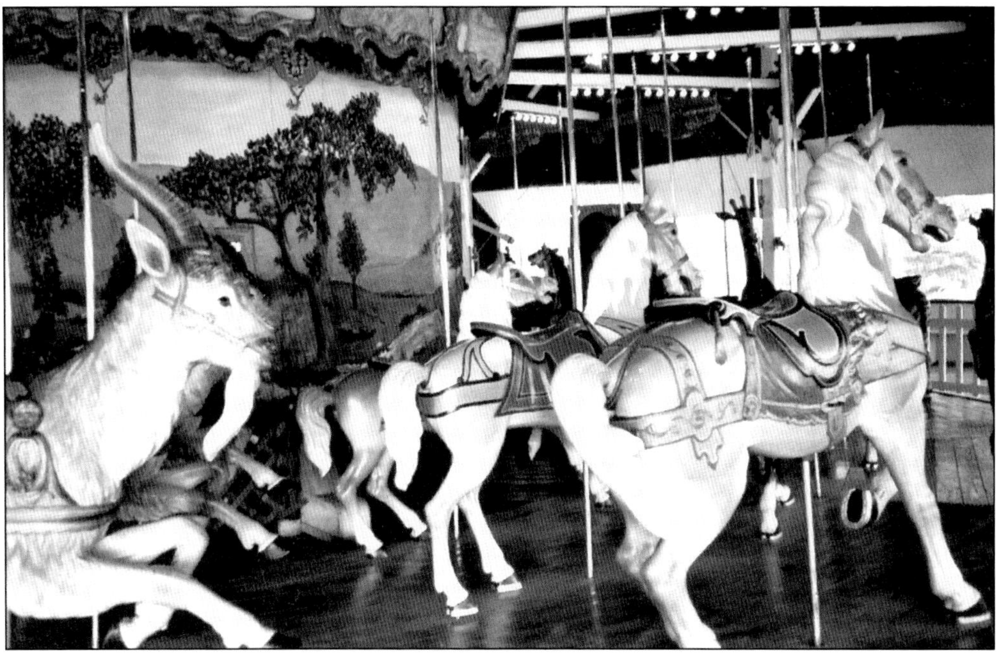

Weona Park is home to a world-famous Dentzel Carousel, purchased from the William Dentzel Factory in Germantown, Pennsylvania, in 1923. It is housed in a specially made, round, wooden building that is supported by concrete piers. The carousel features hand-carved giraffes, goats, deer, a zebra, and chariots, along with horses for a total of 44 animals. (Author's collection.)

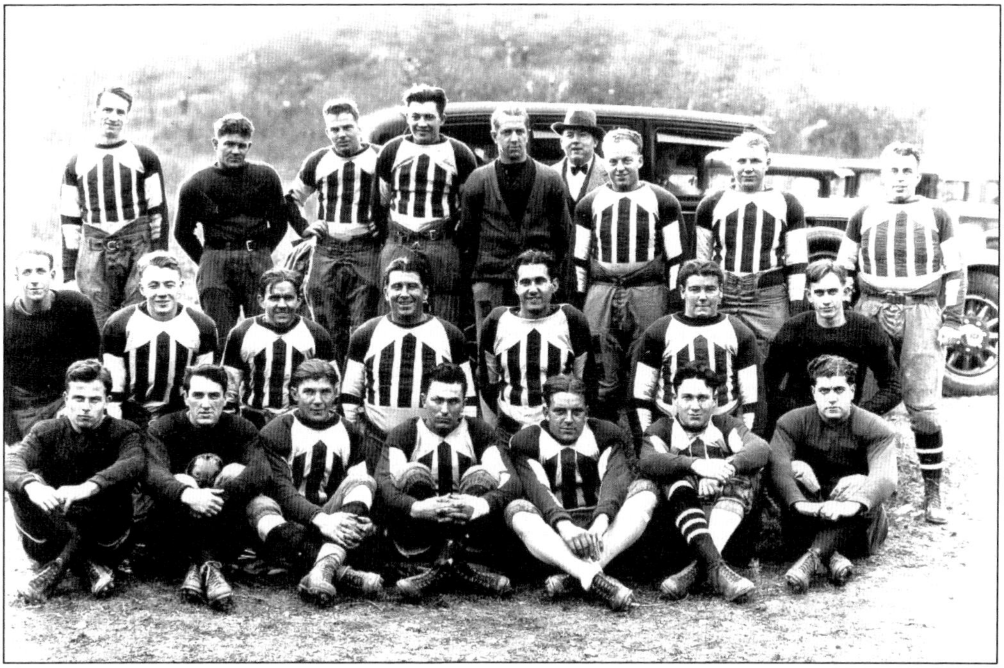

Sports were a big part of life in Pen Argyl, just like they were in nearby Bangor and other Slate Belt towns. Records of the teams and their players were often sketchy, but both baseball and football were popular sports. One of the most popular and successful teams was the Nightriders (above), so named because, in 1933, lights were erected at Weona Park and the team played there in the evenings. In the span of seven years, they played over 112 games. They posted a record of 90 wins, 13 losses, and tied nine games. (Courtesy BPL.)

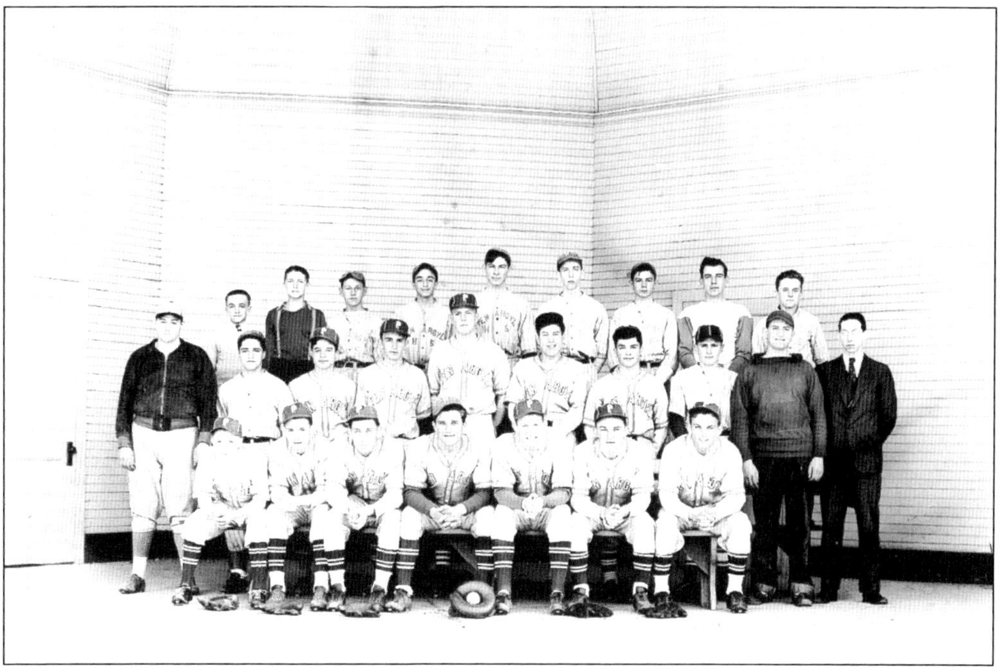

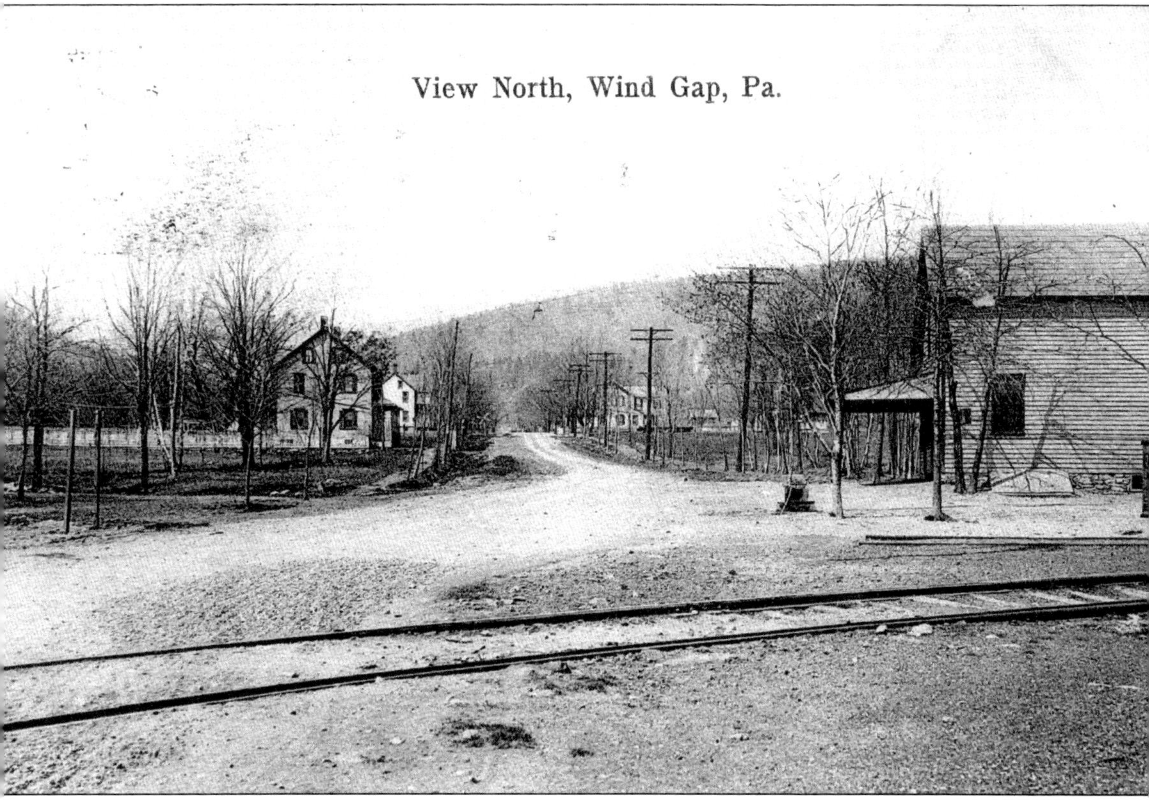

The borough of Wind Gap is seen here in the early 20th century. Wind Gap was originally part of Plainfield Township and was incorporated in 1893, when Ben Miller served as the first chief burgess. Gen. John Sullivan passed through the area on his now famous Sullivan's March during the Revolutionary War. The area was then known as Hellertown, likely named after one of the few families and businesses, Heller's Tavern. Transportation, such as the railroads, helped develop the area to the point where some quarries and silk and garment factories were opened. In later years, Wind Gap became known as "The Gateway to the Poconos" because of its proximity and direct route into the Pocono Mountains. (Author's collection.)

Five

A Star Among Us

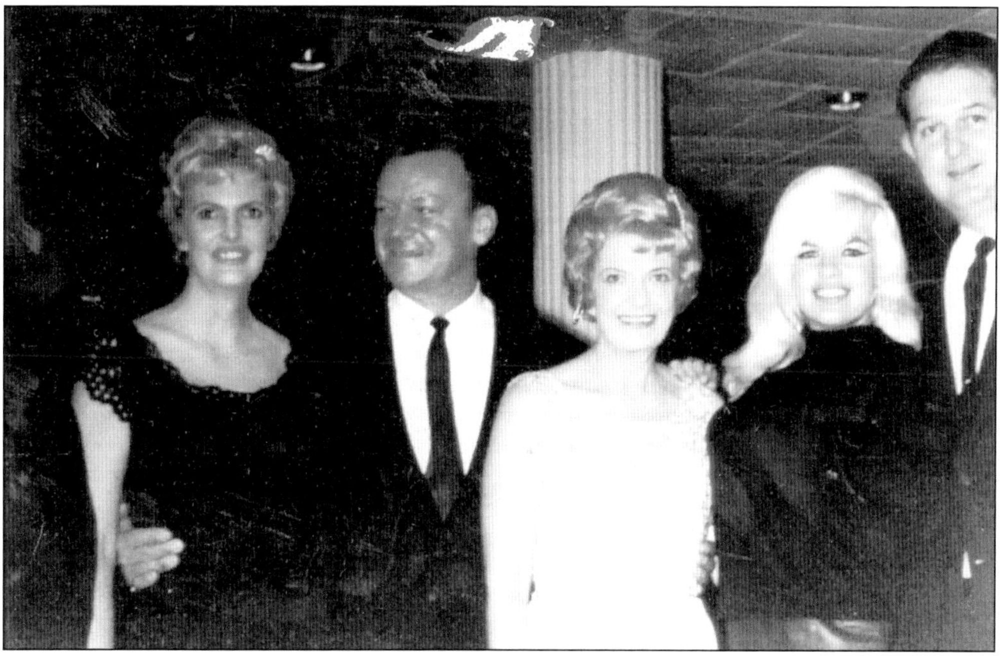

Actress Jayne Mansfield (second from right) is shown here at Mount Airy Lodge in the Poconos in what would prove to be one of her last public appearances. The star of Hollywood screen, stage, and Las Vegas nightclubs, she was raised in Pen Argyl. Shown here are, from left to right, Jayne's first cousin, Cynthia, actor Aldo Ray, Jayne's aunt Helen Milheim, Jayne, and Cynthia's husband, Aldo. (Courtesy Frank Ferruccio.)

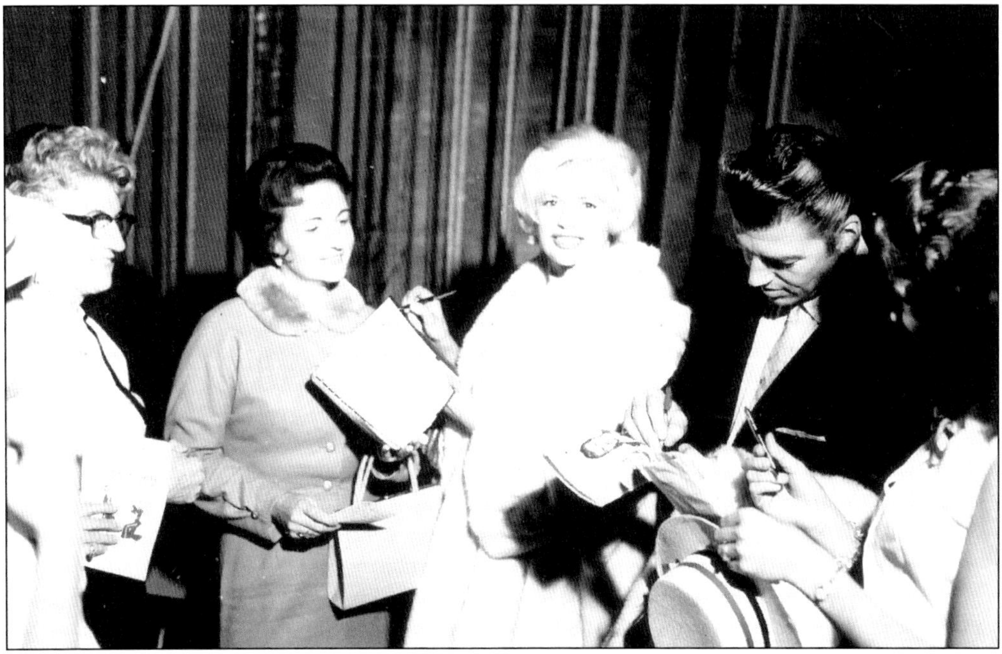

Jayne Mansfield is seen here signing autographs after a show with her husband, Mickey Hargitay, who was Mr. Universe of 1955. Autograph-signing was a frequent activity for Jayne, whose unpretentious personality and down-to-earth attitude earned her the reputation for being "the people's actress." (Courtesy Frank Ferruccio.)

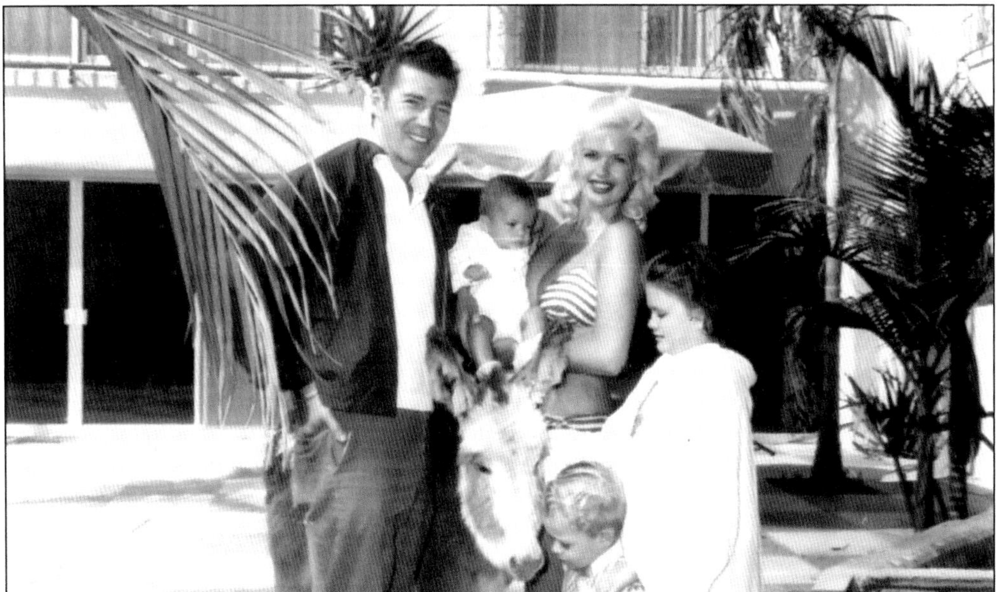

Jayne, who loved animals, frequently took photographs with animals like this donkey. She is seen here in the backyard of her Hollywood mansion, dubbed the Pink Palace due to Jayne's fondness for decorating with the color pink. With her are husband Mickey Hargitay, daughter Jayne Marie, son Miklos "Mickey" Jr., and, in her arms, her youngest son, Zoltan. Daughter Mariska, of *Law and Order* fame, came later in 1964. (Courtesy Frank Ferruccio.)

Jayne emerges, clothes and all, from a swimming pool in Hollywood. The scene was from the Hollywood movie *The George Raft Story*, which was filmed in 1961 and followed up in 1962 with *It Happened In Athens*. Her other films included *Pete Kelly's Blues* and *Will Success Spoil Rock Hunter?* (Courtesy Frank Ferruccio.)

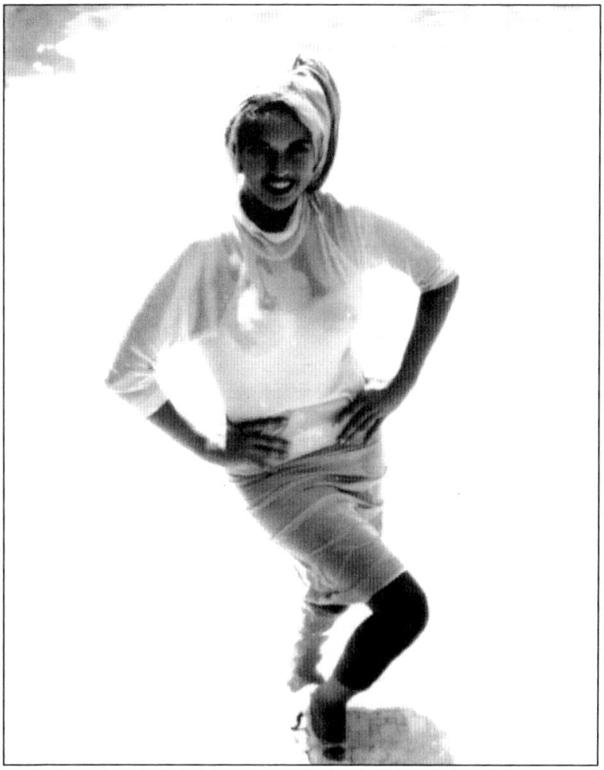

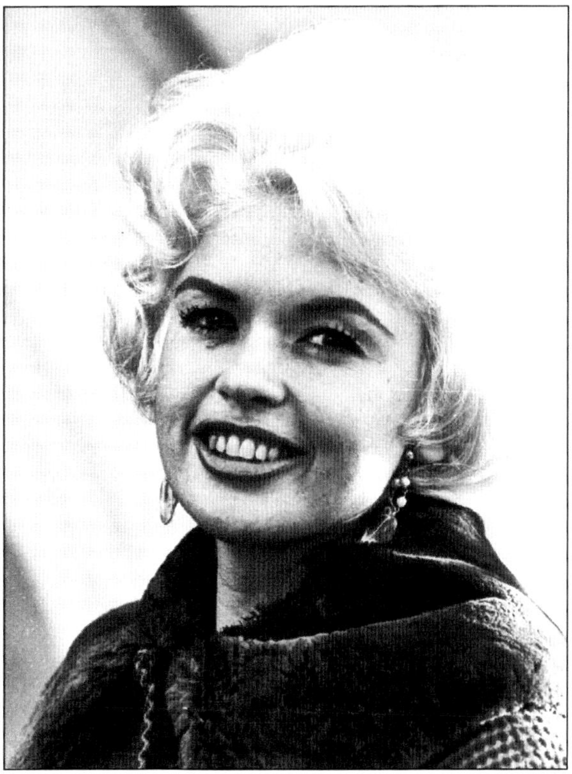

Jayne Mansfield showed a passion for Hollywood movies early in life and excelled in singing and dancing in school. The date and location of this photograph are not known, but it is well liked by many for its natural quality, where Jayne's good looks and girl-next-door quality still shine through. (Courtesy Frank Ferruccio.)

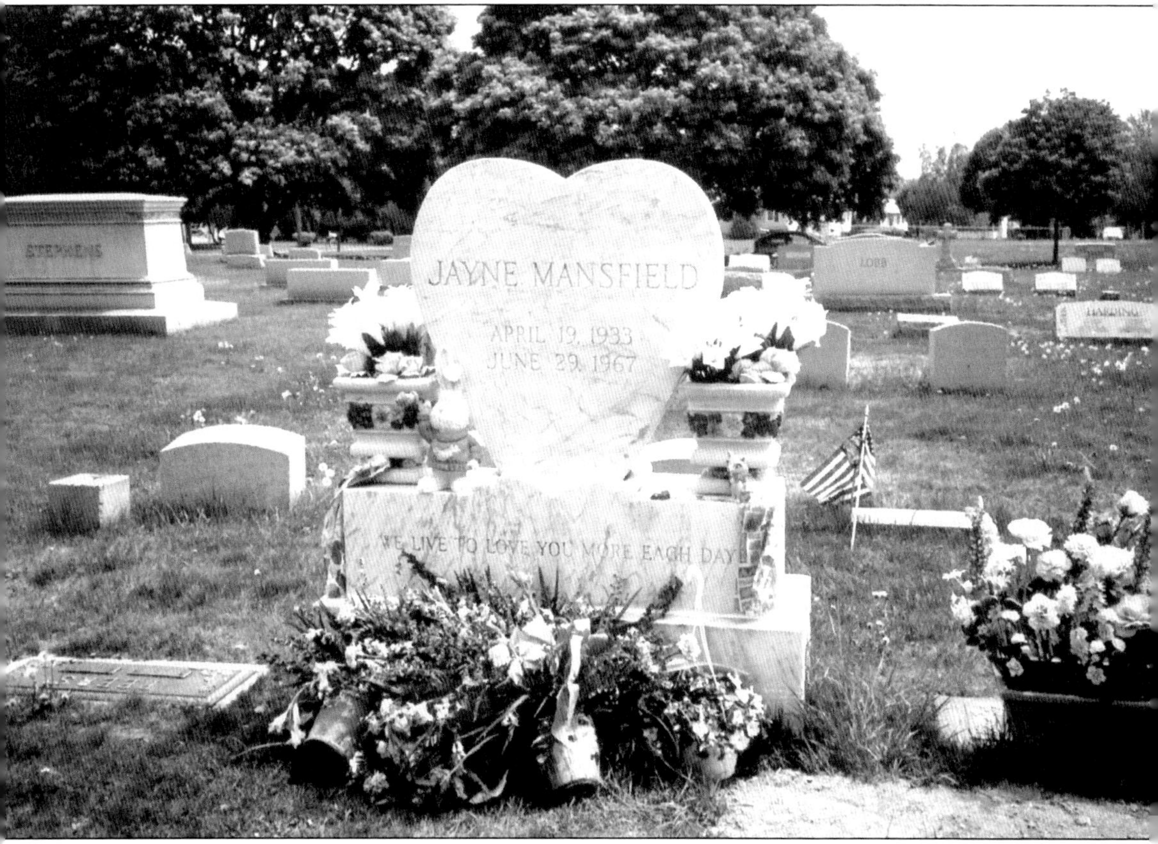

Jayne Mansfield died prematurely on June 29, 1967, at the age of 34, while on her way to a television talk show appearance in New Orleans. The car Jayne was riding in crashed into a slow-moving semitruck. Another truck that was in the area spraying for mosquitoes may have created poor visibility. Mickey Jr., Zoltan, and Mariska were in the back seat and survived their injuries, but Jayne and the other adults were killed. Jayne Mansfield is buried in the Fairview Cemetery in Pen Argyl, near Weona Park. The National Guard was present at her funeral to oversee the more than 10,000 fans who showed up to pay their respect. Her pink, marble gravesite, shown here, is maintained by fans and loved ones who still believe the sentiment "We live to love you more each day." (Author's collection.)

Six

GETTING AROUND

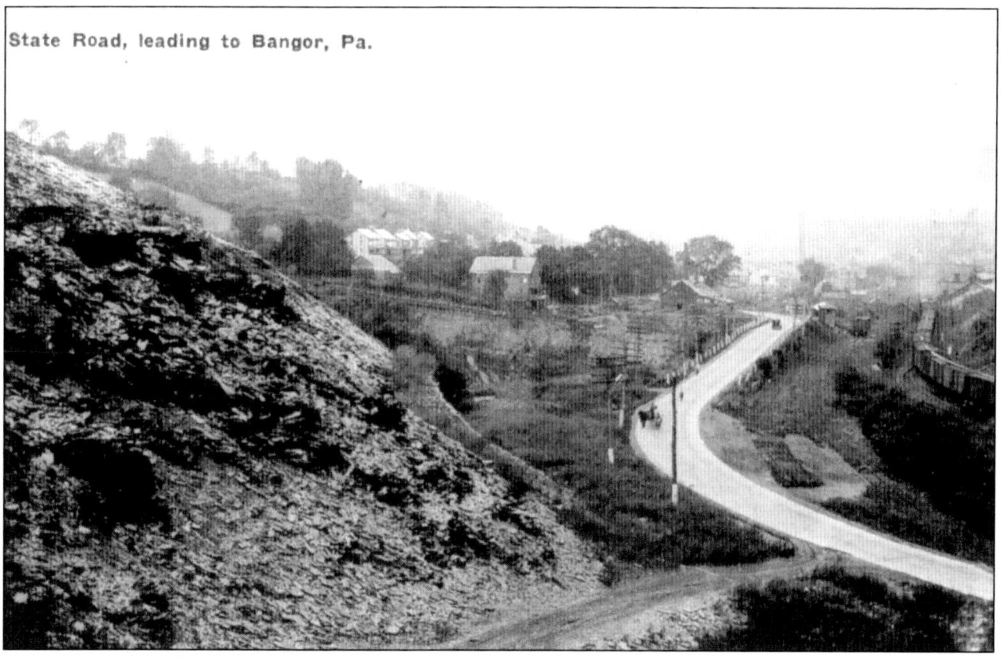

A state road leading to Bangor (now Route 512) is shown here from the east. The old Native American paths throughout the Slate Belt were eventually replaced with dirt roads for traveling by horse and mule. By 1900, there were not many paved roads, but once established, the roads were well paved, drained, lighted, and well maintained. At one point, Bangor owned its own stone crusher. (Courtesy PSA.)

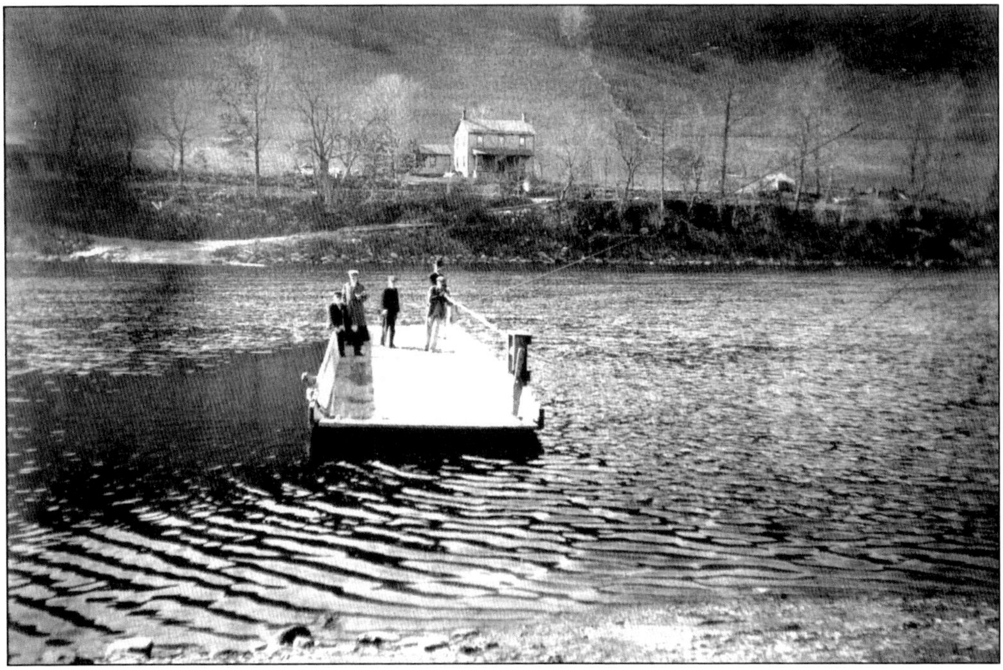

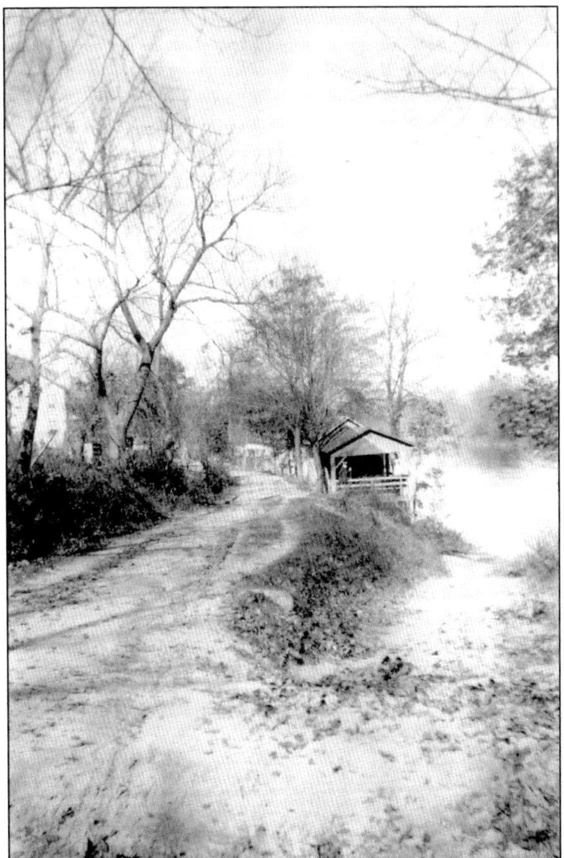

Ferries, like the Meyers Ferry above, were the earliest form of transportation for crossing the Delaware River from 1753 to 1914. The oblong structures were about 40 to 50 feet long, 7 feet wide, and 3 feet deep. They were propelled by means of a long pole. Meyers Ferry was owned and operated by John Meyers in the late 1880s and sold to Joseph Kline shortly after the turn of the century. Other ferries in the area included the Decker, Goodwin, Dill, Kline, Attine, Albertson, and Mack Ferries. The road leading to the ferry house (below), which was located a few miles below Portland along the Delaware River, is shown here. (Courtesy SBM.)

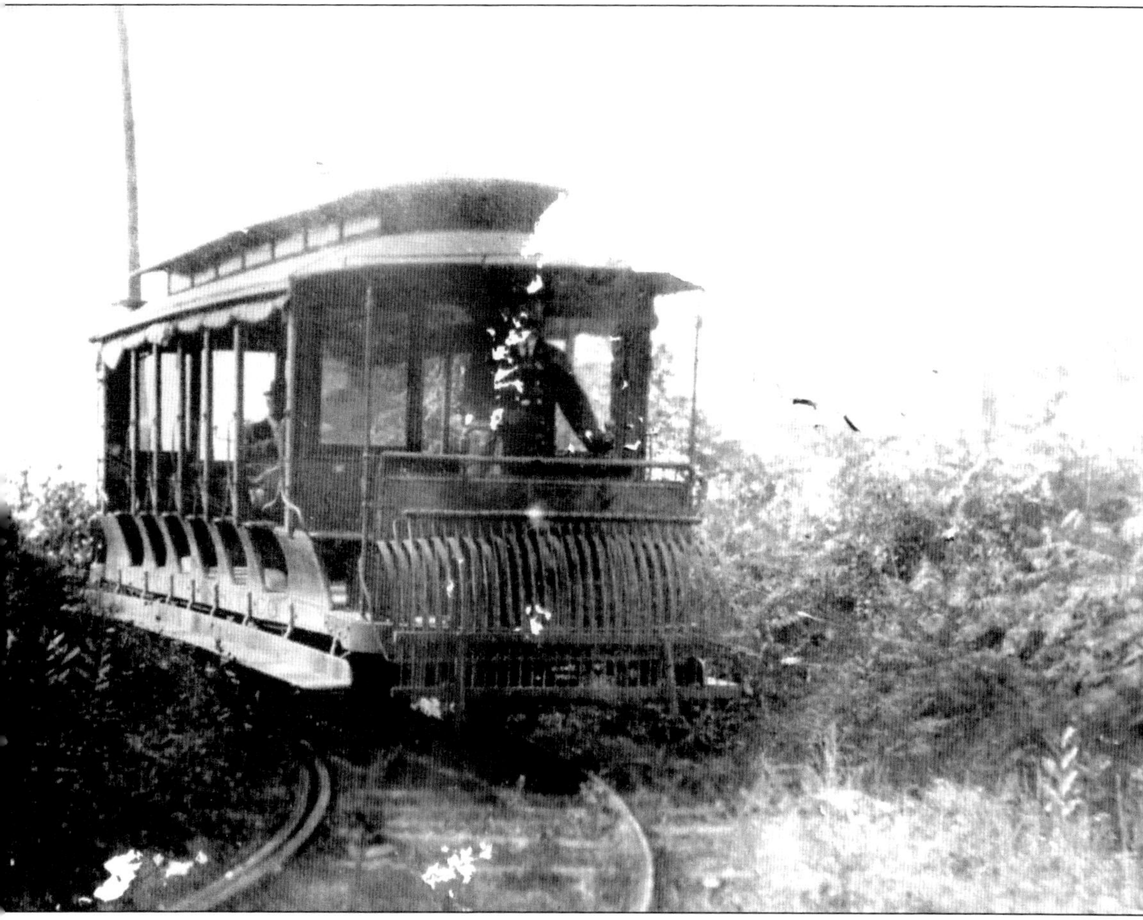

As the area grew and expanded, faster and more efficient means of transportation became necessary and trolleys became popular. The first trolleys were drawn by horse, but wooden, and later steel, rails replaced them. Bangor had three trolley lines servicing the area: the Slate Belt Traction Company, the Hay Line, and the Bangor-Portland Trolley. Service began in 1905 and ended around 1933. The trolleys allowed residents to travel outside their immediate area to neighboring counties. Quarry workers could also buy "quarry time" on the trolleys instead of walking miles to work. (Courtesy SBM.)

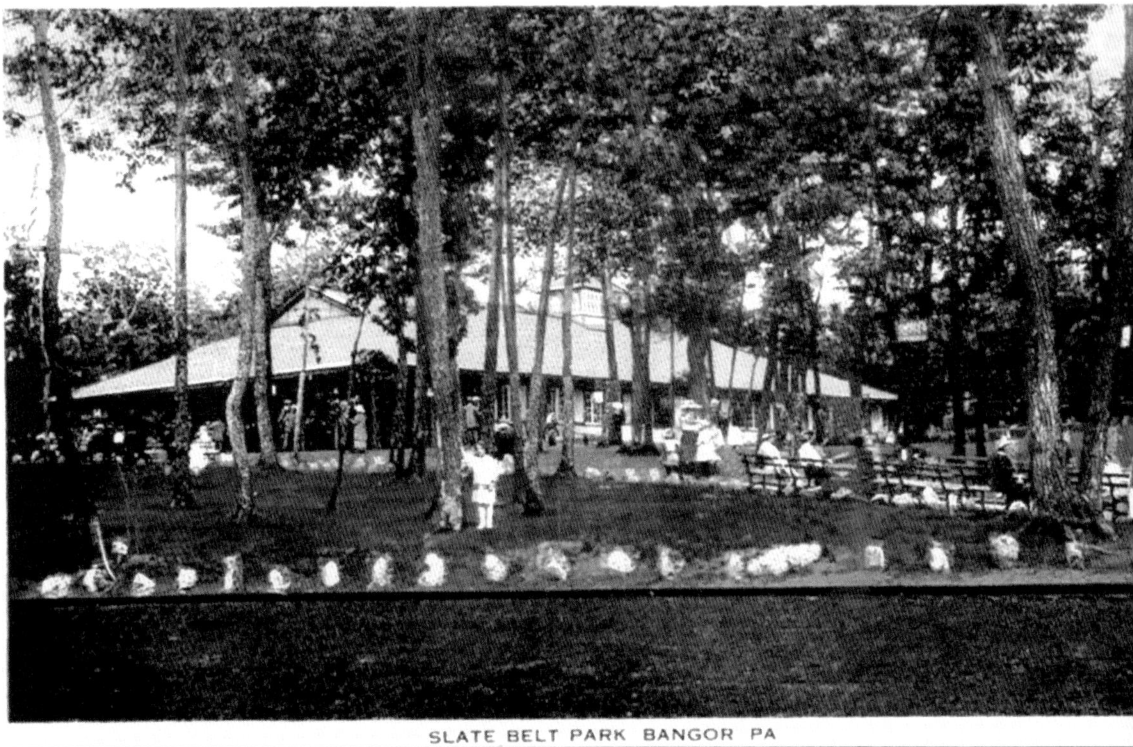

Slate Belt Park was built by the Slate Belt Traction Company to help promote business. Located between Bangor and Pen Argyl, it was a popular attraction that had a merry-go-round and was known for its lively dances. Trolley fare to the park was 5¢. The park burned down in the 1920s. (Courtesy SBHC.)

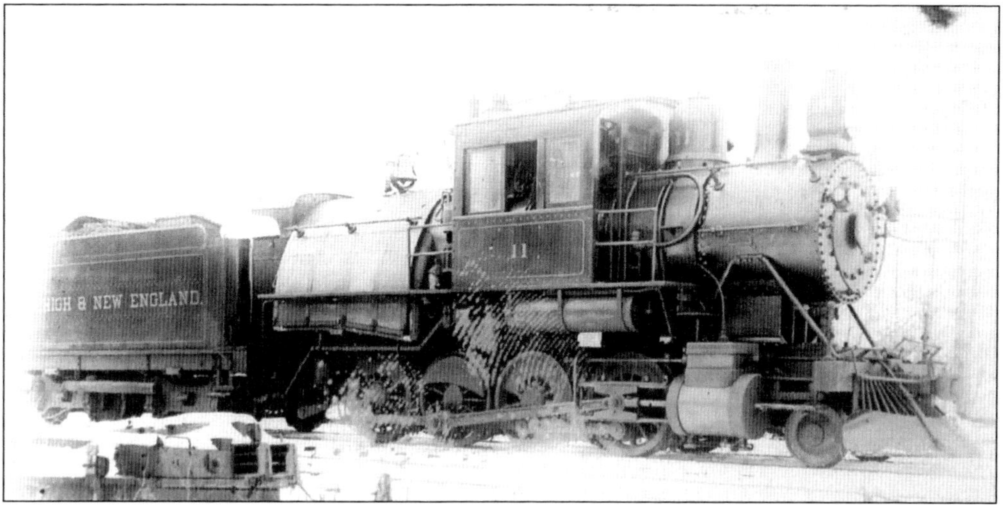

The Lehigh New England Railroad is shown here, along with some of its workers. The town of Pen Argyl would eventually become its home base. The railroad's goal was to connect the Midwest with major New England cities, with Pen Argyl on its proposed route. However, other railroads began servicing the area first, including the Pennsylvania, Poughkeepsie and Boston line. The Pennsylvania, Poughkeepsie and Boston went into receivership and was reorganized into the Lehigh and New England on April 2, 1885. The railroad expanded and flourished for many years, despite setbacks like a fire in its car shop. A new car shop, yard, and engine house were built, providing a financial boom to the area until years after the Great Depression. The last train order was taken on November 1, 1961, at which time operations were abandoned. (Courtesy SBM.)

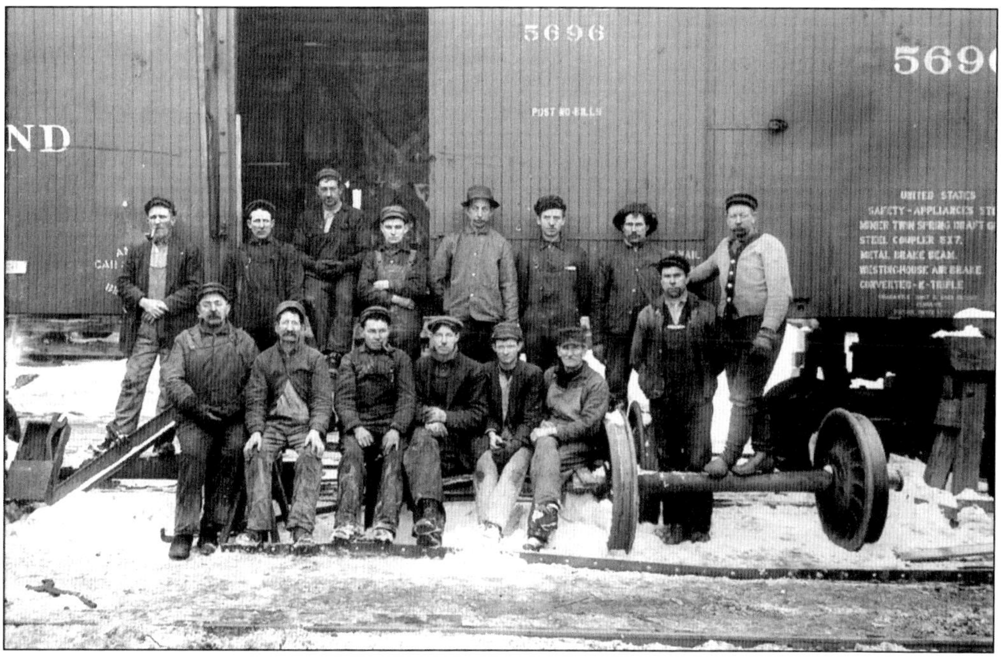

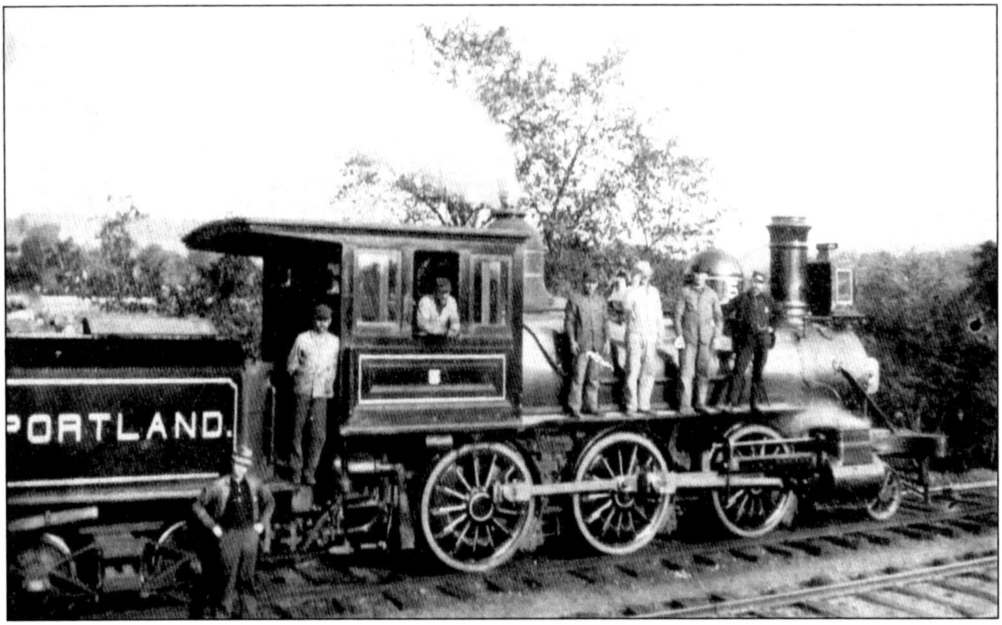

Two railroads serviced the Bangor area: the Lehigh and New England and the area's first, the Bangor-Portland branch of the Lackawanna Railroad, shown here. The Bangor-Portland Railroad was the brainchild of German immigrant Conrad Miller. Miller and his brother, Charles, began construction on July 4, 1879, and expanded it through Pen Argyl, Nazareth, and into Martin's Creek. In 1903, the railroad was sold to the Delaware, Lackawanna and Western Railroad. (Courtesy SBM.)

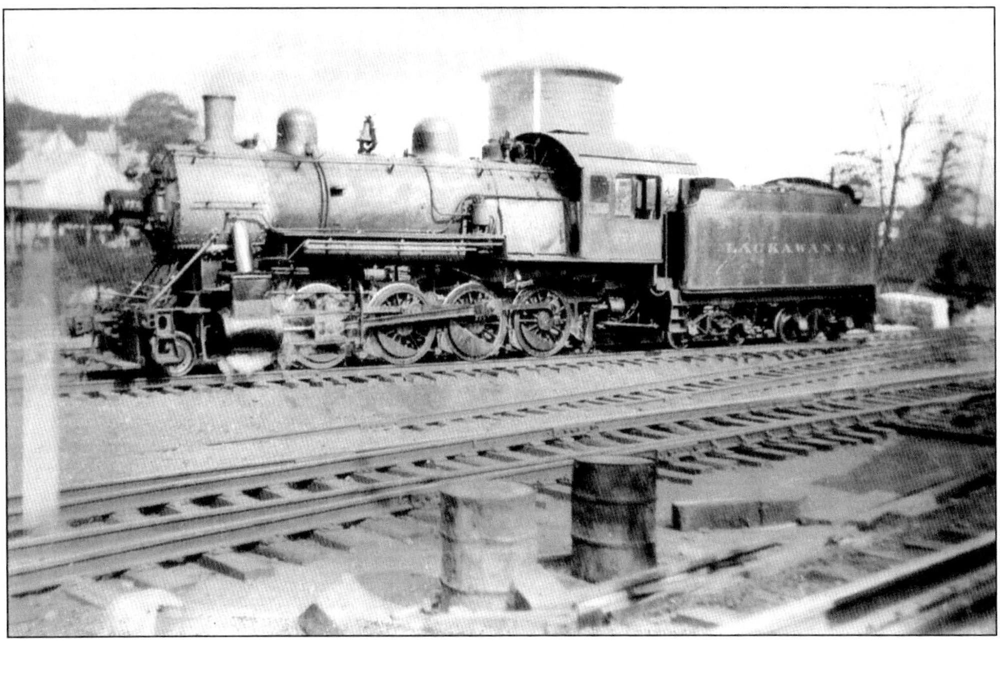

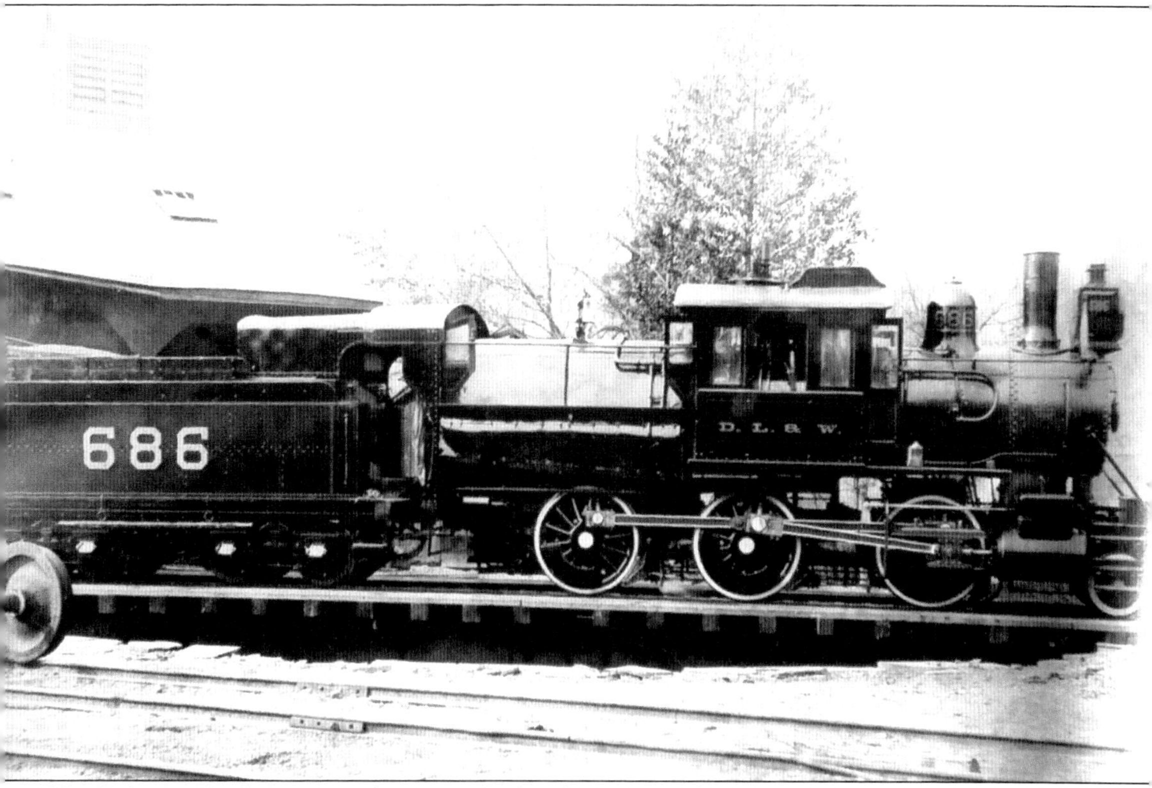

The Delaware, Lackawanna and Western Railroad, Bangor and Portland Division, was the sister railroad of the Lehigh and New England. Many area residents nicknamed it the Delay, Linger, and Wait. (Courtesy SBM.)

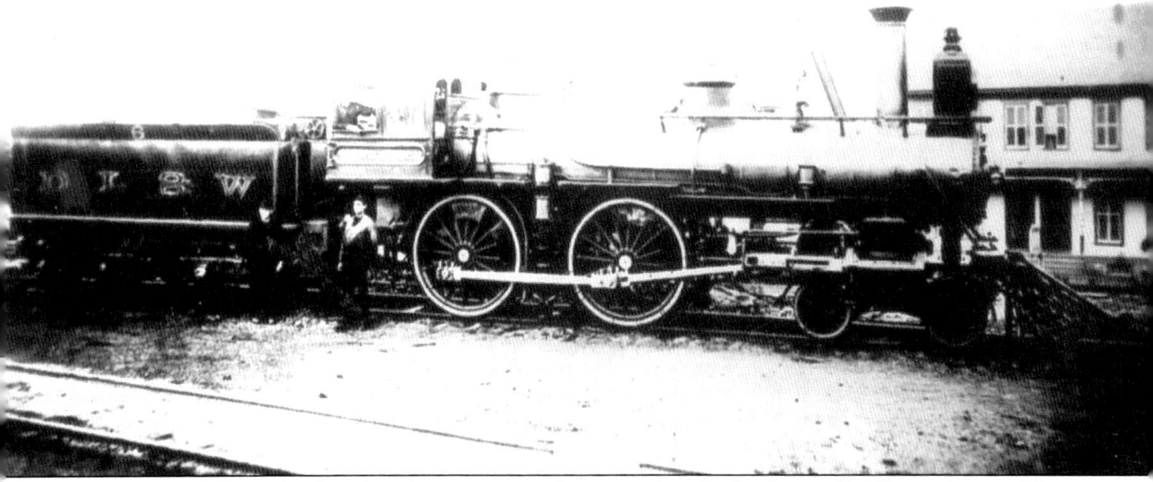

The Bangor-Portland Railroad was organized on May 17, 1879, by Conrad Miller and several Bangor residents. Operations between Bangor and Portland began on December 1, 1880. Lines were later added through Wind Gap, Pen Argyl, Nazareth, and the Cement Belt, Bath, and Martin's Creek. On July 1, 1903, the Bangor and Portland division was bought by the Delaware Lackawanna and Western Railroad and became the Bangor-Portland division of the rail, with headquarters in Bangor. (Courtesy SBM.)

Seven

Faith and Education

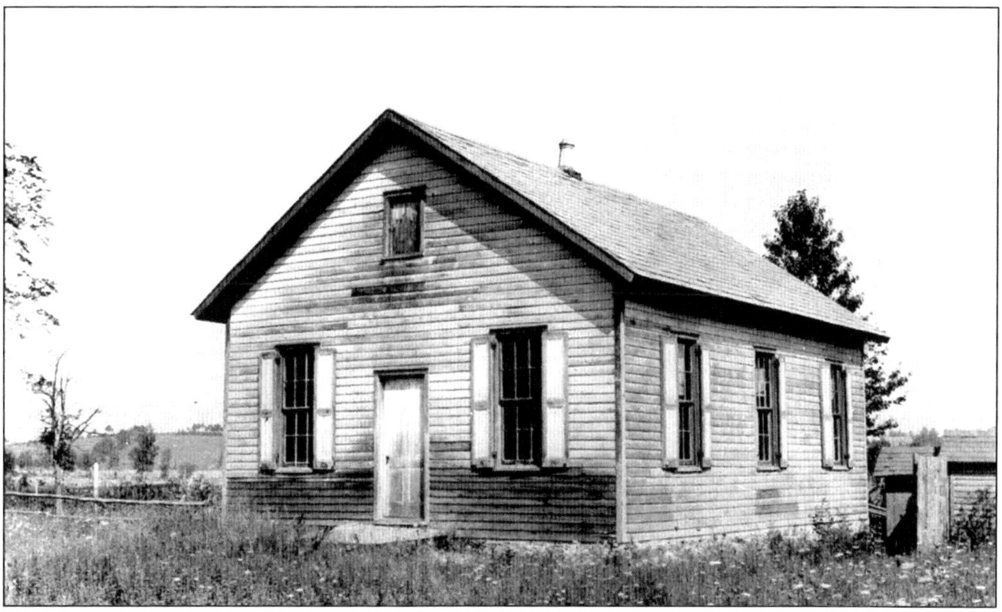

This one-room schoolhouse was located in Flicksville. Records, maps, and deeds from the 19th century show that the one-room schoolhouse was quite prevalent in the area, with Upper Mount Bethel Township alone having 22 such schools. Portland had a one-room schoolhouse, and Bangor had several. A log cabin schoolhouse existed in East Bangor. (Courtesy FHS.)

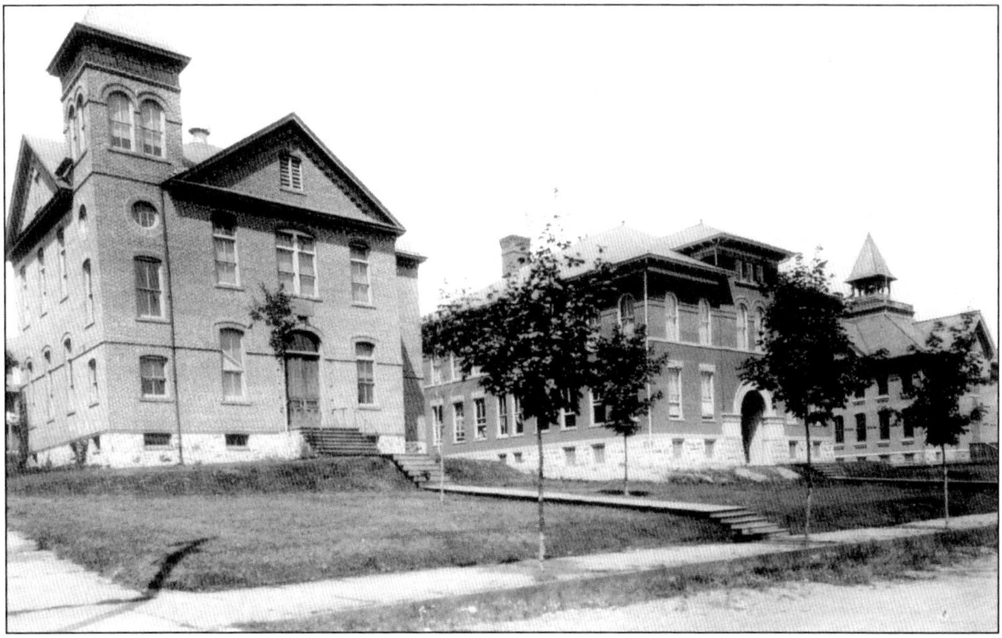

The Garfield and Lincoln Schools (above) and a high school were located on Fourth Street in Bangor. Garfield (right) was demolished to enlarge the high school. All the schools were eventually razed. Students from the class of 1925–1926 pose outside the Lincoln School (below). From left to right are the following: (first row) Alexander DeNadai, Donald Williams, Amelie Scott, William Bellis, Leo Segatti, George Young, Dick Dawe, Joe Shirley, Guy Segatti, and Walter Kneeler; (second row) Buster Porter, Cliff Counterman, Fred Bonney, Leonard Doney, Francis Ford, Dick Correll, Wimpy Harding, George Sandt, Clark Buskirk, and Clint Cornelius; (third row) Maryella Correll, Mafalda Carrer, Hilda Bet, Hannah Blabe, Beatrice Fedon, Sofie Dapkowitz, Eva Saurwine, Inez Harding, Mary Perinotto, and Hazel Bishop; (fourth row) Louis Sigmond, Katie Harabin, Rugh Slater, Emma Palmer, Ruth Bonney, Elenore Doney, Adelaide Guthrie, Vera Parson, Alma Albert, and Paul Harris. (Above, courtesy NCHGS; below, courtesy SBHC.)

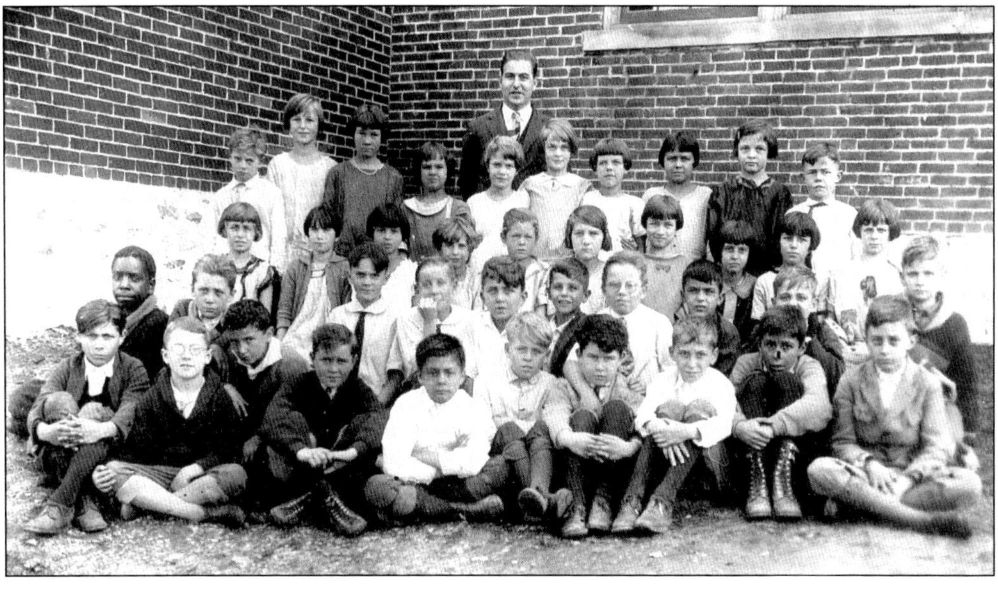

Bangor High School is seen here along with the statue of Robert Morris Jones, which now stands in Founder's Park adjacent to the Bangor Public Library. The first high school was built in 1882 and graduated its first class in 1885. It served grades 8–11 until 1914, when a 12th grade was added. This two-story brick structure replaced the original school building that was damaged by fire in 1919. A new high school was built at Five Points, several miles from town, and in 1954, the schools were consolidated into the Bangor Area Joint School System. Below unidentified students from the class of 1910 pose in front of the high school. (Courtesy NCHGS.)

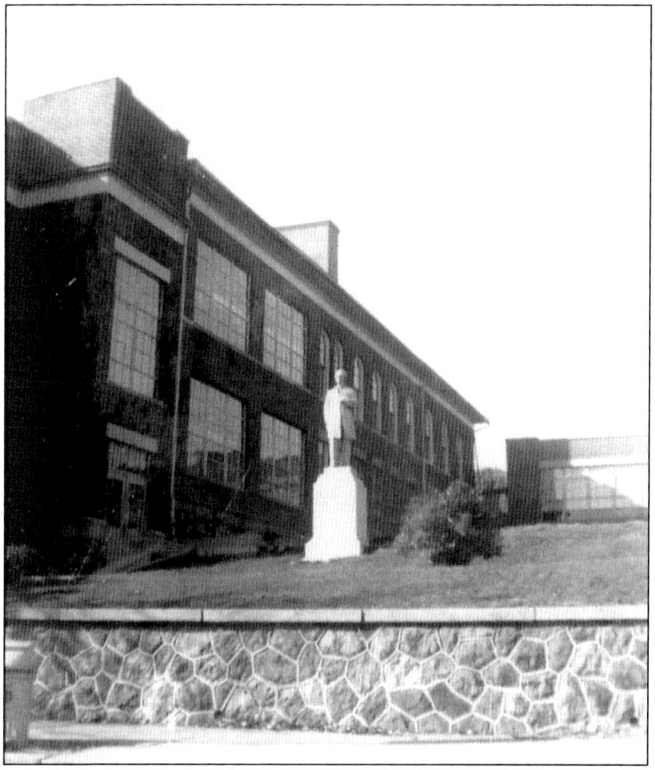

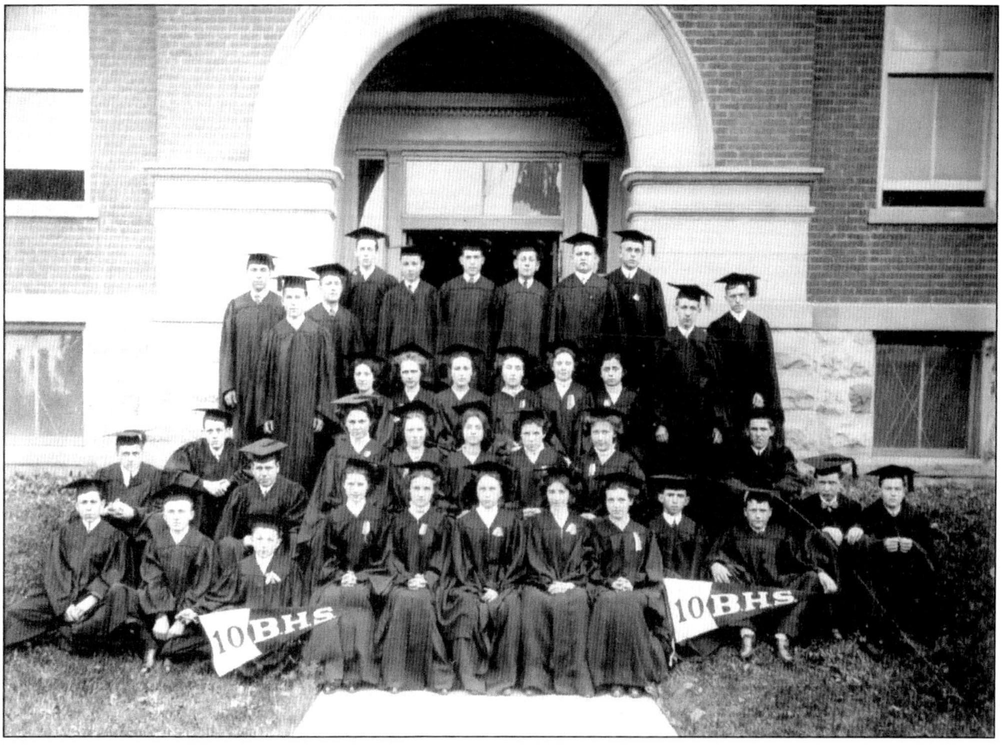

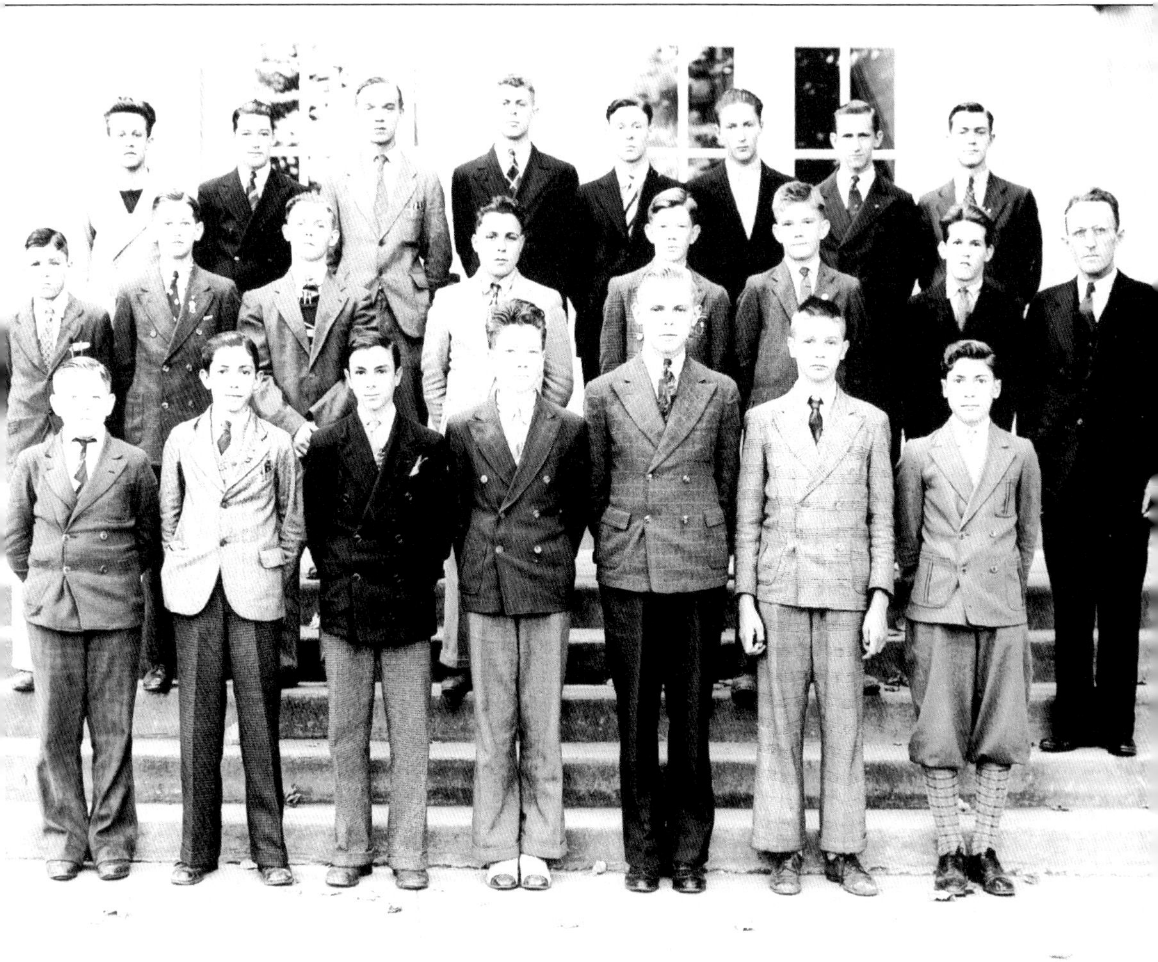

Bangor High School was the first school in eastern Pennsylvania to have vocational agricultural studies in its curriculum. George Ott Sr. began the program in 1935, and students learned about poultry, gardening, fruit growing, farm management, animal and dairy husbandry, and even rural sociology and law. All of the students, like those shown here, were members of the Future Farmers of America. Pictured here, from left to right, are the following: (first row) Raymond Stenlake, Alex Bocko, Michael Sabatine, Clarence Barnes, Arthur Stratton, Robert Ace, and Ralph Falcone; (second row) Chester Gambelli, Delbert LaBar, Leroy Brewer, James Febbo, James Luscombe, Wendell Shafer, Nelson Searfoss, and instructor George Ott; (third row) Earl Messinger, Carl Blitz, Paul Brodt, Robert Stratton, Robert Andrews, Clayton Horn, Donald Finkbeiner, and James Ott. (Courtesy BPL.)

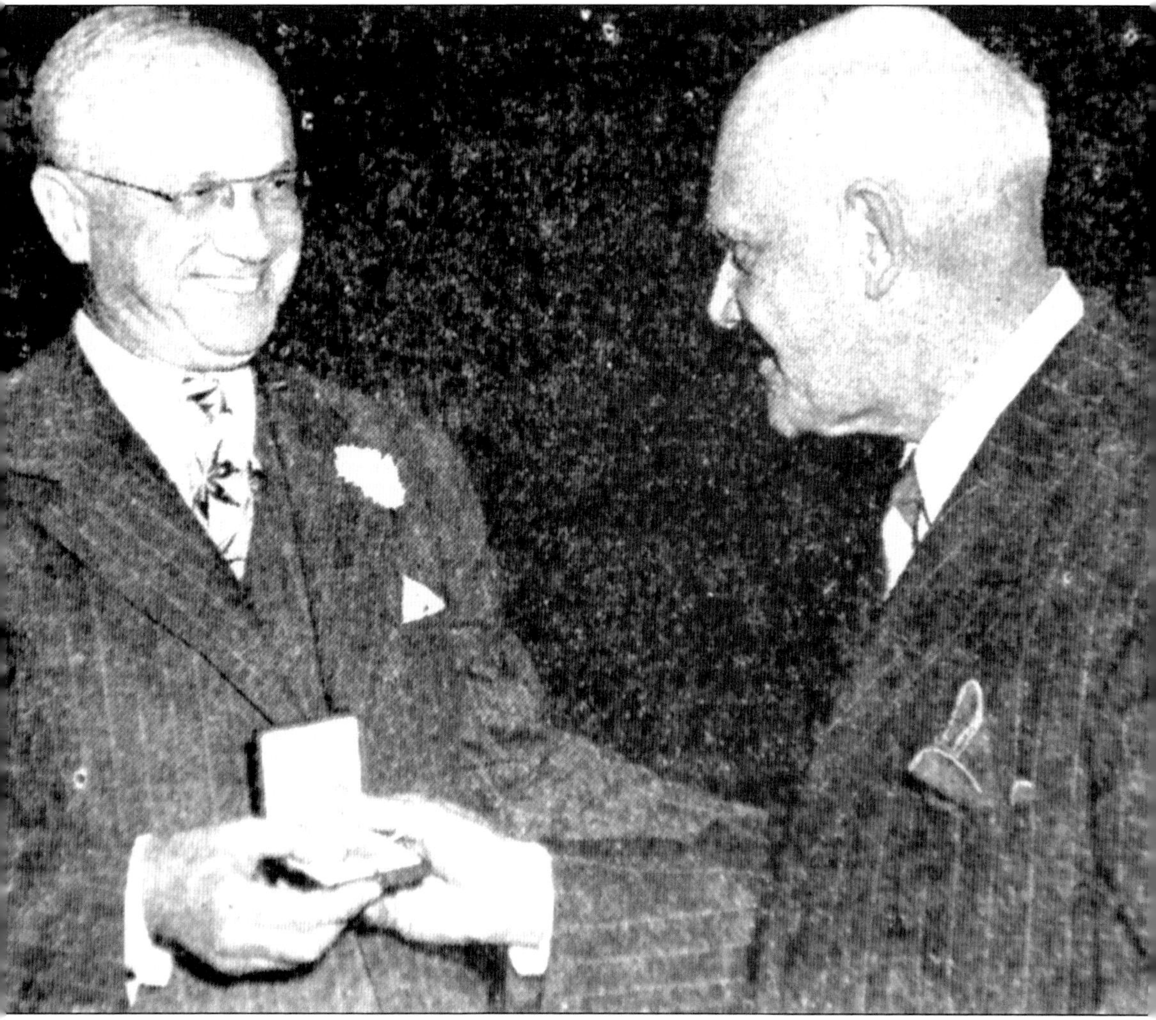

Bangor High School's most famous graduate, Ivor Griffith (left), receives the very first Proctor Gold Medal award from scientist Dr. Charles Vanderkleed (right) for his research with quinine in World War II. The founder of the National Quinine Pool, Griffith also earned the recognition and praise of Pres. Franklin Roosevelt. Born in Rhiwlas, Wales, on January 3, 1891, his family came to Bangor in 1907. Griffith loved nature as a boy and became a pharmacist, graduating from the Philadelphia College of Pharmacy and Science in 1912 and later serving as dean of pharmacy. He was also a chemist who served as an instructor at several colleges and was an editor of the *American Journal of Pharmacy*. He was the author of *Recent Remedies* and two books of poetry and prose, *To the Lilacs* and *Lobscowse*. (Author's collection.)

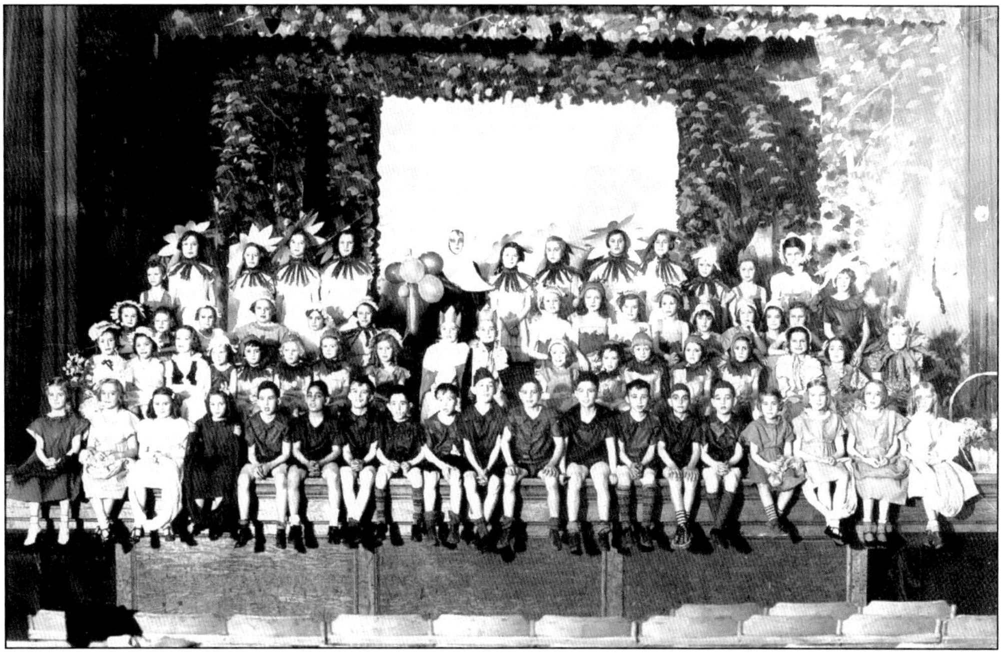

Bangor students perform in a play, with Robert Albert as the king and Joyce Keiser as the queen. The man in the moon is George Pritchard, who would later run a successful clothing business in Bangor and played a role in the start of Bangor Welsh Day. The other students are unidentified. (Courtesy BPL.)

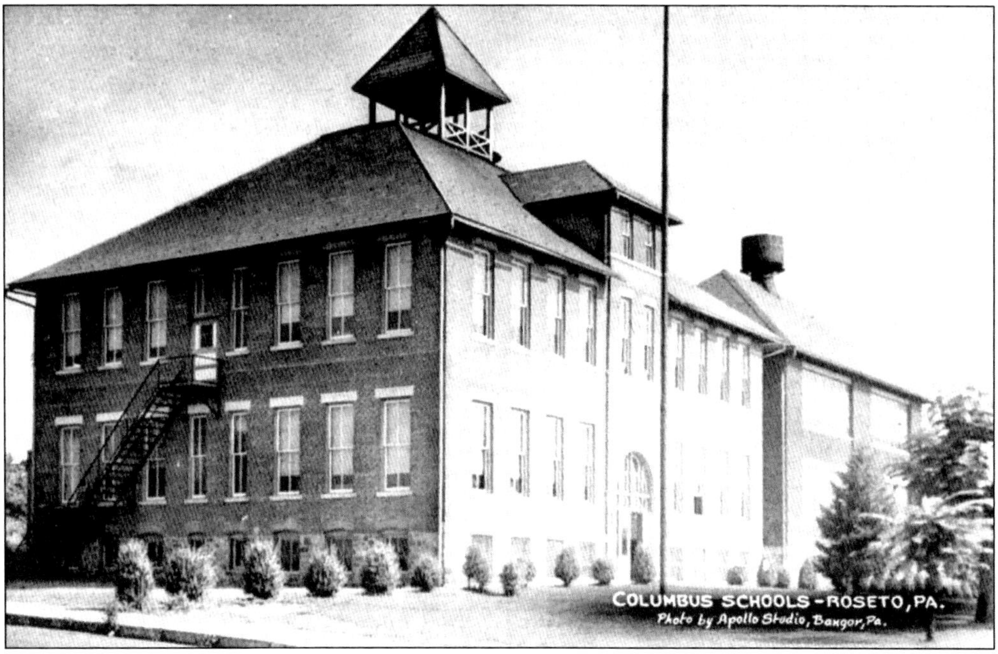

The Columbus School still stands on Dante Street in Roseto. The building was erected in 1913 and served grades one through eight. Philip Ronco was the school's first principal, and Josephine Farace was the first teacher elected by the first Roseto School Board. In 1955, the Roseto Public School became part of the Bangor Area Joint School System. (Courtesy BPL.)

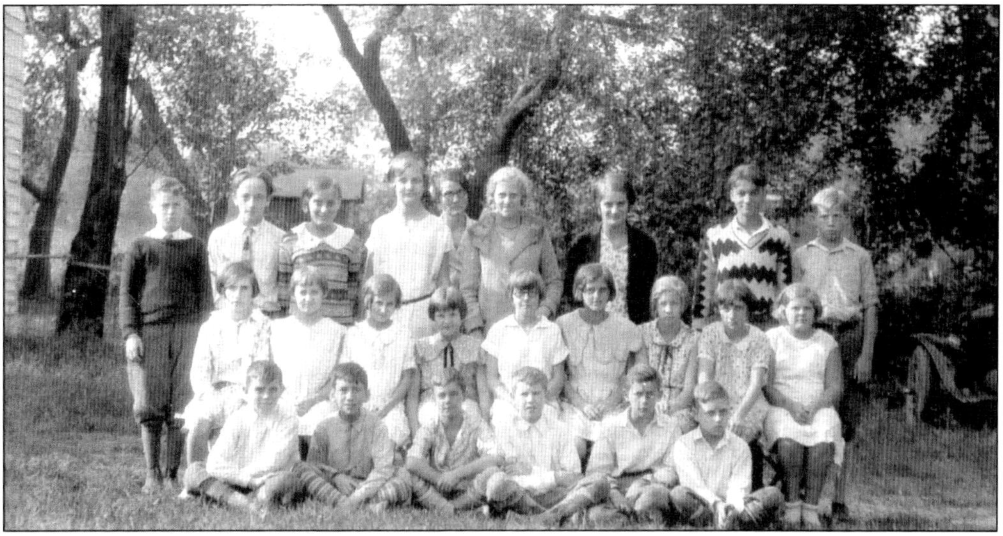

Pictured at the Mount Bethel School are, from left to right, the following: (first row) Charles Fisher, Clarence Albert, Russel Compton, Earl Rasely, Arthur Reagel, and Junior Butz; (second row) Margie Streepy, Vera Hartzell, Pearl Hartzell, Arvella Horn, Lorraine Snyder, Ester Hagerman, Georgeanna Bierei, Pauline Lambert, and Velma Reagle; (third row) Paul Hilliard, Paul Lambert, Virginia Felker, Louise Emery, Lottie Hilliard (teacher), Mary Shuster, Mirian Hunt, Wayne Van Vorst, Paul Cole. (Courtesy SBM.)

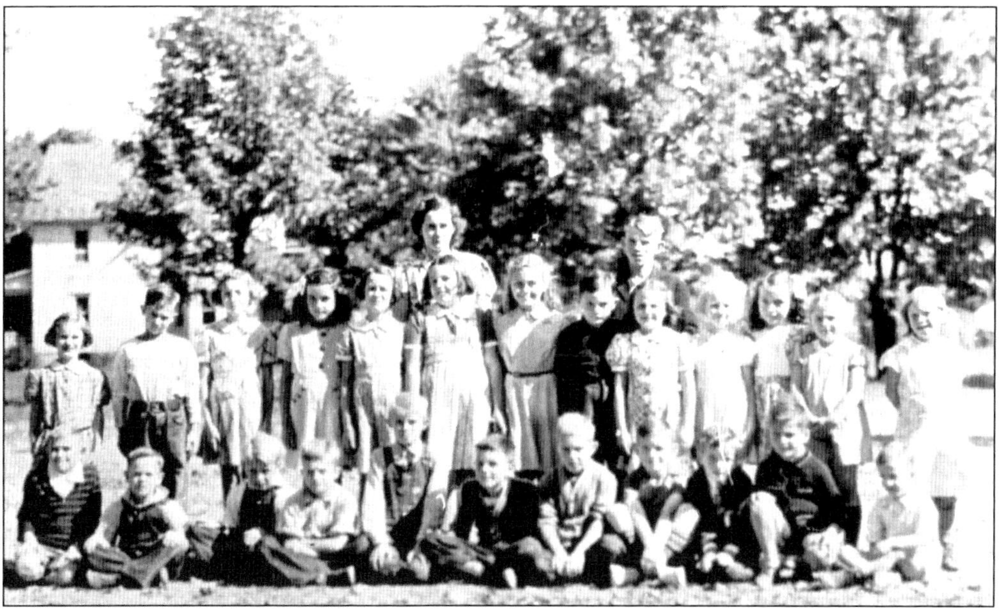

The Williamsburg School in Mount Bethel is seen here in 1940. From left to right are the following: (first row) Ed Resh, Melvin Raisner, Alfred Bush, Douglas Compton, Douglas Bush, Ralph Kneebone, Jesse Hunt, unidentified, Earl Sandt, Robert Compton, and unidentified; (second row) Evelyn Compton, Junior Compton, Doris Weidman, Betty Strunk, Joyce Raisner, Barbara Hartzell, Madge Felker, Charles Felker, Marion Evans, Connie Honey, unidentified, M. Charlotte Bach, and Laura Bell Hunt; (third row) teacher Ruth Rothrock, and Harry Hunt. (Courtesy SBM.)

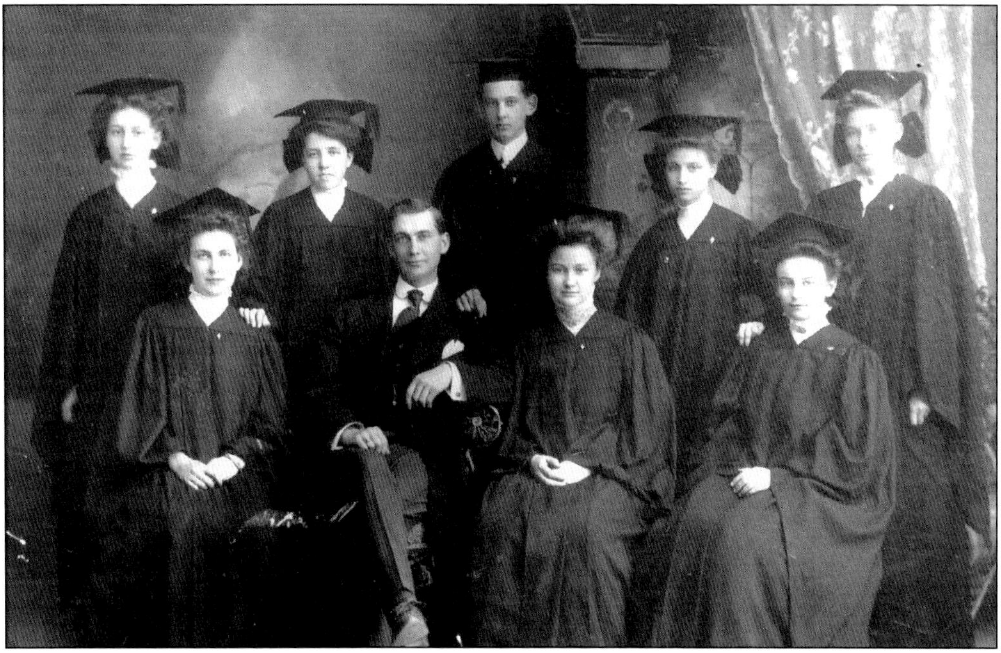

This is the graduating class of 1908 from Pen Argyl High School. The first high school class graduated in 1899 with only four students. From left to right are the following: (first row) Muriel Harris, Principal Nicholas Male, Edna Acker, and Edna Fuller; (second row) Lillian Rundle, Eva Doney, Charles Martin, Lillie Baker, and Edith Richter. (Courtesy SBM.)

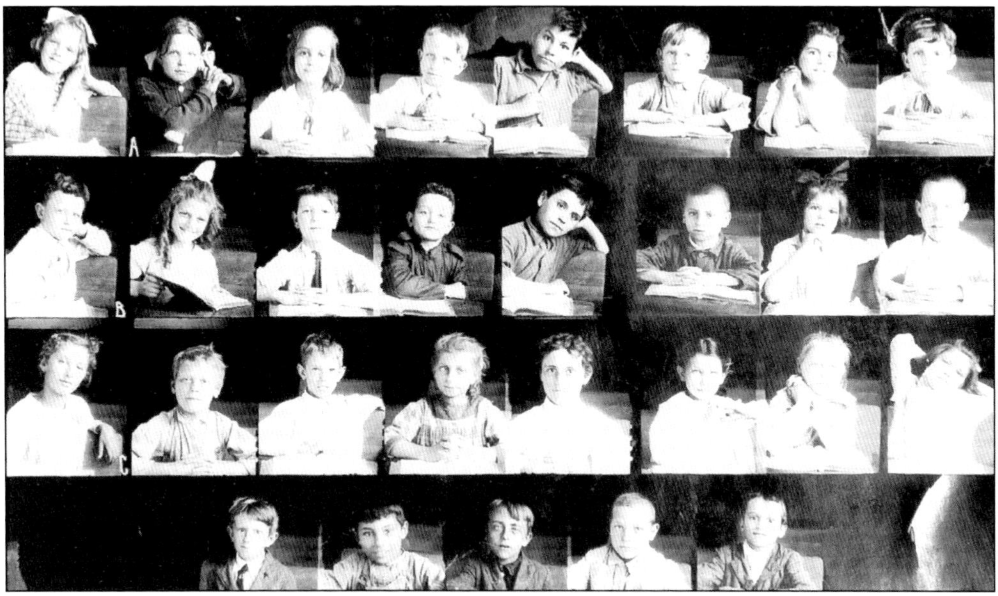

The Centerfield School, east of Martin's Creek, was built around 1905 in the middle of a field, hence the name. Pictured from left to right are the following: (top row) Gladys Gardner, unidentified, Lorna Kindt, unidentified, Joe Gardner, and unidentified; (second row) unidentified, Loretta Young, Ray S?, Burton Rader, Philip Ascani, and unidentified; (third row) Vincene Castelleti, unidentified, Harold Hutchison, Betty Marge, and unidentified; (fourth row) Harry Rogers, unidentified, Louis Papp, Alfred Castelleti, and unidentified. (Courtesy HMM.)

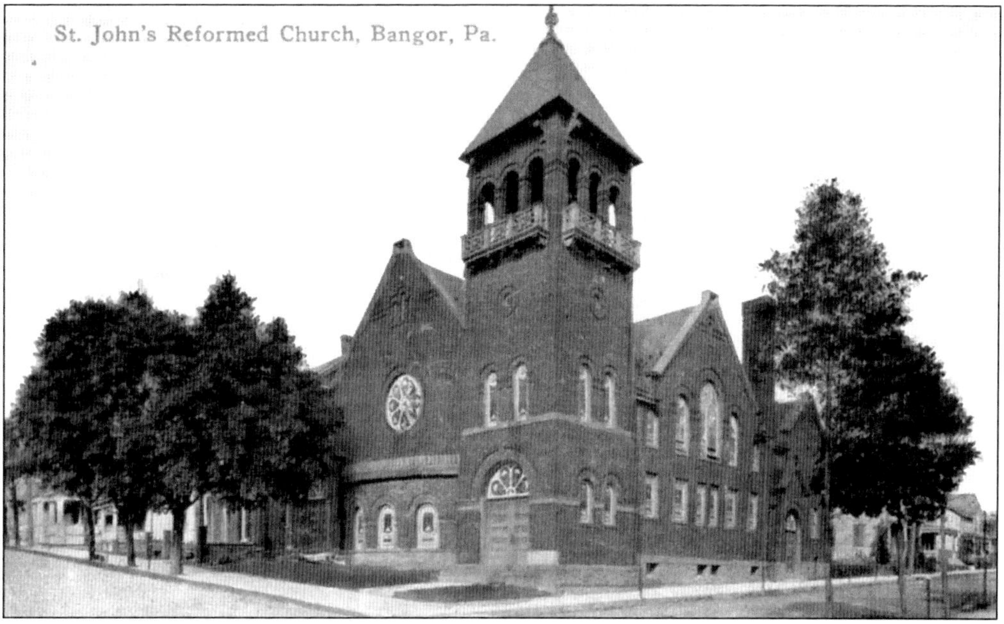

St. John's Evangelical and Reformed United Church of Christ was organized on July 24, 1878. Its first building was opened on August 30, 1879, and construction was completed on a new building in 1903. The Reformed Church believed in sacraments such as baptism and communion, but their churches were generally devoid of religious images, such as statues, and instead contained natural items like flowers and crops. (Author's collection.)

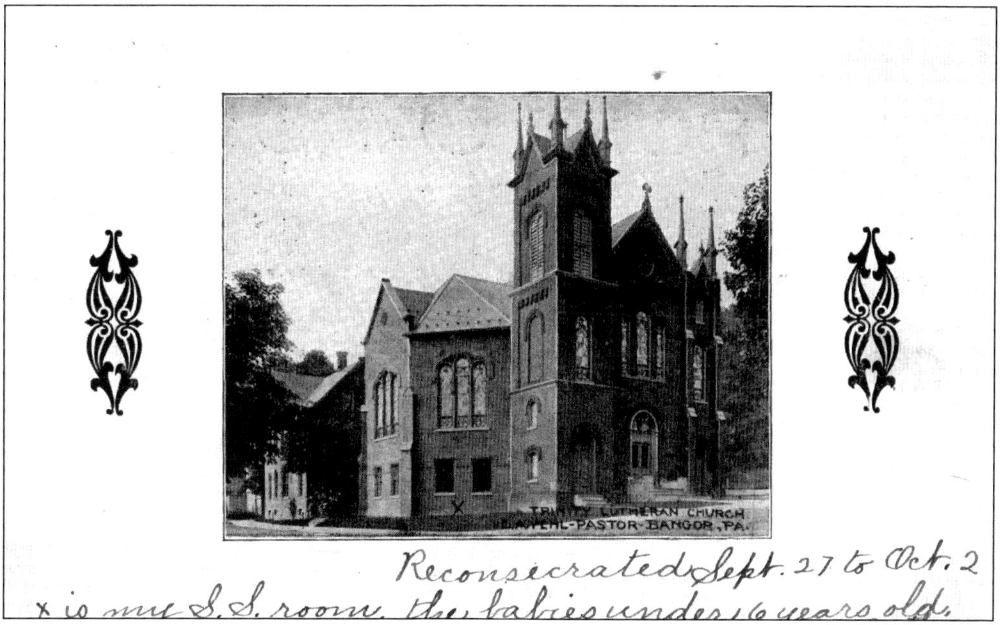

One of the first houses of worship was built of logs in 1804 on the property of the Trinity Church. In 1883, a brick building was constructed thanks to the labor of many church members and the church's pastor, the Reverend B. F. Apple, who secured donations and a gift of a chandelier from his friend Pres. Grover Cleveland. (Courtesy SBHC.)

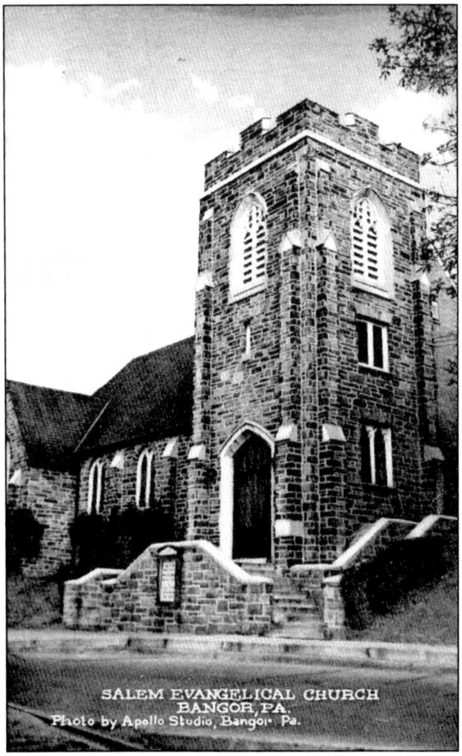

The Salem Evangelical Church, or as it was later called the Salem United Methodist Church, still stands at 125 South Main Street. This building was constructed in 1929, though the Salem congregation met as early as 1822. A division occurred in 1891, which caused many members to form other factions and eventually they became united under Methodism. (Courtesy SBHC.)

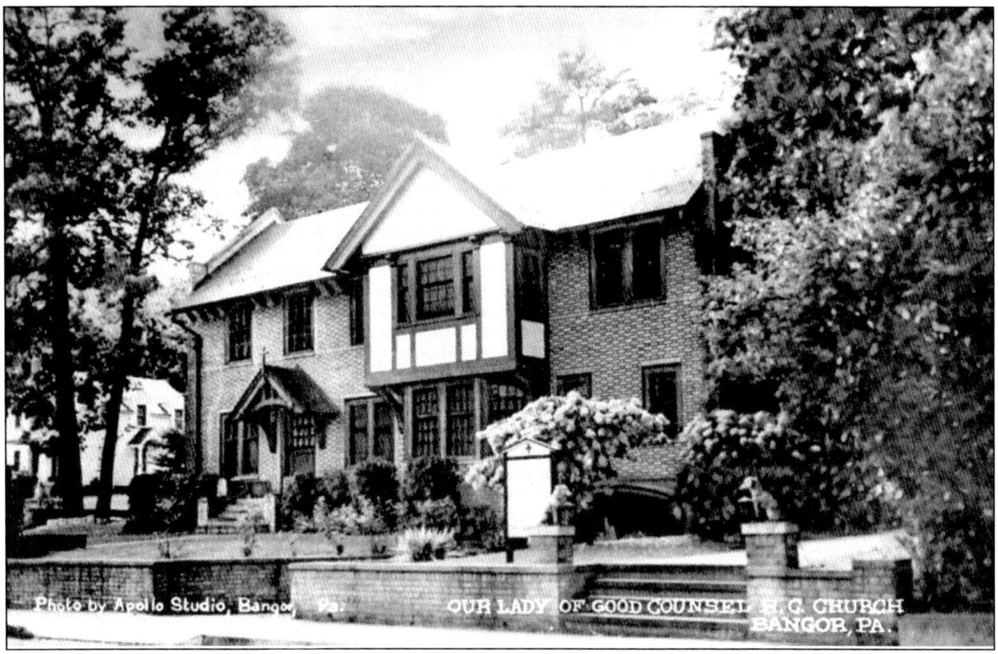

Our Lady of Good Counsel Church was constructed during the early part of World War II and was formally dedicated on September 2, 1917. It was intended to be a center for the area's Catholics, who for many years did not have their own church. It was located on South Second Street, and the Reverend Jeremiah A. Tracy, Congregation of the Mission, was the first pastor. (Courtesy SBHC.)

Mount Bethel Presbyterian Church is shown here and is now the home of the Slate Belt Museum. The Presbyterian church was founded largely by the Scotch-Irish immigrants. The congregation had several buildings and factions. Land for the church was purchased in 1823, and the building was erected in 1836. A very old cemetery adjoins the building. (Courtesy SBM.)

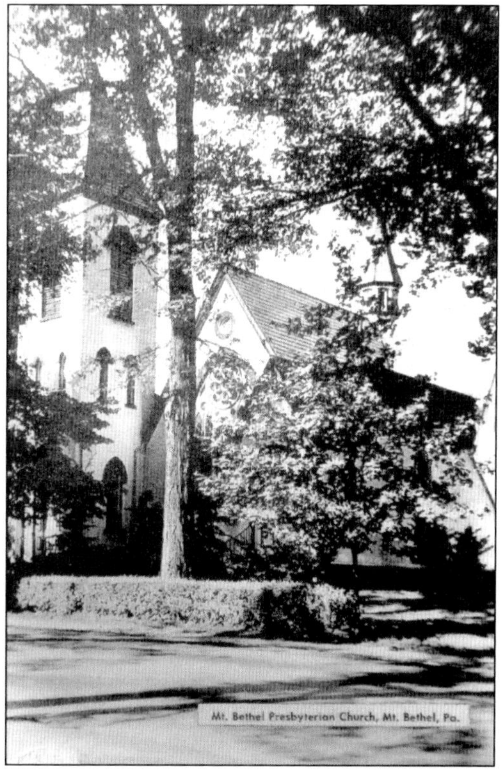

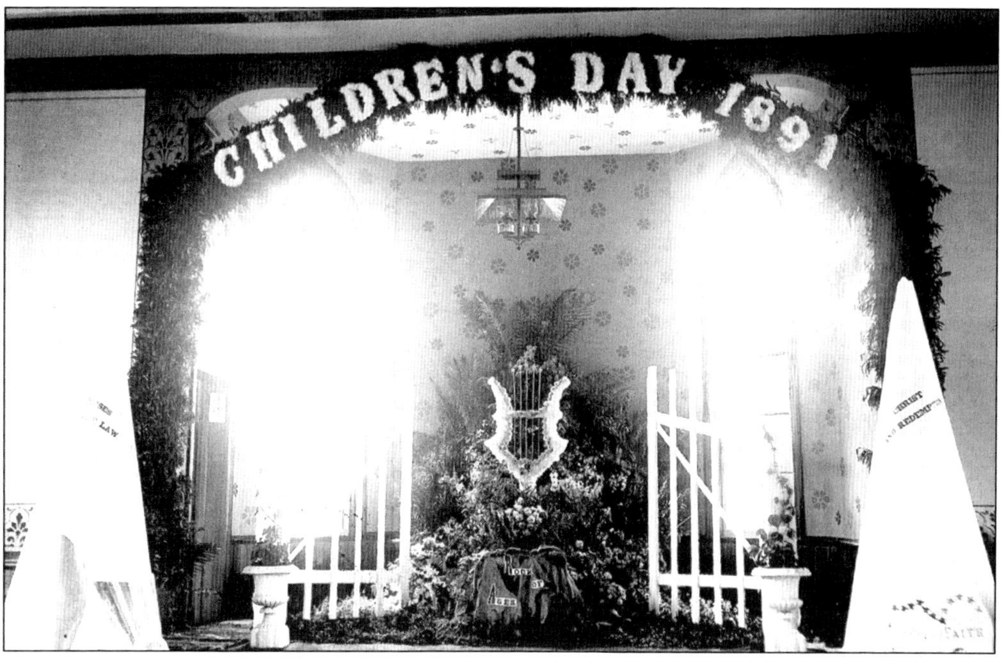

This display was part of Children's Day at the Pen Argyl Presbyterian Church. Many area churches held Children's Day festivities for both children and adults alike. Although the focus of the program had a moral theme, it was intended to be a fun-filled day of skits, recitations, and socialization. (Courtesy SBHC.)

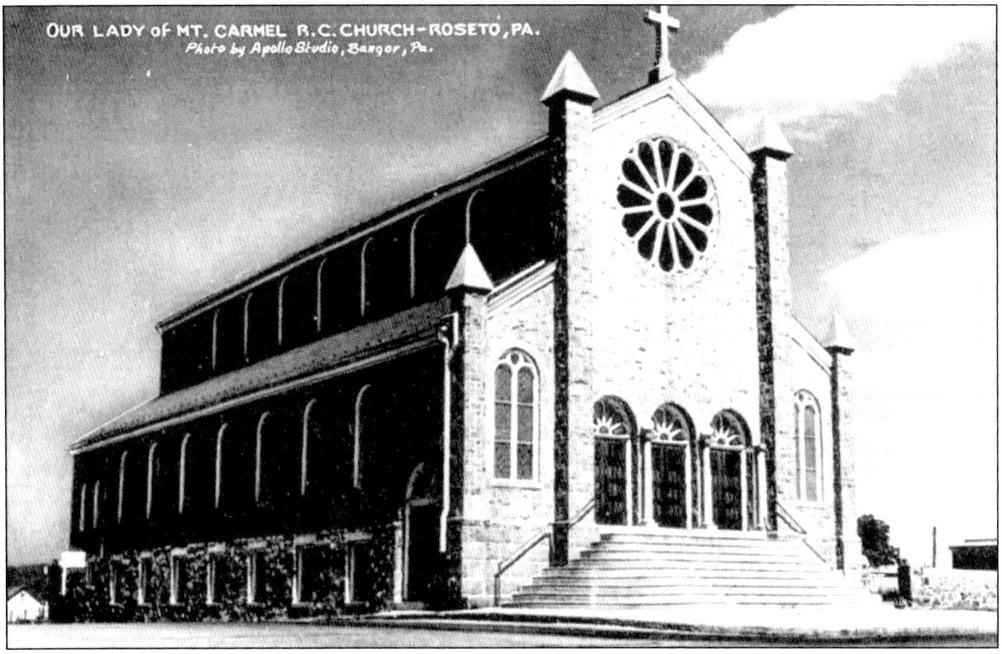

Our Lady of Mount Carmel Church of Roseto was built in 1923. The church came about thanks to the financial support of area residents and through the efforts of the Reverend Peter Montiani. The Reverend Pasquale DeNisco was the church's first permanent pastor and is credited with helping the church and town progress. (Author's collection.)

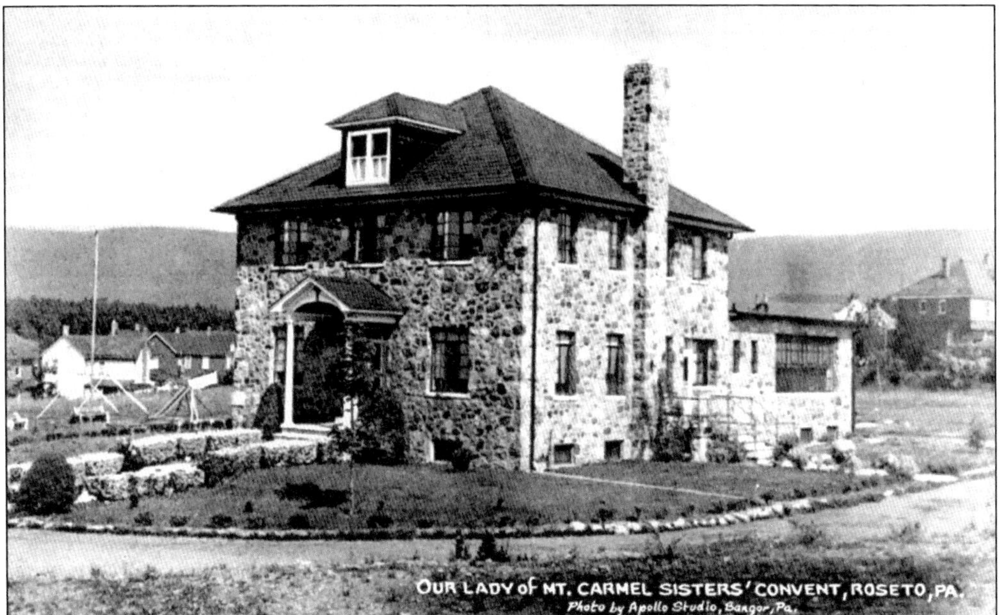

This beautiful stone structure is the Salesian Sisters Convent of Our Lady of Mount Carmel Church. The building was erected in 1940, two years after the Salesians came to the area. Kindergarten classes were held on the first floor. An elementary school serving grades one through eight was located to the right of the building. (Author's collection.)

Eight

Good Times, Bad Times

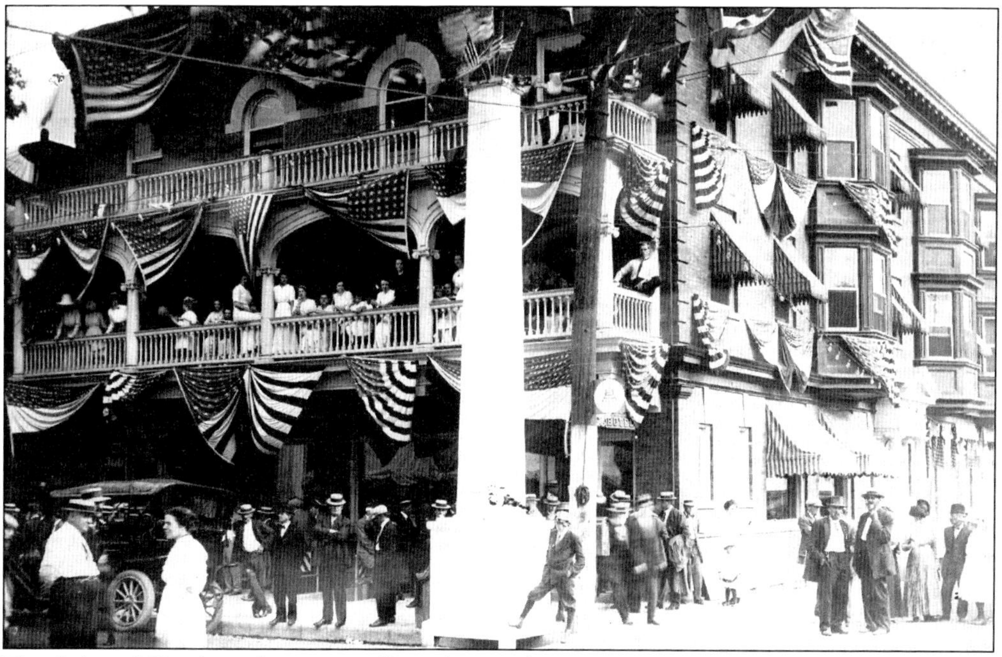

The Colonial Hotel, on the corner of Broadway and Main Street, is seen decorated for Old Home Week, August 18–25, 1912. Old Home Week was organized by the Bangor Board of Trade and was held to celebrate the growth of a "Bigger, Better, Busier Bangor." Parades and athletic and slate-splitting contests were held on the dirt roads, complete with floats, lights, balloon ascensions, and nightly fireworks. (Courtesy SBHC.)

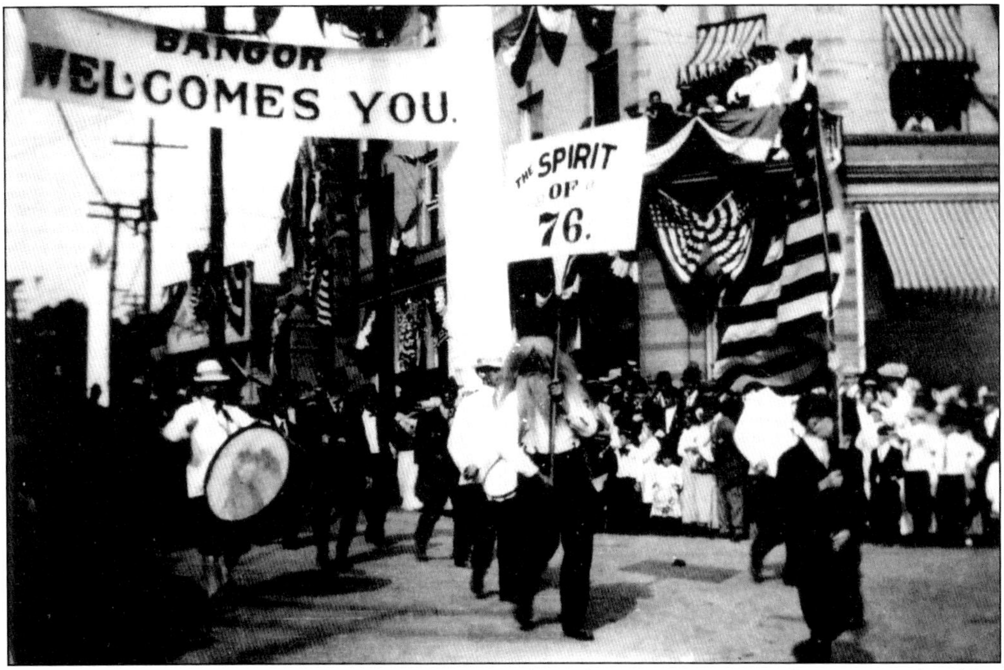

Here are more photographs from Old Home Week, welcoming visitors and townspeople alike. The festivities were divided into different events each day, such as Carnival Day or Religious Day, and included a variety of parades, like the Baby and Industrial parades, or athletic contests. Prizes were awarded such as gold pieces, brass alarm clocks, silk hosiery, or $1 in cash. Milton Flory was president of the board of trade at the time, but S. W. Christine, vice president, was in charge of the festivities. Clara C. Strunk was elected queen of Old Home Week, and George Godshalk was chosen to be the king. (Courtesy NCHGS.)

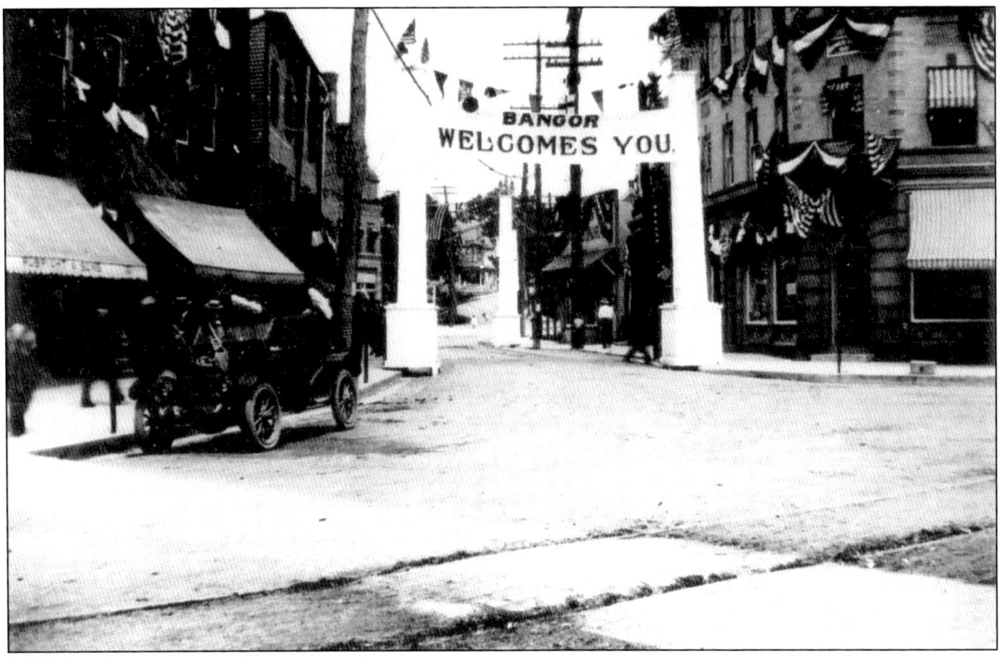

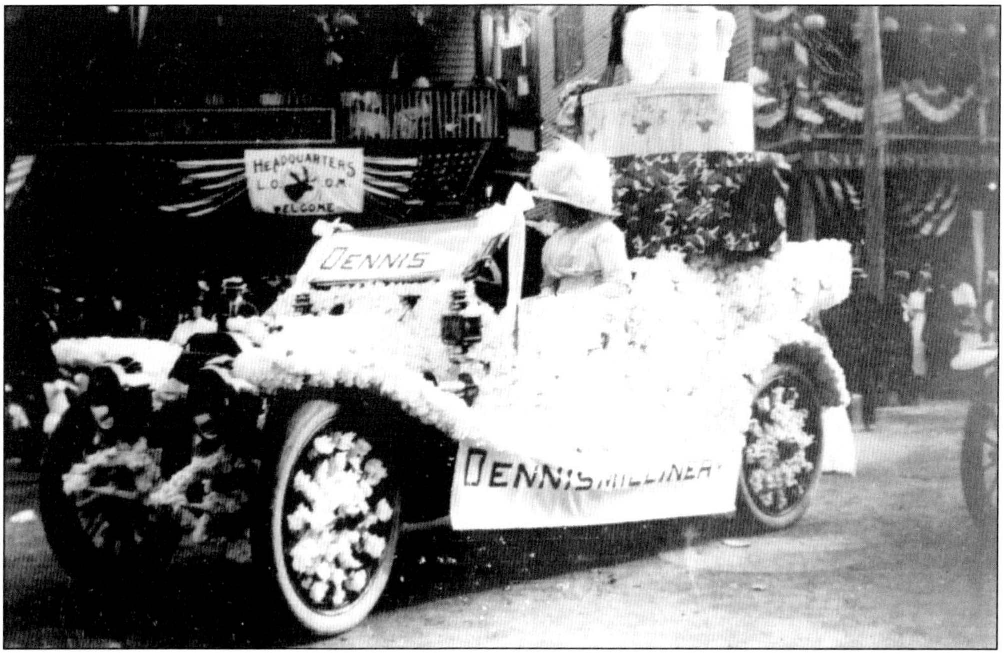

Participants of the Old Home Week celebration are shown here. A float, covered with flowers from Dennis Millinery, is seen above and was likely part of the automobile parade of best-decorated machines held on Historical Day. Modern marathoners have nothing on the man in the photograph below, who, if the signs can be believed, pushed a wheelbarrow of slate from Bangor, Pennsylvania, to Boston, Massachusetts, and back. (Courtesy NCHGS.)

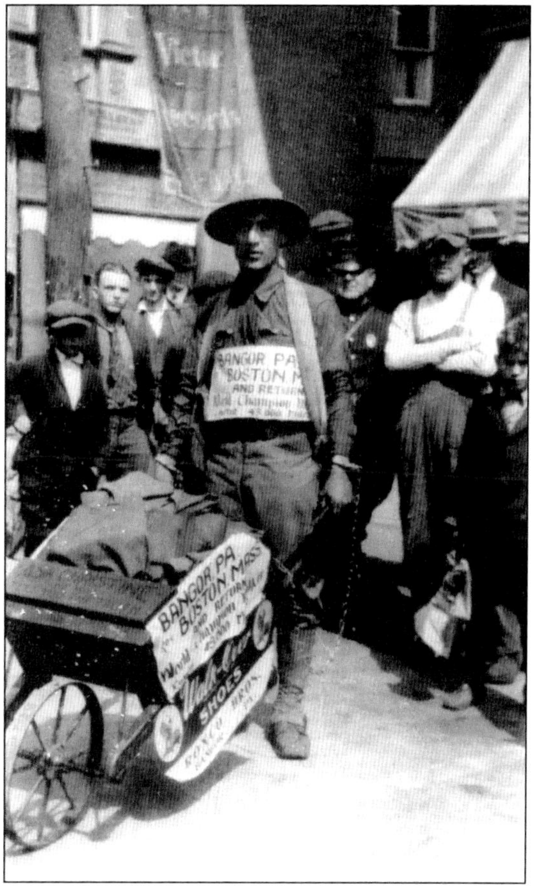

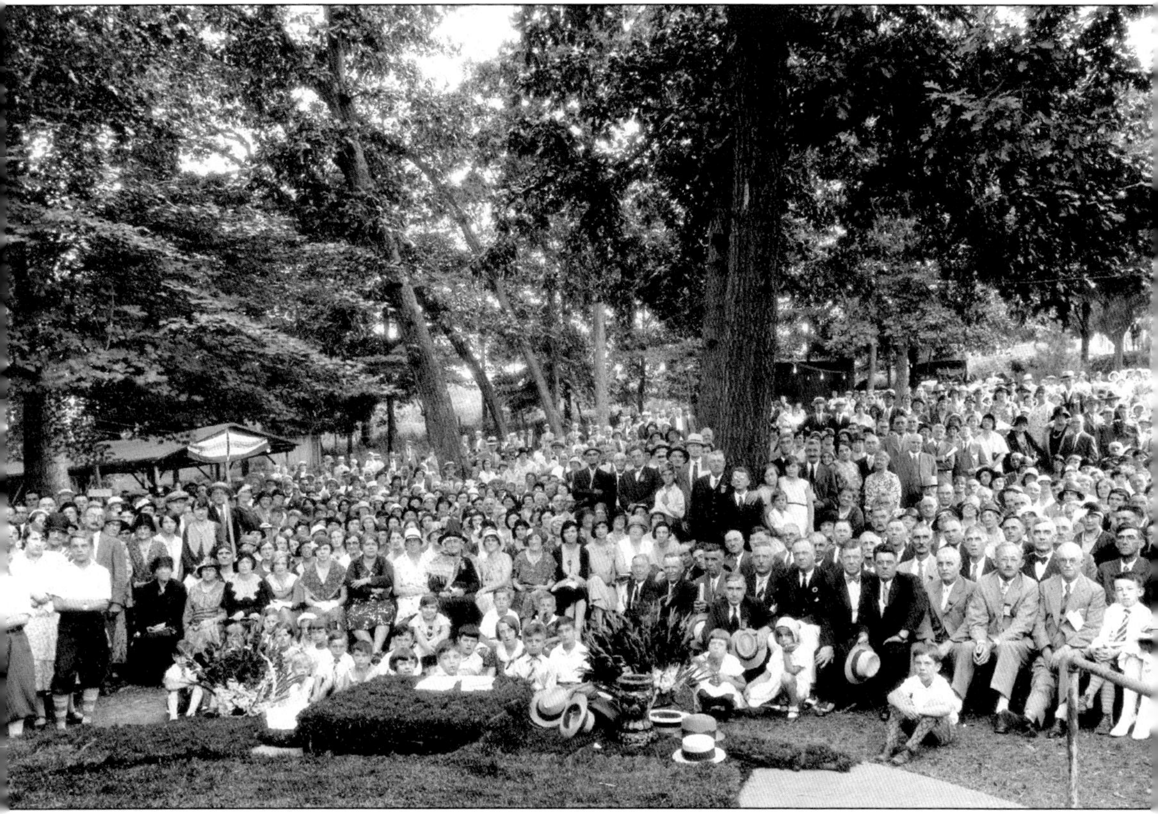

A crowd gathers for Bangor Welsh Day at the grove of the Lutheran church. "Gymanfu Ganu," or Welsh Day, was a religious song festival, usually held on Labor Day weekend, whose purpose was to preserve and celebrate the Welsh heritage. Competitions called "eisteddfodau" were held in music and literature for prizes. Recitations, singing, and slate-splitting contests were also held, and people came from all over to participate. (Courtesy BPL.)

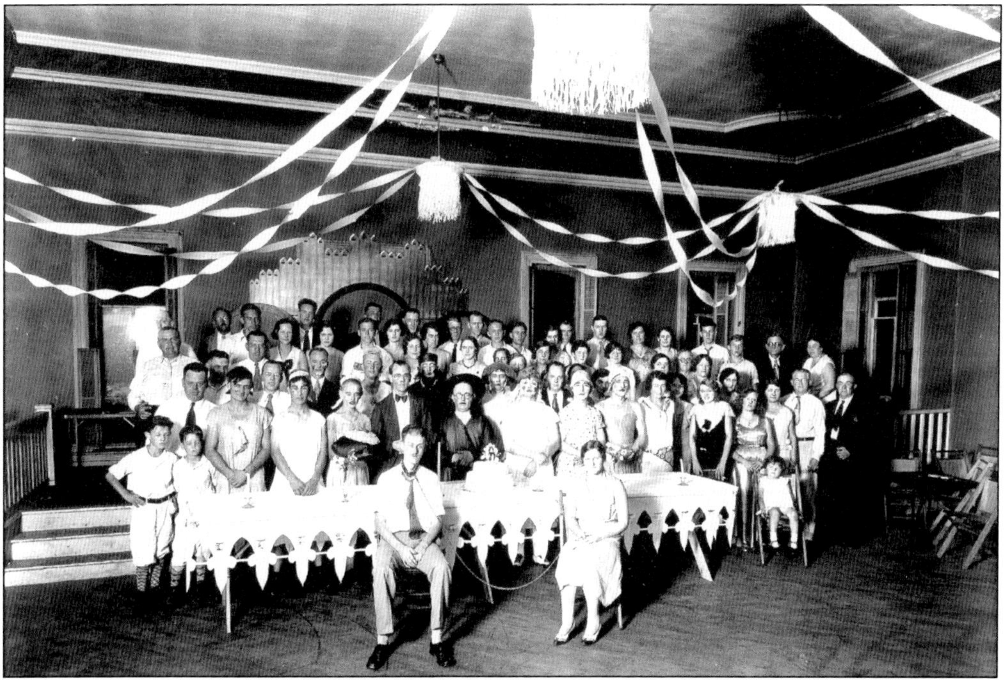

In the early days of the town's development, churches played a prominent role in the social and moral fabric of the community. They were not without their lighter side, as this photograph shows. Here members of the Methodist church on Third Street mug for the camera. This may have been part of the Welsh Day celebration. (Courtesy BPL.)

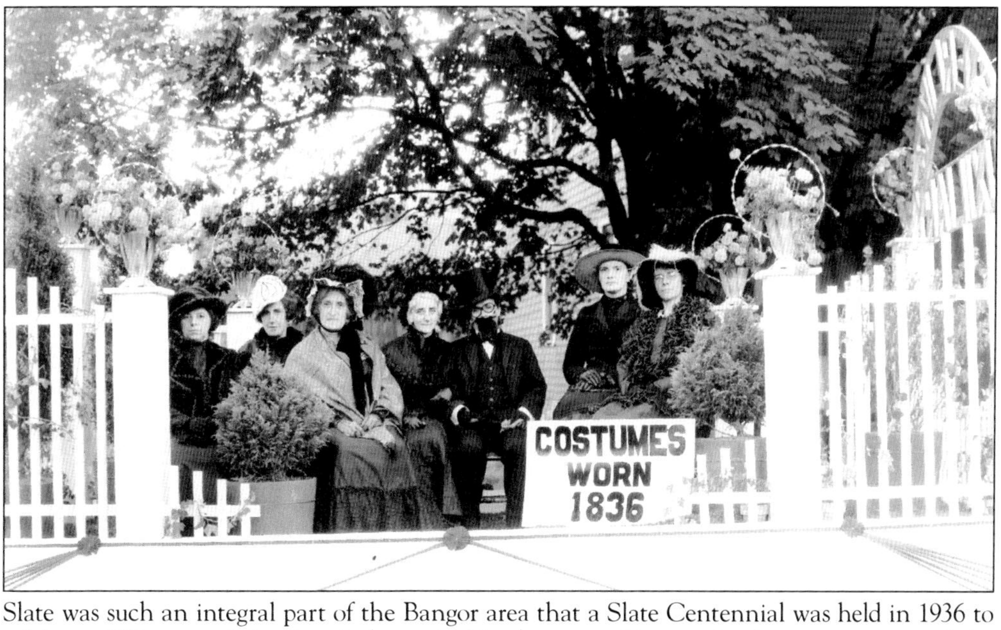

Slate was such an integral part of the Bangor area that a Slate Centennial was held in 1936 to celebrate 100 years of the slate industry in Northampton County. It also commemorated the 50th anniversary of the death of Bangor founder, Robert Morris Jones, and honored past and present quarrymen. Here townspeople pose for the camera dressed in traditional attire of 1836. (Courtesy HMM.)

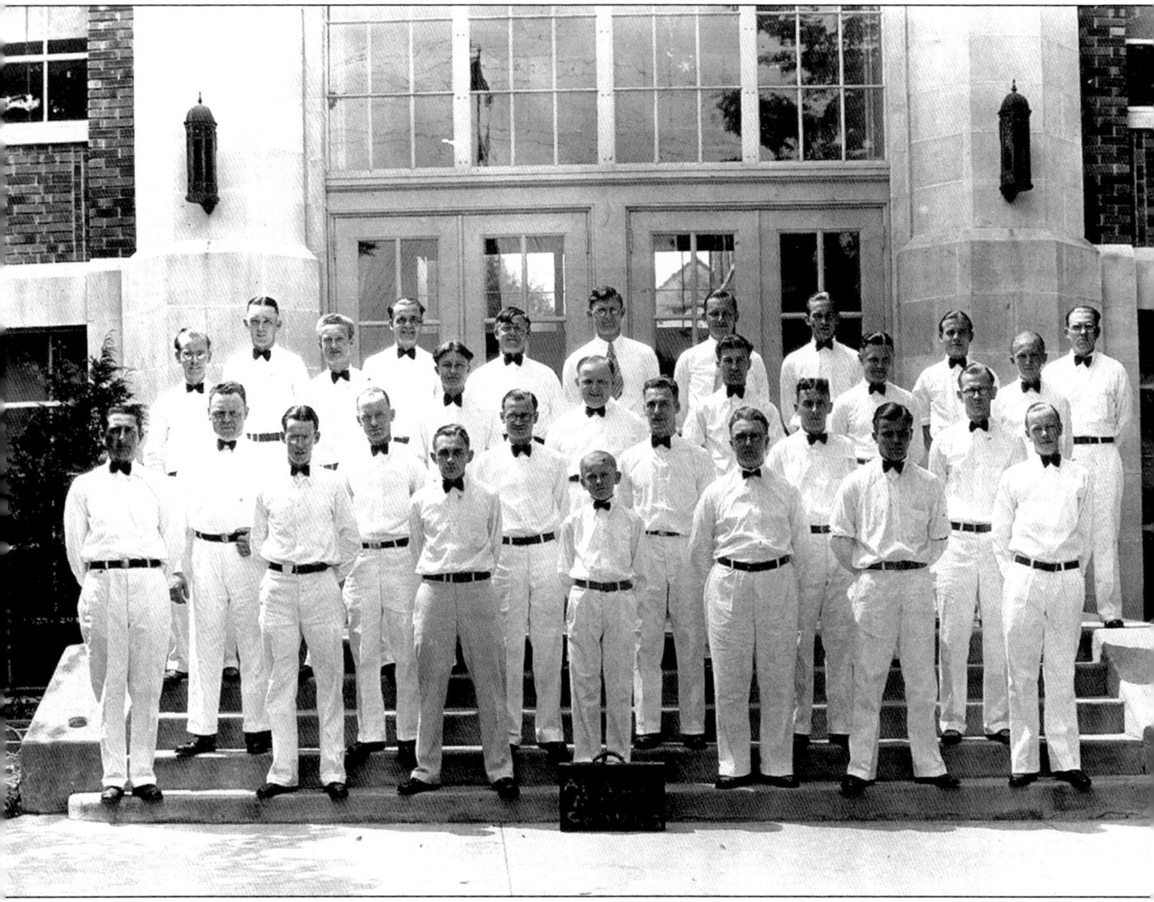

The Apollo Male Chorus started in 1928 under the direction of Ralph Sandercock. Like the Welsh Male Chorus before them, they carried on the tradition of singing and performing that was so important to the early Welsh immigrants. Shown here, from left to right, are the following: (first row) Russell Werkeiser, Edward Avery, Foster Bray, Forest Sandercock, Charles May, Bill Strike, and Walter Sandercock; (second row) Wilson "Brick" Parsons, Russell Kneebone, Elmer Hocking, Dave Beiler, Stanley Lindsey, and Glenwood Sandercock; (third row) Russell Sandercock, Douglas Jones, John Cowling, George Ruth, A. Albert, Arthur Lee, and Charles Strout; (fourth row) John Hughes, Bill Sandercock, Thomas "Zut" Amy, George Parsons, Wesley Jones, Bob Hughes, Nelson Sandercock, and Delmer Wills. (Courtesy BPL.)

Living along the Delaware River was not without its drawbacks. The area has seen several floods over the years, including this one in 1903 at the Cotton Mill in Martin's Creek (above). The Cotton Mill provided its workers with living arrangements in small cabins like the ones seen here. They were often damaged when the river rose over its banks. The Alpha Portland Cement Company, plant No. 3, is seen below during the flood of 1955. The area was hit by back-to-back hurricanes, Connie and the more destructive Diane, which dumped 600 million gallons of water into the plant. (Courtesy HMM.)

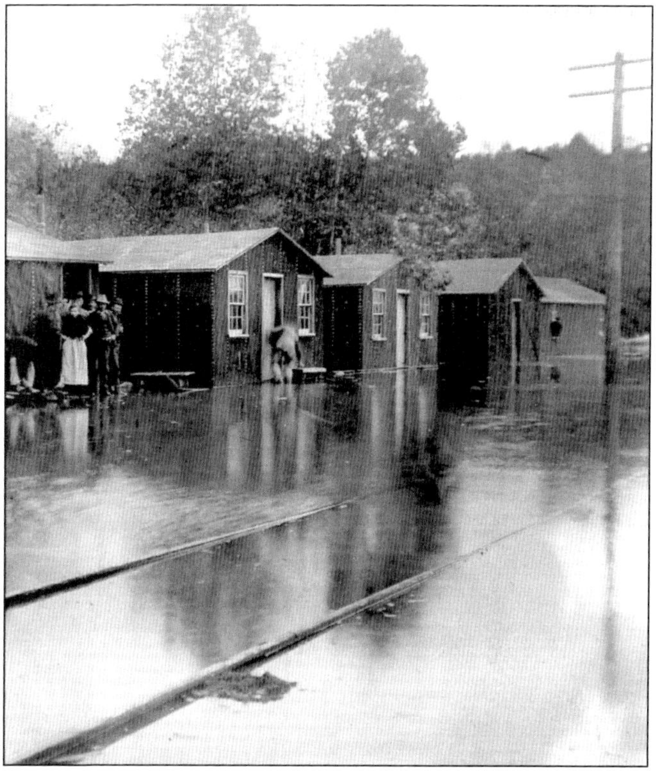

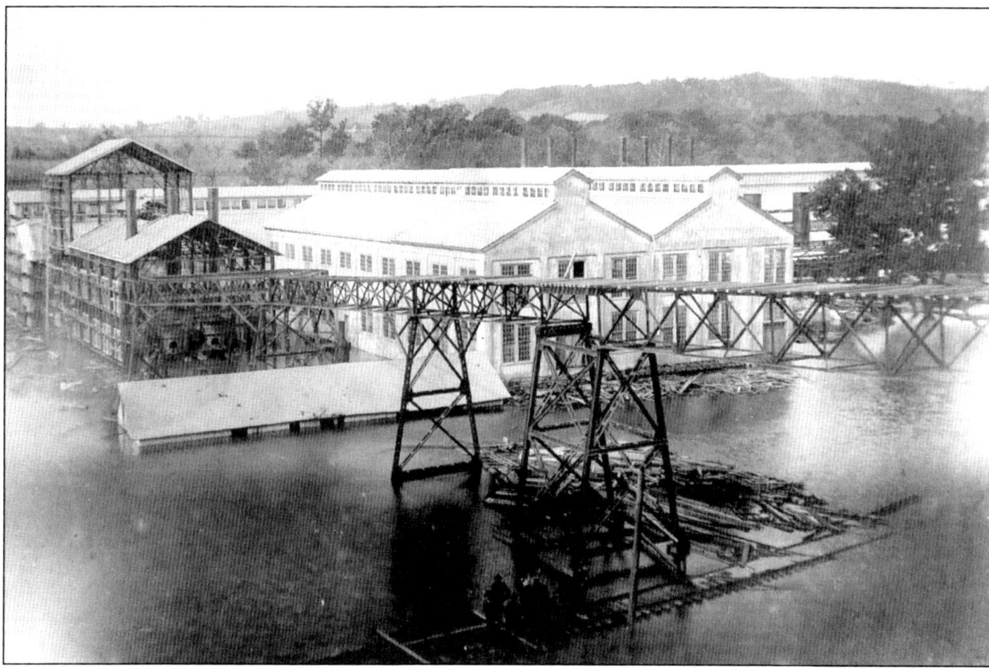

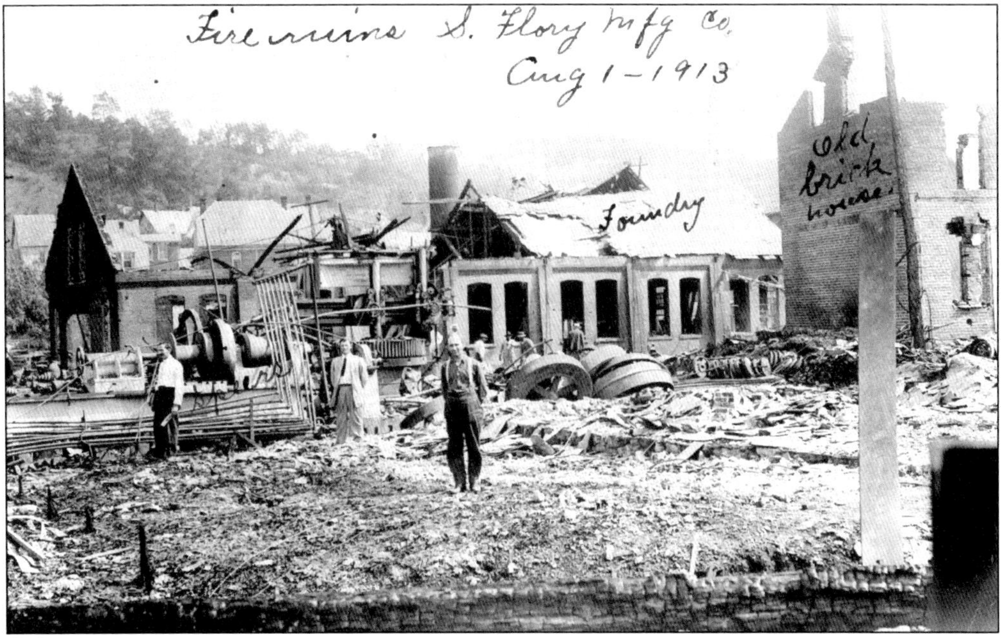

The ruins of S. Flory Manufacturing Company are shown here on August 1, 1913. The fire destroyed much of the plant, including the foundry and electrical plant. A previous fire is said to have occurred on February 26, 1900, which was responded to by the Rescue Fire Company No. 1. That fire and one at the Wise Lumber Company in 1927 were two of the largest fires fought by the company. (Courtesy SBHC.)

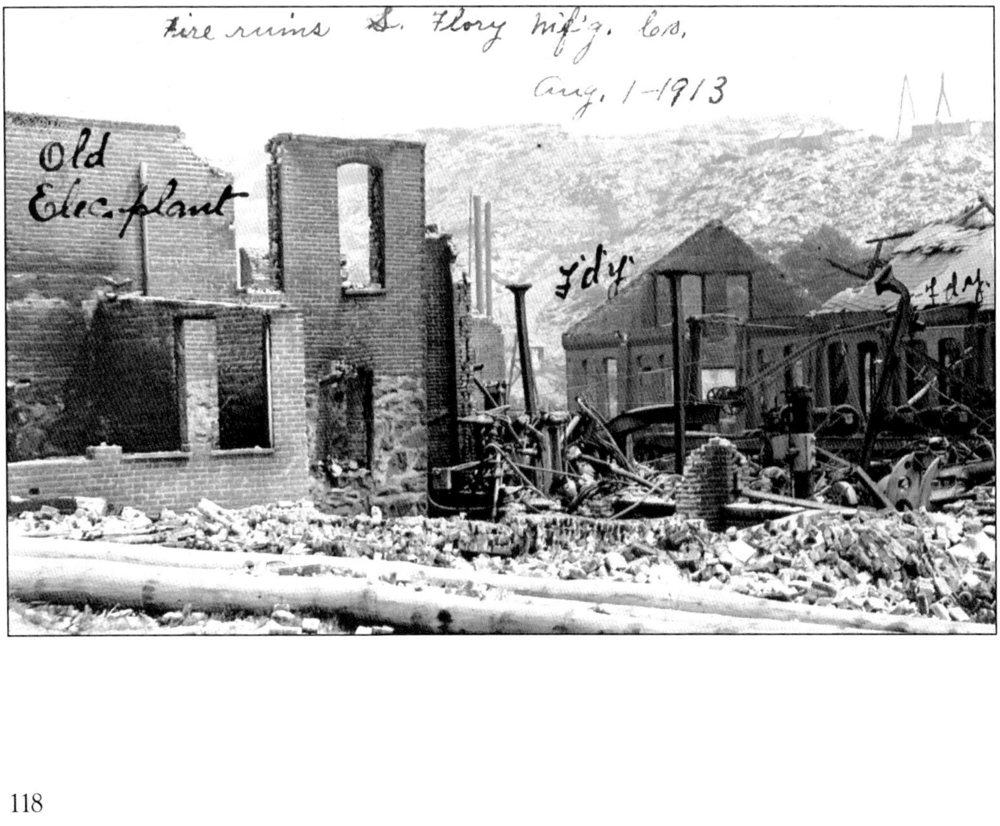

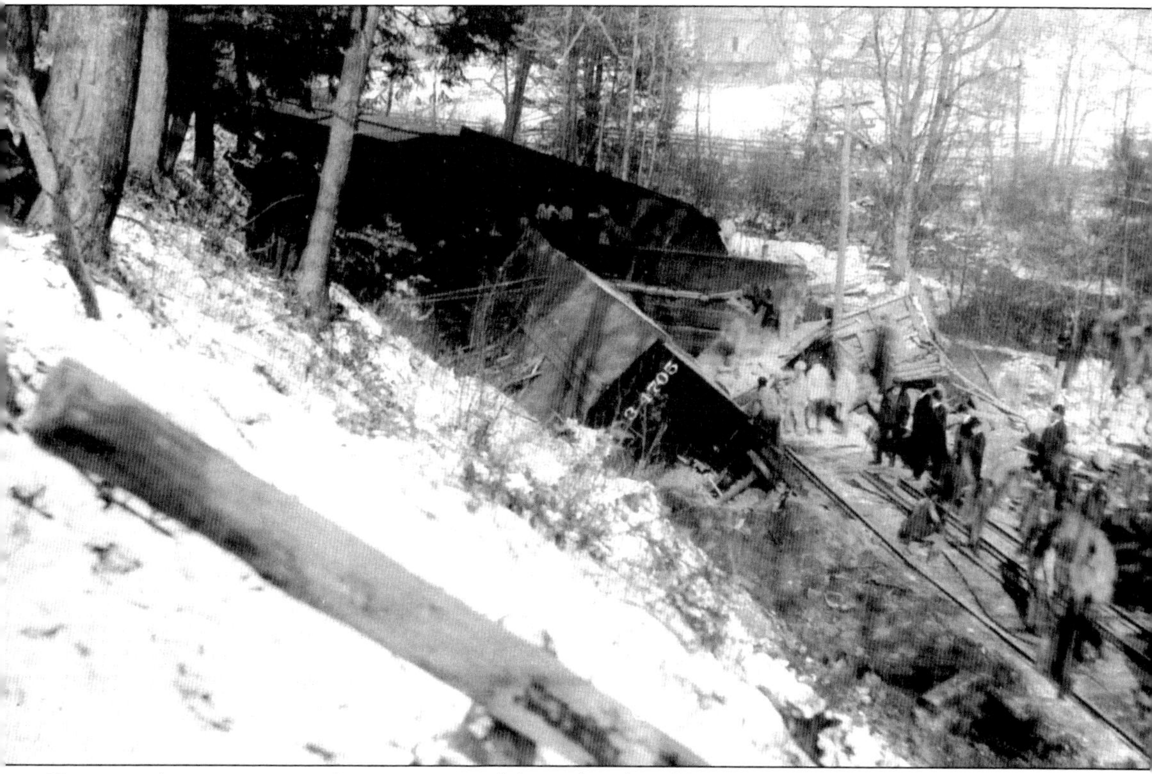

Train accidents were an unfortunate part of the railroads. Although the train wreck shown here is unidentified, the area had several mishaps in which lives were lost. Three men died in July 1919 in a head-on crash of two trains near Pen Argyl. In November 1903, 14-year-old Leanora Diorio and 70-year-old James Thomas were killed near Ackermanville, when a train car, the Tatamy, was struck by another train. Several New York teachers were also burned and killed in an accident along the Delaware River tracks. (Courtesy SBM.)

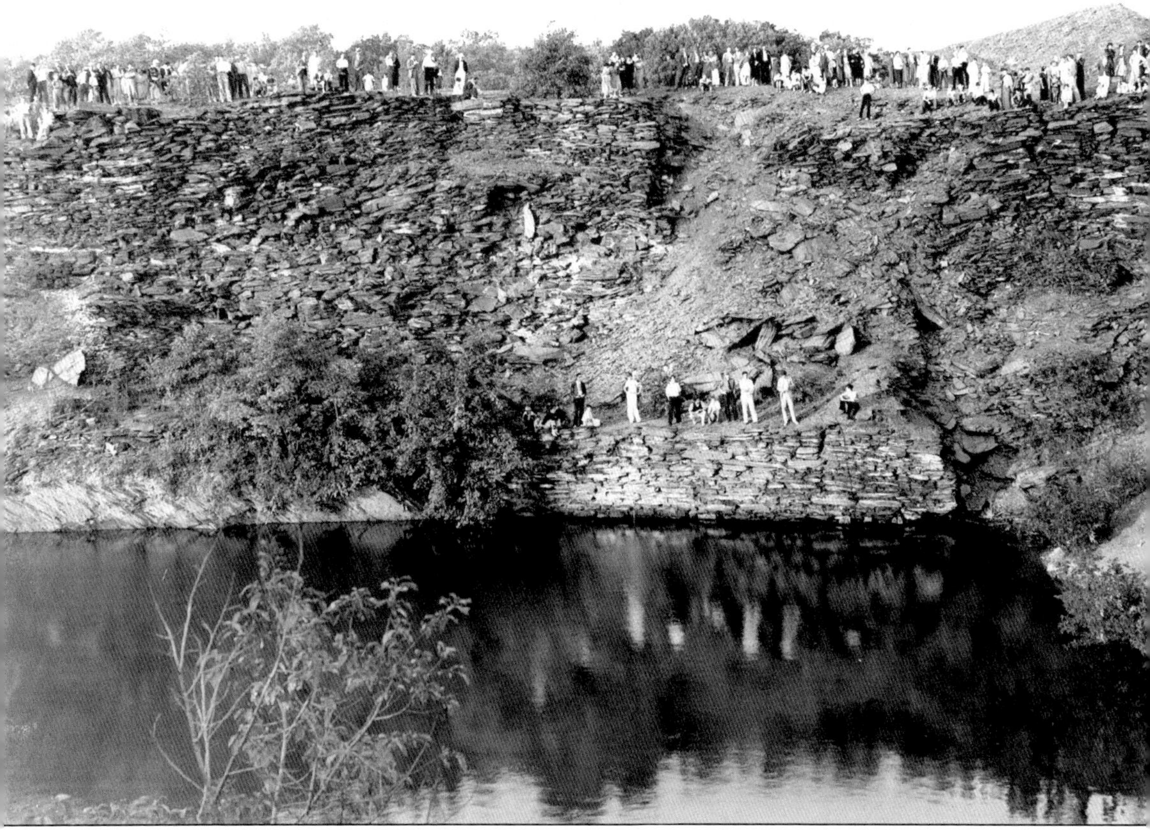

Not everything about the quarries was positive. Many people met their deaths from falls or from dynamite blasts that did not go off as planned and later exploded. Drowning occurred, too, because many people liked to swim in or explore the dark, cold water. Here rescue workers search the Pennsylvania Quarry in Pen Argyl for the body of William Cesare of Wind Gap. The drowning occurred in September 1936, when the quarry was known to be full of water. It was not uncommon for hundreds, even thousands, of people to show up to help or watch. (Courtesy BPL.)

Nine

PEOPLE AND PLACES

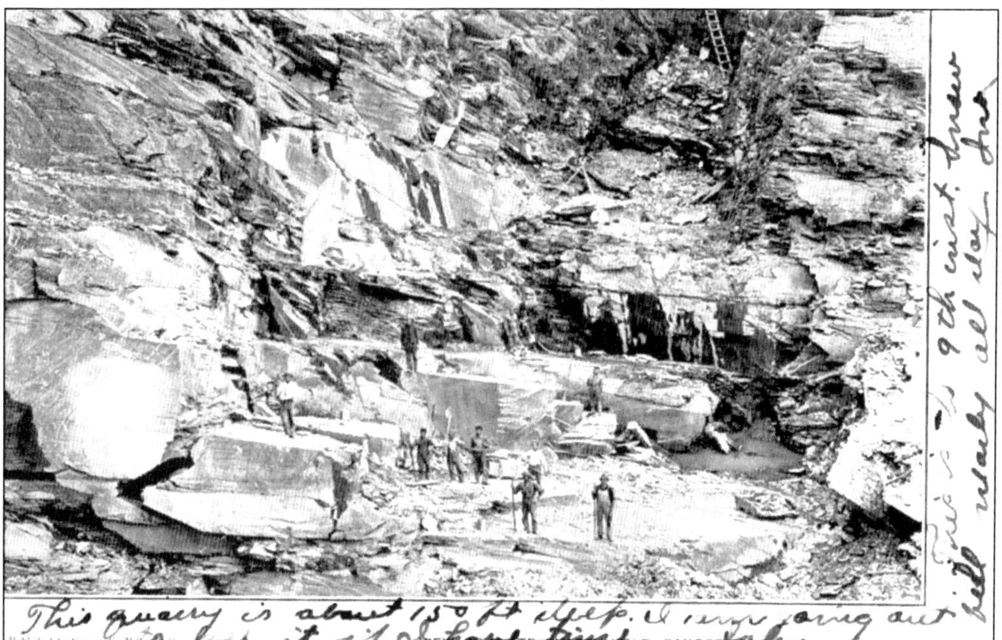

Men work in a quarry, possibly the Bangor Excelsior Quarry, which was about 150 feet deep. (Author's collection.)

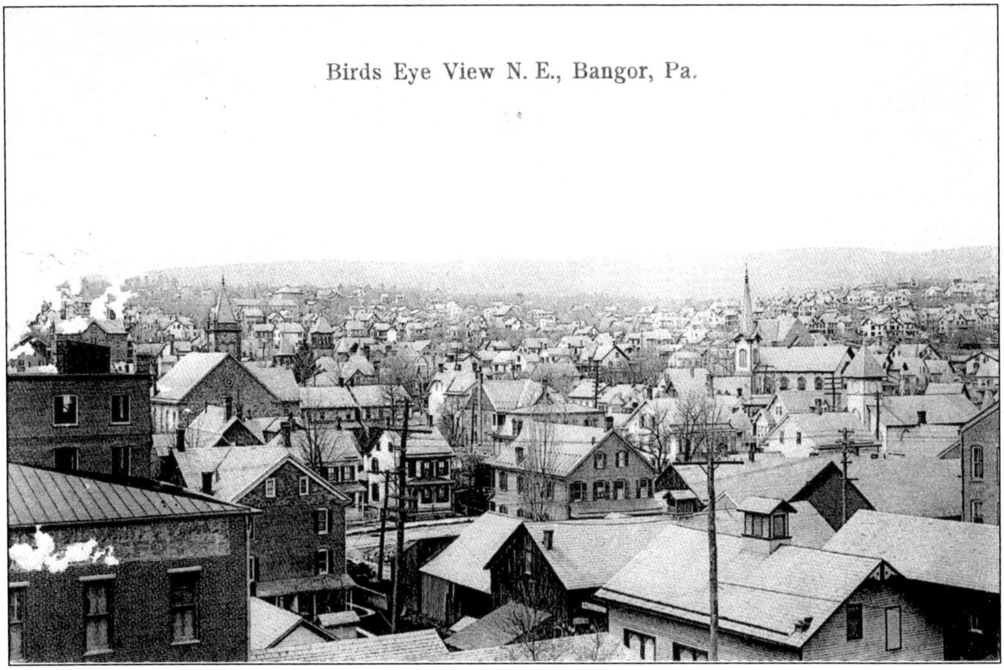

This is a bird's-eye view of Bangor from the northeast, date unknown. As early as 1896 Bangor was known as a town of houses, with a real estate value of approximately $1.5 million. (Courtesy SBHC.)

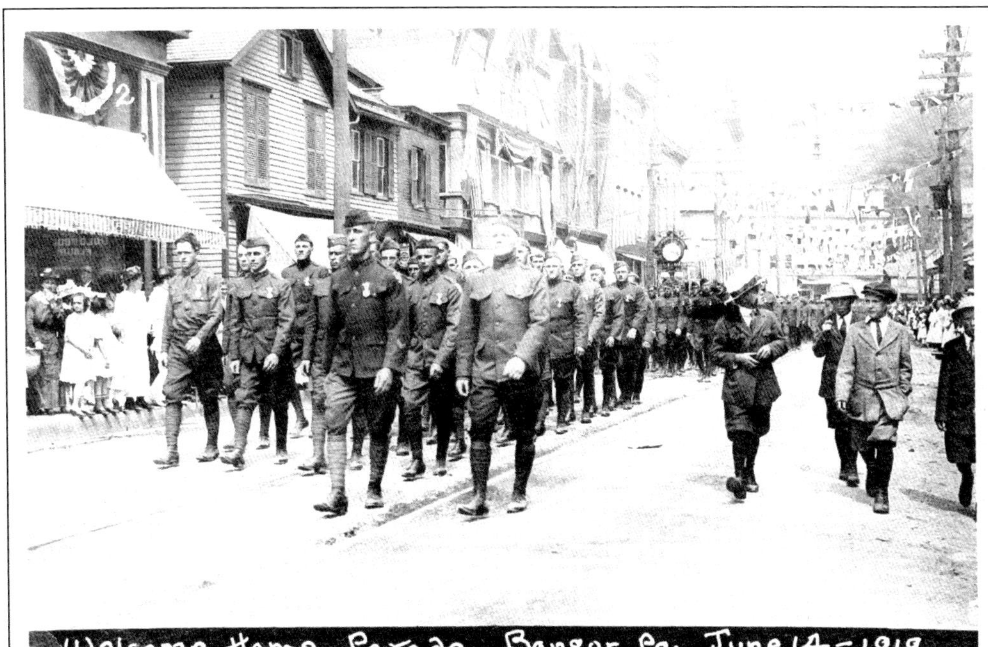

Bangor has a long tradition of honoring its veterans. Here veterans of World War I are welcomed home with a parade on June 14, 1919. (Courtesy SBHC.)

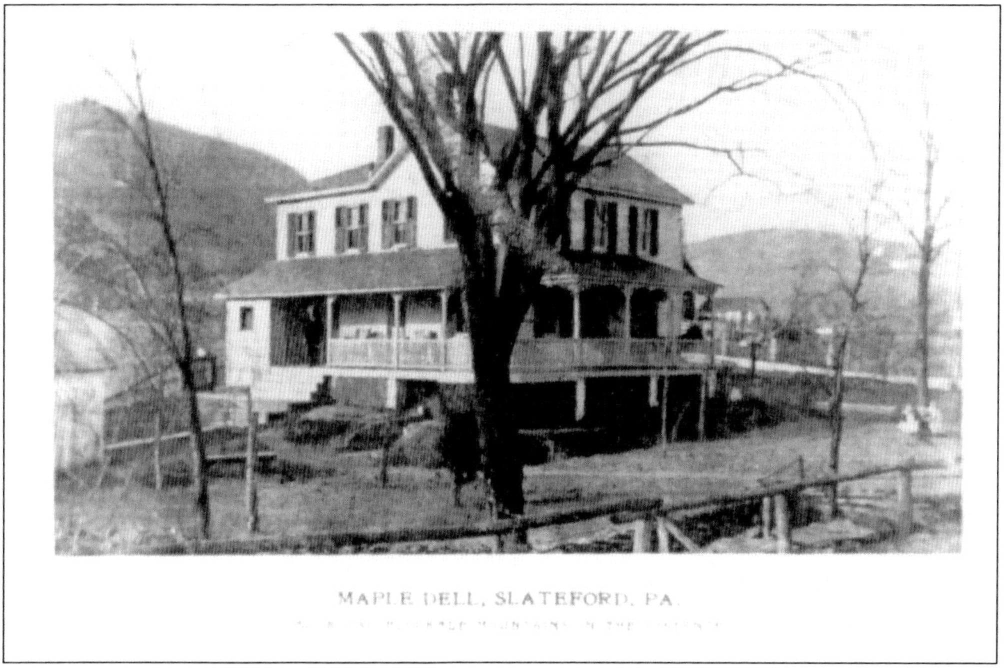

Shown here is the Maple Dell House in Slateford. They rented out rooms and were located near what is now the Delaware Water Gap National Recreation Area. (Courtesy SBM.)

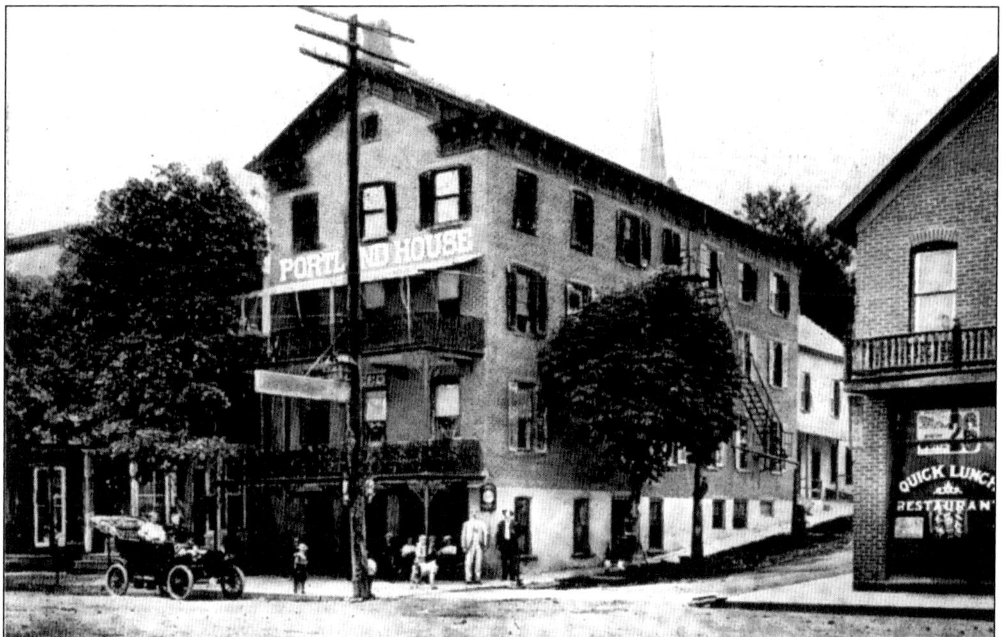

The Portland House is shown here. The facility had a bar and J. A. Wise was an early proprietor. (Courtesy PSA.)

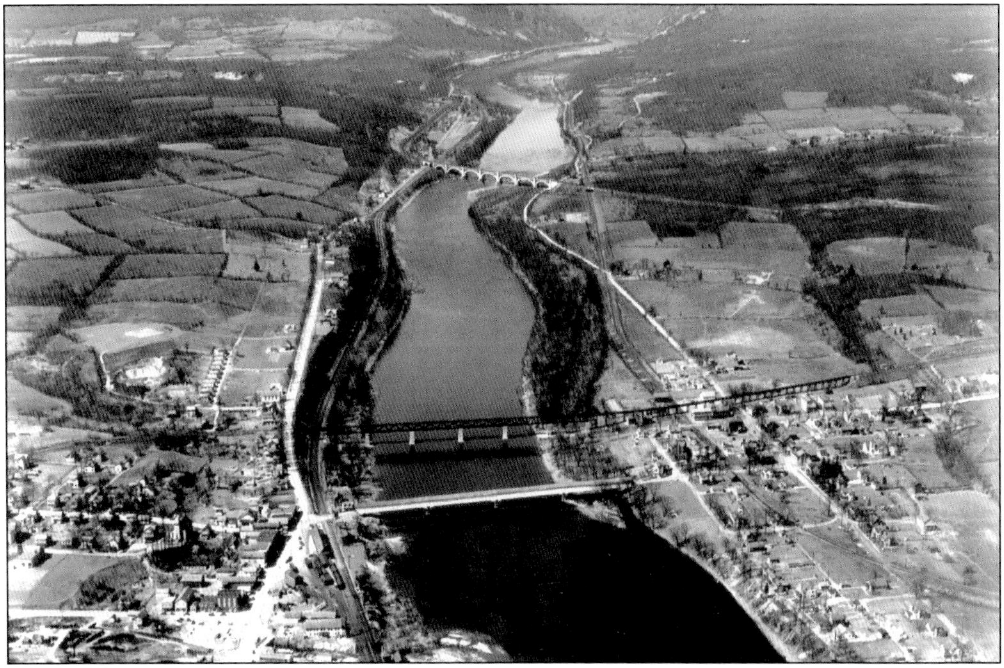

In this aerial view of Portland, the Columbia-Portland Covered Bridge can be seen in the foreground with a steel railroad span behind it. An old, concrete railroad bridge from the Lackawanna Railroad is in the background. (Courtesy PSA.)

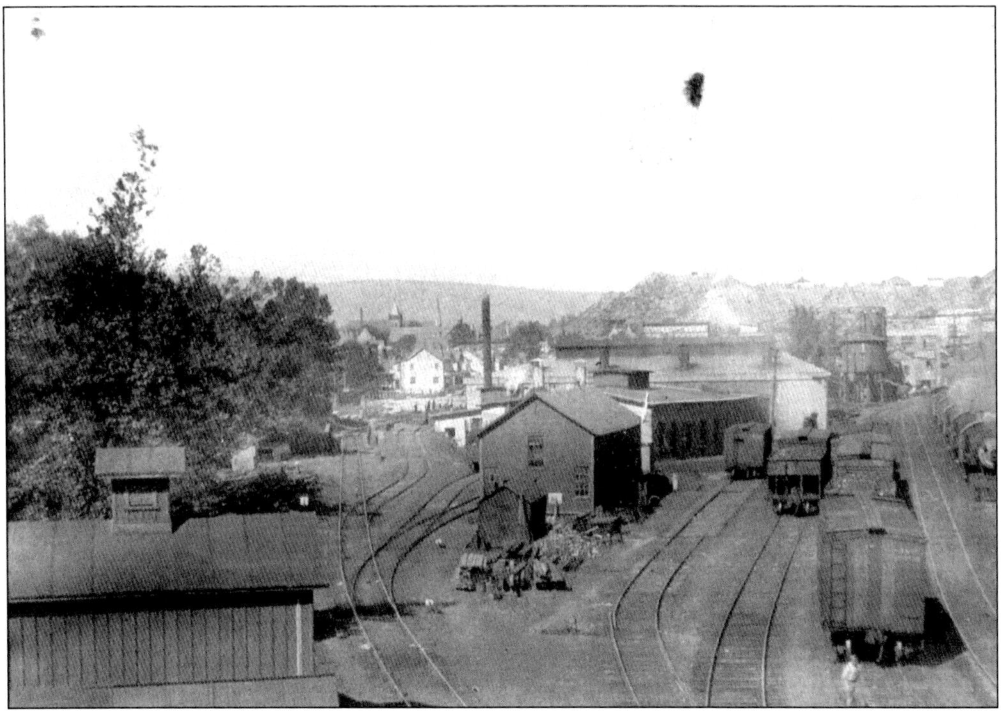

This is a view of a railroad yard in Bangor. (Courtesy SBM.)

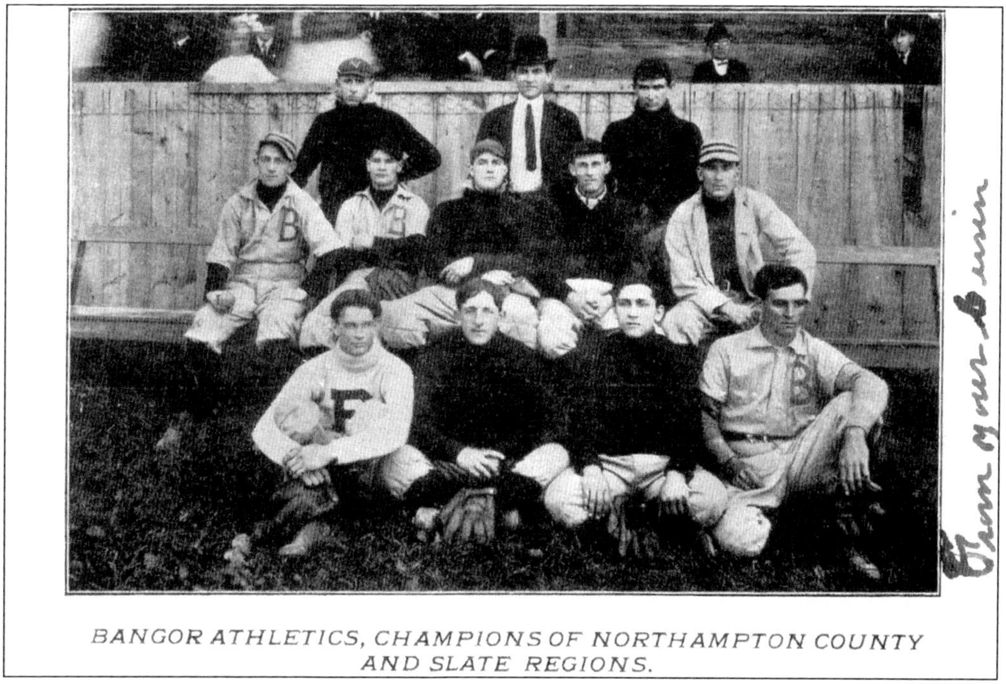

The Bangor Athletics, Slate Belt champions, are shown here. (Courtesy PSA.)

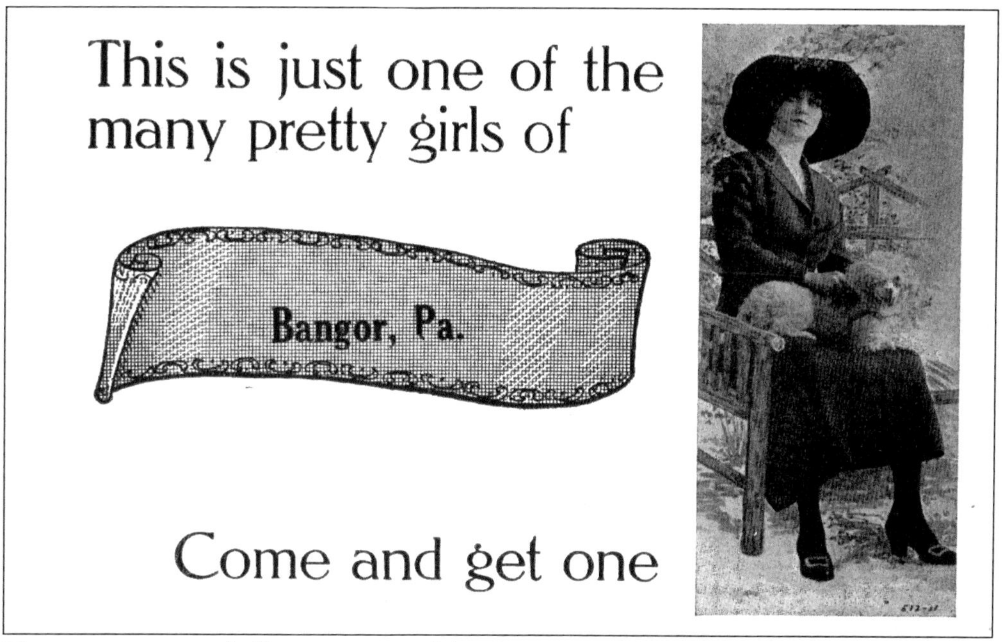

This pennant postcard offers positive proof that Bangor earned a place in the world, or at least was known well enough to be featured on the postcard. (Author's collection.)

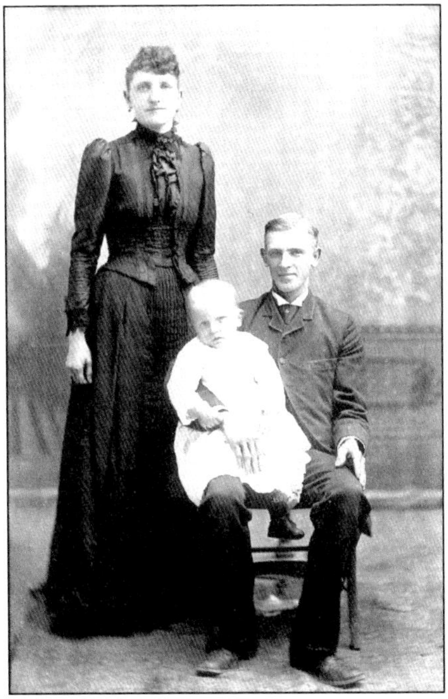

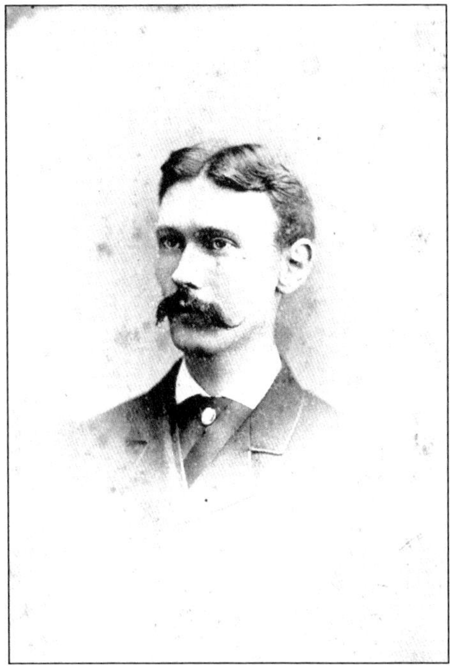

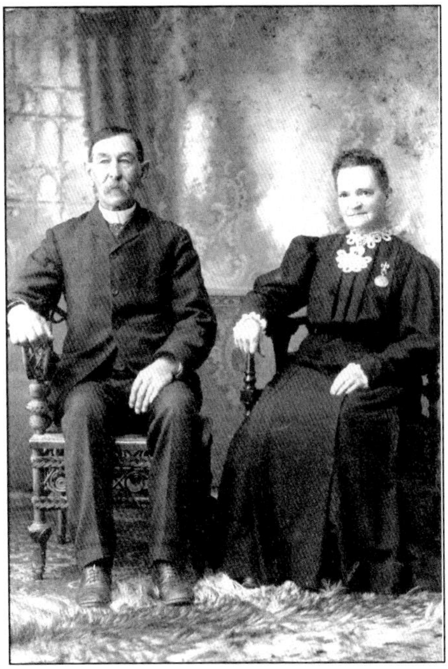

Few details are known about these individuals other than that they were members of the community. They may have been the original immigrants to the area or, more likely, their descendents. (Courtesy HMM.)

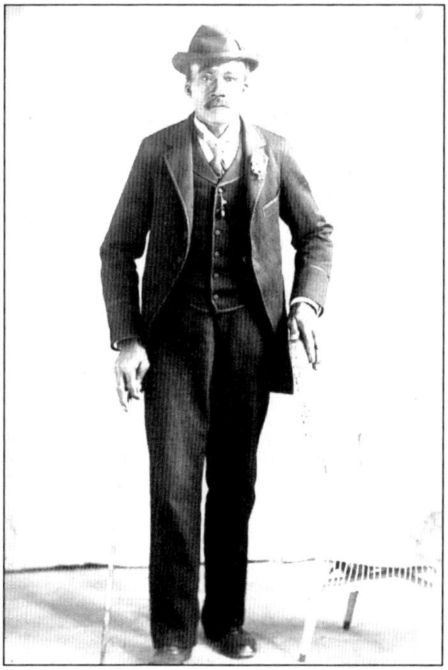

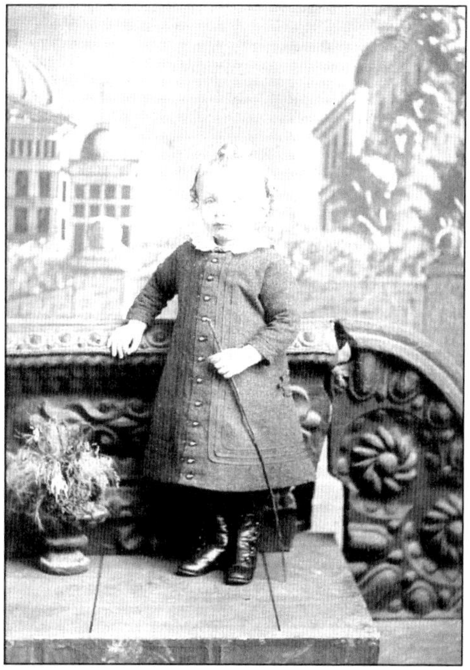

These are all examples of the common style of formal portraits in years past. The gentleman in the upper left-hand corner is African American. Bangor had a small but significant African American population, including Gertrude Mary Smith, who, in 1904, was the first African American to graduate from East Stroudsburg Normal School, now East Stroudsburg University. (Courtesy HMM.)

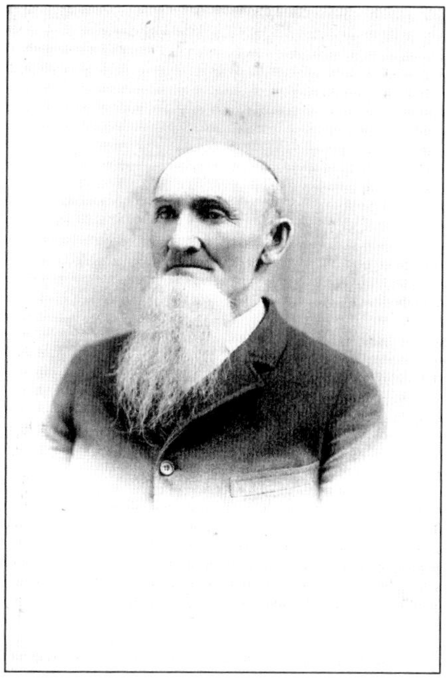

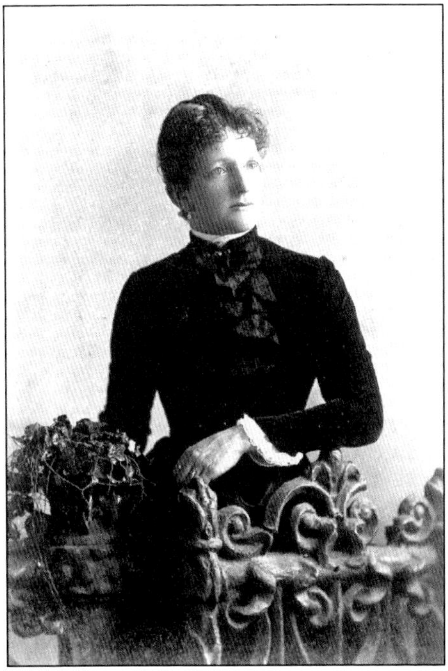

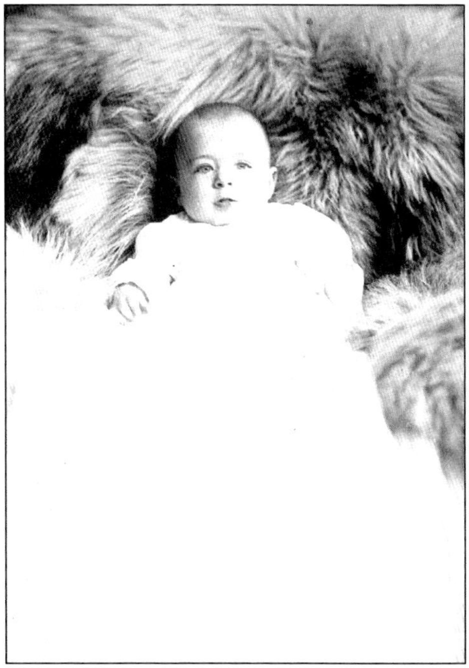

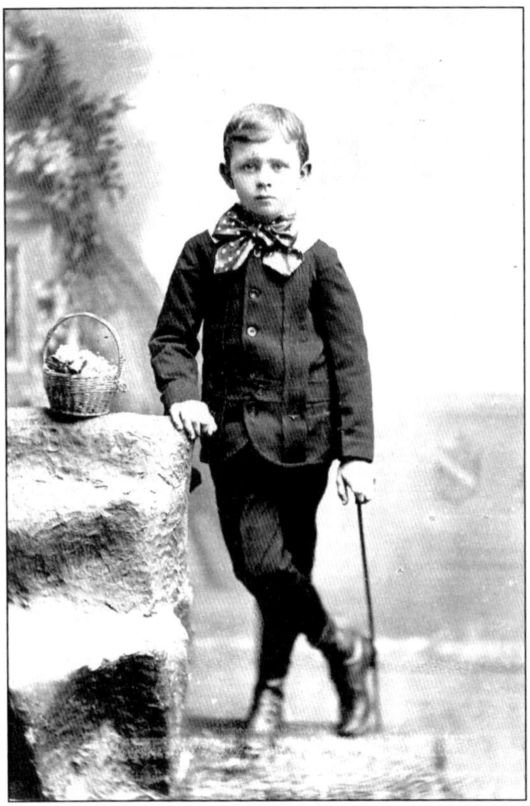

These individuals are all unidentified, though they are all a part of the history of Bangor. They may be someone's son, daughter, sister, or other loved one. Regardless of their identities, they are all a part of the spirit that was Bangor and the Slate Belt. (Courtesy HMM.)